SKILLS FOR EFFECTIVE COMMUNICATION

COMMUNICATION

A Guide to Building Relationships

RAPHAEL J. BECVAR

Department of Education
St. Louis University
St. Louis, Missouri

John Wiley & Sons, Inc.
New York • London • Sydney • Toronto

Library of Congress Cataloging in Publication Data

Becvar, Raphael J   1931-
  Skills for effective communication.

  (Wiley self-teaching guides)
  Bibliography: p. 195
  1. Interpersonal relations.   2. Communication--
Psychological aspects.   3. Role playing.   I. Title.
(HM132.B37)   301.14   73-19914
ISBN 0-471-06143-3

Printed in the United States of America

74 75   10 9 8 7 6 5 4 3 2

To my sisters, Mary and Lois

and to the memory of
my father, Jacob;
my mother, Mary;
my brother, Francis.

Preface

In several years of conducting human relations training with counselors, teachers, parents, students, business executives, and employees, I have used a variety of models. My comfort with sensitivity or encounter group models has gradually decreased. Although self-satisfaction and good feelings resulted from the training process, the effects were transitory. Little learning transferred to the real world where the participants were confronted with interpersonal problems that detracted from their enjoyment of life. Adding to my discomfort was the realization that many participants had previously sought assistance from a variety of sources—classes, group experiences, and reading. Why did the training not provide functional, practical learning to build the desired relationships with others in the real world?

Because of the above considerations I began two complementary activities. First, I redesigned the human relations workshops to promote practical applications as well as understanding of self and of theory. Instead of the euphoric, emotional high of previous workshops, I sought a learning environment where people might learn skills to build better relationships, therefore achieving greater personal satisfaction in living.

The laboratory focus on skill learning produced a different emotional atmosphere—a task orientation, a realistic perspective on the difficulty of the task, but an optimism that the task could be accomplished. Self-report questionnaires and personal interviews with participants indicated that for the first time in their lives many felt the ability to influence the quality of their interpersonal environments and reported greater satisfaction as a result.

I then explored the possibility of a written version which would be as successful as the formal workshops. The written form could be an alternative to workshops, but could also be used before and during workshop training. This book is the result of that translation. Hopefully it captures the essence of the workshops—practical training for transfer to daily living.

This book is not a scholarly treatise. It was designed for practical learning and application, consistent with current theory and research. Ideas were borrowed from many sources. To improve readability they are not identified in the text. The bibliography contains lists of the references used in one form or another—some for ideas and some for inspiration. All are quality publications to which the reader might refer if he wishes greater depth of study in human relations. To aid the reader, references relating to specific topics are presented in a separate list.

The learning model used in the book reflects a strong behavioristic approach—focusing first on interpersonal behavior (what you do) rather than the intrapersonal behavior (what you think and feel). One might call it a behavioral-humanism. The learning focus is on behavior, not denying or minimizing the importance of attitudes or feelings but assuming that attitudes affect relationships only as they are expressed.

A further assumption of the model is that intrapersonal behavior (self-concepts, attitudes about self and others) changes as interpersonal behavior changes. In role-playing exercises the reader will experience his own feelings and attitudes toward others as he observes his partner and will experience his own feelings as he does the exercises and observes the reactions of others to the behavior. Thus, new insights about self and others will result. Hopefully, sufficient awareness will be created so that the reader will attempt the "more effective" behavior in ongoing relationships. It is assumed that the experience of influencing relationships (rather than reacting to them) is what brings changes in self-concept, attitudes, and feelings.

The word "effective" used in the title of this book is a relative term, reflecting specific values and goals of interpersonal communication. Throughout this book, I assume that the prevailing norm of communication in societies in the Western culture is less than satisfying, effective, and productive. The skills you will learn here should help you achieve greater openness, confidence, trust, respect, and understanding in your relationships with others. Such relationships should produce more satisfaction, productivity, and psychological health for all those involved. The reader should weigh his own goals and values with those presented here.

I am particularly grateful to Donald Blocher, Alan R. Anderson, Virginia Satir, Sidney Jourard, John Krumboltz, David W. Anderson, Joseph Luft, Robert Carkhuff, John Wallen, Margaret Hoopes, Addie Fuhriman, and Lynn Scoresby. Their ideas were particularly influential and appear frequently in the book, often in different language and form.

I especially appreciate the contributions of my students and colleagues. Their willingness to ask questions, experiment, be the subjects of test runs of various exercises, test the early drafts of the manuscript in their work settings, and make suggestions, were invaluable.

St. Louis, Missouri   Raphael J. Becvar
February 1974

Note to Students

Skills for Effective Communication is appropriate for people who want to
improve their communication skills and build better relationships—
married or engaged couples, families, new counselors, teachers, work
teams, student groups, employers, employees, instructors, and students.
This book is not intended as a substitute for a closely supervised group
experience in communication. Ideally the book would be used along with
a group experience. It is designed to provide sufficient skills and knowledge for two people to work together to improve their relationships with
themselves and with others. The suggested learning experiences can
make reading in communications more meaningful and human relations
training experiences more profitable.

By no means are these exact and precise skills. They represent a
beginning. The skills help you influence relationships—by communicating
how you truly feel and by building on a sincere desire to help the other
person or your relationship with him. The skills could be used to fake
people out—to manipulate people and to enhance oneself with no regard
for others. But if the skills are used for these devious purposes, then
the desired relationships will not be obtained.

I urge you to learn the skills and to use them in your own unique way
in all groups to which you belong. Be sensitive to the effects of the skills
on people and make adjustments to accommodate unique situations and
the learning of the people in the situation.

Note to Instructors

This book can be used as a preliminary learning activity in discussion courses. Many teachers believe in group discussion as a classroom learning method and they often desire open instructor-student interaction and student-student interaction. Unfortunately many instructors presume their students know how to communicate effectively and efficiently. These expectations are, more often than not, unrealistic. If you wish to use a group discussion method, you may first have to become an instructor of communication and group process. This is no easy task.

If you wish your students to be actively rather than passively involved in their classroom learning, you may wish to use this book in one of two ways: (1) Complete the learning experiences with a colleague and then use the first three or four class meetings to give your students an opportunity to learn the skills in class under your supervision. (2) Complete the learning experiences together with your students.

How you use the book may depend upon the subject you teach. If the course is focused on the subject matter of communication and human relations you have a great deal of latitude in how the book might be used. In these classes one can assume that the students are "choosing" to take the interpersonal risks that necessarily accompany this subject matter.

In other courses, the problem becomes more complex. Students may see training in communication as irrelevant in a history, English, or science class. In any class, learning is facilitated when the students feel a need. Thus in courses other than human relations courses, readiness for formally learning the skills may come only when attempts at group discussion are not successful or when interpersonal problems emerge in the class. "That didn't go too well. Would you be interested in learning to communicate more effectively?" You can promote learning of more effective communication indirectly through your modeling or through your interventions to promote more effective communication. This latter approach is discussed in detail in Chapters 7 and 8.

In most schools there is a resource person you might call upon to assist you. Your school counselor has extensive training in human relations and communications and he might help you identify the best strategy to develop more effective communication in your classroom. The counselor could (1) assist you in formal training activities, (2) give you feedback on your modeling and interventions, or (3) conduct formal training while you participate with your students.

However you choose to proceed, plan your activities well. Try to anticipate the probable reactions to each exercise. Plan how you will deal with various reactions. This always entails using the skills you would have them learn. In brief, if students are to perceive these skills for effective communication as functional, they must experience the skills. For example, rational arguments to emotional concerns are neither functional nor consistent with what you would have them learn. Do what you would have your students do!

How to Use This Book

This book explains principles of effective communication and allows you to experience the effects of specific interpersonal behavior—both ineffective and effective. The skills presented were suggested by research, theory, and observation because they effectively build close, trusting, satisfying, helpful relationships. The skills may seem unrelated to each other, but they gradually build from relatively simple skills to more complex skills that combine to form an effective interpersonal style.

Chapter 1 provides both a brief background to common communication problems and a frame of reference for developing more effective communication skills. Chapter 2 introduces some basic principles of communication underlying the interpersonal style presented in this book. In Chapter 3 through 7, the skills become the focus for your learning. Each of these chapters is divided into the following sequence: (1) explanation (rationale); (2) exercises in which you experience the behaviors described; (3) post-experience discussion blending experience and explanation; (4) a decision-making exercise about which behavior you and your partner will use in your relationships; (5) questions testing your knowledge of principles and probable effects of specific behaviors illustrated; (6) a self-observation form to assist you in systematic, consistent interpersonal growth.

The primary learning device in this book is role-playing between you and your partner. The role-playing activities supplement the logical explanations and help you (1) become aware of the desired behaviors, (2) identify the components of the new behaviors, (3) recognize situations in which you might practice the new behaviors, and (4) create a situation where you receive feedback from your partner about how well you are doing the behaviors. With practice in a wide variety of situations you will soon be able to integrate the behaviors into your own unique, personal style.

By following the sequence of readings, experiences, and questions you can increase your interpersonal effectiveness as you (1) examine your values and behavior intimately and specifically, (2) explore the consequences of various behavior alternatives, (3) evaluate your behavior in the light of your values and anticipated and experienced consequences, and (4) modify or accept your behavior as a result of your evaluation.

You should complete each chapter of the book at one sitting. The approximate time you will need is given on the first page of each chapter. Try to allow more time if possible. If you try to rush through a chapter, the desired learning may be reduced considerably. Care enough to devote the time and energy to do the task well.

PRECAUTIONS FOR THOSE WORKING THROUGH THIS BOOK

Ideally this book should be studied by two or more people who want to improve their relationships with others. Another result can occur; your relationship could be hurt and/or your relationships with other persons could become uncomfortable. This "negative" side effect need not happen, but since it may, it requires a special understanding on your part.

There are a couple of fundamental attitudes that you must have to reduce these negative side effects. First, your learning goal must be to build better future relationships rather than to focus on past interactions. For example, after one of the exercises you are reminded of a behavior you dislike. Your partner may have done this behavior quite frequently in the past. While before you accepted it as the "way the person is," you may now be uncomfortable with this particular behavior. If you follow an inclination to criticize you may hurt your relationship. In the past your partner was only doing as he had learned to do. To punish your partner for this is akin to punishing someone for not speaking French when he only knew how to speak English. This inclination to criticize is tough to set aside, for in all relationships people do irritating little things that we have learned to tolerate. The skills in this book will be most helpful in building a relationship if the focus is on the future—on the solution. You can help each other do more frequently the behavior that helps your relationship and do less frequently the behavior that produces tensions in your relationship(s).

You can head off the negative side effects if your expectations are realistic. Sometimes both you and your partner will fall back on the old habits. Of course, "having realistic expectations" can be a cop-out. "Oh well, I'm not perfect." "I'm too old to learn." "This just isn't working. I feel phony; it's not me." Each time an old habit creeps into the situation it should be talked about—with the goal of helping the other person and the relationship.

The challenge for you is to have the courage to be imperfect, to accept yourself and your partner as people who make mistakes at times—and as people whose behavior may hurt a relationship. Old habits die hard, but they die. In times of tension in relationships—when the skills are most necessary—the old habits pop up. Each time an old habit recurs it should stimulate renewed effort. The old behavior becomes less and less frequent because it is replaced with more effective behavior.

Is this book for you? Possibly. Take the short quiz on the next page and score yourself with the answers that follow. If you score 1-3 or 4-6 on the Individual Involvement Inventory, I recommend that you work through the book alone before trying it with someone.

Special Note to Persons Working Through the Book Alone

As you study this book alone, you may gain many insights into your behavior and the behavior of others, but unfortunately the amount of learning "to do" effective communication is reduced. To get the best of two worlds, read the book alone and then select another person to work through the book with you.

INDIVIDUAL INVOLVEMENT INVENTORY

T   F

( ) ( ) 1. I try new procedures rather than discount them.

( ) ( ) 2. I take responsibility for my own learning.

( ) ( ) 3. I laugh at my own mistakes.

( ) ( ) 4. I listen discriminately to what I hear and its relevance for me.

( ) (✓) 5. I value openness to change in others and expect it of myself.

( ) ( ) 6. I am willing to take risks in learning situations.

( ) ( ) 7. I approach old tasks in new ways.

( ) ( ) 8. I am willing to alter my expectations when I learn others have different expectations.

( ) ( ) 9. I am an active learner rather than a passive learner.

( ) ( ) 10. I try to learn in all situations.

( ) ( ) 11. I am patient with other people as they learn although at times it is very difficult.

Your responses to these statements indicate your readiness to profit from the learning experiences presented in this book. On the next page are the "desirable" answers. Score yourself, total your correct responses, and find your readiness status.

Answers to Individual Involvement Inventory

1. T; 2. T; 3. T; 4. T; 5. T; 6. T; 7. T; 8. T; 9. T;
10. T; 11. T

Judge your readiness for these learning experiences as follows:

Number of trues
in your score

1-3	Perhaps this book is not for you. You may wish to return it to the shelf. Otherwise, I recommend that you read the book alone first before working through it with a partner.
4-6	You may be ambivalent about this kind of learning experience. You may want to discuss it with a friend before you decide to continue. Consider reading the book alone first.
7-9	You are the type who can participate in and profit from this kind of learning experience but you may be a little uncomfortable doing it.
10-11	Your answers have implied a readiness to profit maximally from the learning experience.

Although this book was written for two people to read together, it is also rewarding for one person to read on his own. Even if you scored 7 or above, you may find it rewarding and more beneficial to read the book alone first.

If you choose to work through the book with a partner, your next task is to select this person. Who should it be? It could be someone you know well. Even if you have a good relationship, you may feel a need to improve it or to help each other improve your relationships with others. It could be someone you don't know well but would like to know better. It could be a colleague at work, a fellow student, another parent. It should be someone with whom you come in contact frequently. It should be someone who scores at least 7-9 on the Individual Involvement Inventory. But most of all, it should be someone who will commit himself to the learning contract presented on the next page. (This person should also read the preceding pages.)

A LEARNING CONTRACT

I understand that the learning experiences presented in this book will be meaningful to me and my partner(s) only as I follow the prescribed sequence.

I understand that at times I will feel phony, awkward, and self-conscious. Even if I feel that a given concept is self-evident, I agree to follow the sequence of the book, do the exercises, and complete all after-exercise discussions as directed. I care about my partner(s) and value my relationship with him (her). I desire to learn to communicate more effectively. I affirm my desire to improve my interpersonal communication skills and build a closer relationship with my partner(s).

I understand that both my partner(s) and I have learned certain ways to communicate in the past. Neither of us can be blamed for doing things the way we have learned to do them. I agree not to punish or berate my partner(s) for past behavior.

I understand that as we use the skills presented in this book with each other, there will be times when we will be less than perfect as old habits may return from time to time. I ask for patience and understanding from my partner as I will be patient and understanding. I shall make a sincere effort to learn from the conflict that we will experience and attempt to develop more effective ways of working through our conflicts.

Name: _____

Name: _____

Date: _____

Chapter Objectives

Chapter 1   WHAT IS EFFECTIVE COMMUNICATION?

After completing this chapter, the student will be able to give an explanation of the following:

(1) why persons are not successful in forming the kind of relationships they desire
(2) how the norm of communication was acquired
(3) how one can build more effective relationships and the fundamental attitude one must have to be successful in building these relationships

Chapter 2   KEY CONCEPTS IN HUMAN RELATIONS

After completing this chapter, the student will be able to give verbal explanations and examples of the following concepts in human relations:

(1) the modes of communication
(2) the behavior paradox
(3) perceptual validity
(4) communication cause and effect
(5) communication as a mutually influential process

Chapter 3   ATTENTION FOR BETTER RELATIONSHIPS

After completing this chapter, the student will be able to demonstrate and give an explanation of the probable effects of each of the following behaviors on another person:

(1) inattention as listener
(2) inattention as speaker
(3) polite attention as listener
(4) punishing attention
(5) nonverbal empathetic attention
(6) active listening
(7) deferring attention

Chapter 4   UNDERSTANDING VERBAL MESSAGES

After completing this chapter, the student will be able to demonstrate and give an explanation of the probable effects of each of the following behaviors on another person:

(1) irrelevant conversations
(2) pseudo-relevant conversations
(3) paraphrasing for understanding of thoughts
(4) paraphrasing for understanding of feelings
(5) requesting paraphrase
(6) mirroring
(7) paraphrasing in summary

Chapter 5   EXPRESSING FEELINGS EFFECTIVELY

After completing this chapter, the student will be able to demonstrate and give an explanation of the probable effects of each of the following behaviors on another person:

(1) expressing feelings indirectly
(2) expressing feelings physically
(3) direct expression of feelings
(4) giving a behavioral description
(5) giving a behavioral prescription
(6) rewarding effective behavior
(7) delayed expression of feelings
(8) immediate expression of feelings

Chapter 6   CONFLICT RESOLUTION, FEEDBACK, AND
            NEGOTIATION IN RELATIONSHIPS

After completing this chapter, the student will be able to:

(1) demonstrate and give an explanation of the probable effects on another person of expressing feelings directly to deal with conflict arising from
     (a) feelings expressed physically
     (b) feelings expressed indirectly
     (c) ambiguous or incompletely expressed messages
     (d) messages sent without perceptual qualification
(2) label and explain several strategies to deal with an impasse in negotiations to resolve differences

(3) explain the rules for giving and receiving feedback and the underlying assumptions behind the rules
(4) demonstrate and explain the probable effects on the receiver of
    (a) direct questions
    (b) facilitative questions
(5) explain the effects on a relationship when argument is the means employed to resolve conflict
(6) demonstrate and explain the probable effects on the receiver of two interventions to stop an ongoing argument

Chapter 7   INTERVENTION IN YOUR SOCIAL SYSTEM

After completing this chapter, the student will be able to:

(1) give an explanation of how the effectiveness of a social system can be enhanced by
    (a) respecting individual rights
    (b) using the resource of individuals in the social system
(2) explain the probable effects on the receiver and the social system if someone intervenes to promote change in the norm of communication
(3) explain the probable effects of establishing the following conditions in a social system
    (a) setting specific measurable goals
    (b) establishing a common set of procedures
    (c) separating understanding from evaluation in discussions
(4) explain the probable effects on a social system of each of the activities at the close of a group meeting
    (a) review progress toward goals
    (b) review the common set of procedures
    (c) share self perceptions and give feedback to individual members

Chapter 8   APPLICATION FROM DIFFERENT PERSPECTIVES

After completing this chapter, the student will be able to:

(1) give an explanation of how the skills might be used in one or more of the following roles:
    (a) student
    (b) teacher
    (c) parent
    (d) administrator
(2) give an explanation of possible difficulties that might be encountered in effecting change in the ongoing norm of communication in one or more of the above role settings

Contents

CHAPTER ONE

What Is Effective Communication?

Before you begin, be sure to read all the introductory suggestions (pages v-xix). You will need approximately 45
minutes to get the maximum learning from this chapter.

The greatest source of satisfaction or dissatisfaction in living is often
found in relationships with other persons. Despite our best efforts
many of us feel frustrated, angry, or disappointed with the quality of
our relationships with others. For many of us relationships seem tol-
erable at best, yet they are not enhancing our lives as they might. In
rare moments we experience the way things might be; we meet people
who interact in ways that communicate respect, care, understanding,
love, trust, and concern. Perhaps these moments keep alive the
romantic in us. However, the interactions in our daily lives make these
desired relationships seem like things that just happen to other people.

It is somewhat ironic, but I have found that many of us neither know
the kind of relationship we are looking for, nor how to develop good
relationships. For many it is a search for the "right" person, the person with whom we can be comfortable and whose presence somehow
mysteriously enhances our lives. At times we think we have found this
person only to discover that the person was not the way we wanted him
to be. After a few such encounters and disappointments, many of us
give up the search and become "reconciled" to less than satisfying relationships.

We sometimes start by asking the wrong questions. We tend to view
people (ourselves included) as static or unchanging. "That's the way he
is." Therefore the search is for people who are "compatible." Even
more stringently, we search for people who will accommodate us. Thus
the search is based on selectively judging "right" or "wrong," "fits" or
"does not fit," and ultimately "acceptance" or "rejection." But society's
"common sense" psychology fails to recognize that people constantly
change and that people can be influenced to be different if they can experience more freedom in the process.

The lack of satisfaction in relationships can be attributed to the norm of interaction (general social expectations) that we have acquired. As we grew up, we were encouraged to repress feelings. "You don't hate your sister." "Of course you like the gift." "Big boys don't cry." "Little girls should be seen and not heard." We began to feel guilty for feeling angry, disappointed, and curious. The feelings persisted, but we could not show them. Our models (parents, teachers, siblings) did not seem to feel what we felt. Thus, when we felt what we were "not supposed to," we felt guilty, inadequate, frustrated, powerless. In time we learned ways to deal with our feelings when we could not repress them further.

Since we learned that feelings are bad we also learned to project responsibility for our feelings to others. We could not do this openly, but had to be sneaky about it. We learned to play "games." For example, if we are angry at someone we do not tell the person. Instead we snipe, we tease, we tantalize in a way that keeps the person off guard. In this way should the person confront us directly, we can always deny anger and take on an air of innocence, catching the accuser in the ambivalence of what he feels and what you said. Of course, he reciprocates when he has the opportunity. Then you must respond similarly. Game playing is in full bloom.

We learned too that with those in power positions (teachers, parents, supervisors) our games had to be more sophisticated than with those we control. Recall the anecdote of the company president who having been reprimanded by the board of directors proceeds to berate his vice-president, who chews out his unit supervisor, who attacks the foreman, who puts down the employee, who goes home and criticizes his wife, who in turn yells at the kids, who kick the family dog.

Game playing by sending ambiguous messages projects responsibility for accurate interpretation to others. If others do not interpret these vague messages correctly we can punish them by a show of indignation. This is not too bad if one has a power position of authority or if one is able to keep the other on the defensive. However, most of us are usually on the receiving end—pressed to interpret ambiguous messages accurately, not willing to admit our discomfort and to ask for clarification.

Further, we learned as children that people do not listen well. When we really wanted attention we had to do something disruptive. "Now they can't ignore me." A by-product of this process is lowered self-esteem. "If they think what I say and feel is not important, then I must be worth very little. They are important people; they must be right." One result could be an exaggerated form of self-expression in reaction to this lowered self-esteem. "They don't think I'm worth much? I'll show them. I'll dominate the situation and not give people a chance to put me down."

Where in the above set of interactions is there room for the quality relationship we seek? Others in our society and culture learned similar things. In this society the search for the "right" person seems quite

futile if you use these rules as the tools for your search. To be successful this old norm must be set aside and a new norm of interaction
acquired.

Who is the "right" person that each person seeks? We hear and
read words like love, trust, care, understanding. None of these words
includes conflict, a necessary part of human interaction. People who
expect relationships to be free from conflict are setting an impossible
goal. And yet one hears people equate "no conflict" with a good relationship. Two unique persons who form a relationship will experience
conflict. This is not only unavoidable but desirable behavior. Out of
conflict can come growth; out of conflict can come a new understanding
of the uniqueness in each person that no relationship should destroy.
Would you describe a relationship as showing love, care, understanding,
and trust if it cost either person his individuality? The ideal relationship should enhance each person.

But let's set aside how we got the way we are and let's see if we can
get where we want to go. Satisfying relationships with others are possible, and they can be developed. The key is in learning to communicate
more effectively with realistic expectations.

Learning to communicate effectively means changing the norm of
communication (the way we have always communicated) in particular
groups (family, work, school, peer, social). The norm of communication may not be effective, but people in these groups have accommodated
themselves to roles prescribed by the expectations of others. When
someone new enters a group, members are quick to point out directly
and indirectly what is acceptable and what is unacceptable. Group
norms are seldom openly questioned, despite dissatisfaction. Once
indoctrinated, seldom does anyone challenge the way the group communicates. You may learn to communicate effectively, but the groups
of which you are a part may not like the new you. "Let's keep things
the way they are, the way they're supposed to be," they may say. Thus,
as a person learns new skills, he encounters a problem that confronts
all trainers in the area of interpersonal communication—the transfer of
learning to the real world. Just because you have learned a new and
perhaps better way to communicate, you cannot expect that others (who
have not) will immediately share your excitement. Most people will
appreciate their new relationship with you, and in the absence of game
playing they will feel understood and important. But some will feel
threatened by the "new you" and will seek to change you back to the old
way of communicating, especially if they were controlling the relationship before you changed to promote equality in the relationship.

You can learn to be more effective in all your relationships, but
there is a fundamental attitude that you must have before you can be
markedly successful: Your efforts must stem from a desire and a
commitment to improve your relationship with others. Communicate

effectively with people about whom you care, with people whose relationship is important to you. Each relationship in your life may improve as you increase the frequency of behavior that says "I care," that makes people feel closer to you, that builds trust. Likewise, each relationship in your life may improve as you decrease the frequency of behavior that says "I don't care," that makes people draw away from you, and that builds distrust.

The basic model used in defining effective behavior comes from counseling. The counselor's initial task is to build a close relationship with the client. He must communicate that he cares; he must build a trust relationship with his client. Many years of research have provided a fairly clear idea of behaviors that develop this desired relationship. The irony is that counselors exist because society's norm of communication creates casualties. If you can change the norm of communication with persons in your world, your and their need for counselors and "purchased friendships" may be reduced. Even though you cannot change society all at once, you may wish to change your private society by learning more effective communication behavior. In so doing you and those "significant others" in your life are less likely to become casualties.

Can your relationships be improved? Do you want to improve your relationship with your partner? Get together with your partner and do Exercises 1.1 and 1.2.

Exercise 1.1

Get together with your partner. Take one minute to think about the ideas that we set forth in Chapter 1. At the end of this minute look at your partner. As you look at him ask yourself these questions:

    (1) Is this person significant to me?
    (2) Do I care about our relationship?
    (3) Do I wish to improve my relationship with this person?
    (4) Am I willing to learn to communicate more effectively to improve my relationship with this person?

If your answers to these questions are yes, in some manner communicate this to the other person. You might want to say, "You are significant to me, I care about our relationship, and I'm willing to learn to improve our relating." You may wish to communicate this nonverbally—a smile, a touch.

Take a few minutes to share these things with your partner:

(1) How you felt during the exercise.
(2) How you feel now.
(3) How you feel about the other person.

Exercise 1. 2

Take a couple of minutes to think back on the significant relationships you have in your life. You probably won't need to go back beyond a couple of days or a week.

(1) Recall a time when you have held back when you really wanted to say something.
(2) Recall a recent incident involving a person with whom you have had a disagreement and how you looked away from him when you met him in the office, in the hall, or in your home.
(3) Try to remember an incident this week when somebody was doing something that almost drove you up the wall, but you didn't know what to do about it.
(4) Recall when you felt hurt, angry, or misunderstood.
(5) Recall how you may have vowed never to take a risk again when you attempted to "help" someone.
(6) Recall the hard work it was and discomfort you felt when you "needed" to smile while actually you were seething inside.
(7) Recall your discomfort when you saw someone giving what you felt was a phony smile.

Take a few minutes in silence to think back on these situations. Think specifically about what you felt, what others did, and what you did.

(1) Now share your thoughts with your partner. Describe the situation as you saw it, how you felt, what you did, and what what you wanted to do in each of the above situations.
(2) After you have both shared your thoughts with each other, ask yourself whether these kinds of feelings are desirable in your relationship and relationships with other significant persons.

Each of the situations you have just recalled and discussed detracts from your deriving satisfaction in your relationships. You may feel powerless to do anything about the situations. Very possibly you may want to punish others for making you uncomfortable. Chances are you have tried this before with little success, or perhaps you even made the situation worse. Clearly what you have done has not always been successful. Let's try an alternative. Learn the communication skills in this book and change what you do. This just may affect how others around you behave.

SUMMARY

For most people the degree of satisfaction experienced in life depends largely on the quality of their interpersonal relationships. Ironically, the norm of communication we learned in societies derived from the Western culture often precludes the quality relationships that we desire, relationships that include trust, love, respect, concern, openness, and understanding. We learned not to express feelings openly, thus a basic distrust of motives results. We learned to assume meanings and to assume others would not make a deliberate effort to understand our messages. We learned to compete for attention to the point of engaging in disruptive behavior. We learned to judge people as "the way they are" and ourselves as "the way we are." This view obscures the constant change that is the reality. This view obscures the possibility of influencing and being influenced to approximate a reasonable match between the way two people relate.

Attempts to build relationships using the existing norm of repressing feelings, not seeking greater understanding, competing rather than cooperating, wanting accommodation without a corresponding willingness to accommodate is futile. A new way to communicate must be learned if our desire for better relationships is to become more than wishful thinking. The task will not be easy. It will require great patience with yourself as you unlearn old habits and learn new communication skills. It will require great patience with others as they adjust to your new behavior. The habits you learned and the norm of interaction in relationships you have built over the years will be tough to change, but the quality relationships that you desire may well be worth the effort.

Summarizing Exercise

For this set of questions (and for the exercises and questions that follow in this text) it would be useful to identify each of you in some way so that I can communicate to you with greater efficiency. One of you take the designation "A" and the other "B." This doesn't personalize it much, but it is considerably better than your social security number or "Hey, you!"

Now, A and B, alternately respond to each of the following statements. As you respond include (1) the concepts you may have learned, (2) the meaning of these concepts for you personally, and (3) the implications of these concepts for you in your relationships. The other person should listen carefully and when the speaker has finished should add what he remembers and the personal meanings and implications for him.

A. Explain why people are not successful in forming the kind of relationships they desire.

B. Give examples of how we learn society's norm of communication and the consequences of this norm of communication on people.

A. Give an explanation of how one can build more satisfying relationships.

B. Give an explanation of the fundamental attitude one must have to be successful in building more satisfying relationships.

Now, each person should tell his partner how he feels about the task undertaken in committing himself to work through this book.

FOR FURTHER READING

References are grouped by subject on pages 208-215. For further reading on the concepts covered in this chapter, see references under these headings:

Communication Theory: Norms, Roles, Expectations, Interaction
Human Development and Normalcy
Idealized Relationships: Respect, Dignity, Values
Perceptions of Self and Others

CHAPTER TWO

Key Concepts in Human Relations

You will need approximately 50 minutes to get the maximum learning from this chapter.

There are several key concepts in communication you need to understand for the exercises in the following chapters to be more meaningful. Read with your partner (silently or aloud).

2.1 There are two modes of communication: verbal and nonverbal.

The verbal mode refers to the words you use as you communicate, the literal content of a message. The verbal mode is more precise in communicating ideas and observations than the nonverbal. Just imagine what it would be like to live our daily lives without the symbols we call words. (Recall the frustrations of playing charades.) Even people who cannot speak have their own special alphabet and words. Without words we would need to do a great deal of communicating in person. One alternative would be to draw pictures of the ideas we wished to communicate. In fact, the development of word-symbols grew out of the object-symbols that we find in the caves of our ancestors.

However great the precision of words, they are not specific in communicating feelings. The nonverbal is the most important mode in building relationships. As used here the nonverbal mode refers to body movements, facial expressions, tone of voice, etc. It communicates what we are feeling about ourselves, what we are feeling about the topic, and what we are saying about our relationship with another person. We communicate nonverbally what we are feeling about the message we are saying in words. Nonverbal communication is a commentary about our word messages and relationships.

What is significant about the nonverbal mode of communication is the power it has in building or destroying relationships. Implicit in the nonverbal mode is a command or request placed upon other persons by their learned reactions to these nonverbal signals and symbols. Have you observed the reactions of a conservative person upon seeing a "longhair" type? Have you observed how your own reactions to others differ depending on whether they are dressed formally or casually? Have you noticed your reactions when someone either shouts at you or turns away from you when you meet him in the corridor?

Nonverbal communication does not appear solely in the context of word messages. Recall the raised eyebrow, the frown, the clenched fist you have observed. Recall the clothes, the hair styles, the make-up that you have observed others wear. Recall the walk of other people, the toss of the head, the telephone call you did not receive. Each of these is nonverbal communication.

Experience the power of the nonverbal mode of communication by doing Exercise 2.1. This exercise combines verbal and nonverbal modes.

Exercise 2.1

Beginning with B, alternately say the following statements aloud in the manner described.

(Angrily and impatiently) "Of course, I love you!"

What message did you interpret from the words? What was the message you interpreted from the nonverbal part? Which message did you believe? Try another one.

(Angrily and impatiently) "Damn it, I'm not angry!"

Did you get a similar reaction? Try one more.

(Haltingly and hesitantly) "Oh, no . . . no . . . no . . . I'm not nervous. I, I, I'm okay."

Do you see the difference between the verbal and the nonverbal?

> Take a few minutes to discuss these two modes of communica-
> tion and the different effects of the verbal and nonverbal.

What was your reaction as you did Exercise 2.1? In each of these examples you probably experienced what is called incongruence—words and nonverbal signals that do not fit together. You received a double message. Incongruence produces a feeling of ambiguity in the receiver. What did the nonverbal message command you to do? What was your learned reaction to the nonverbal message? What did you do? What did you feel? In situations like this you may also behave incongruently in response by saying "Okay" while thinking "You say it but I sure don't believe it"—and perhaps feeling angry, frightened, insecure, or vulnerable. You probably found yourself attending more to the nonverbal mode. You probably also noticed that the nonverbal mode is not restricted to just the tone of voice, but may involve a change in facial expression, posture, and/or arm movements as well. This exercise may have reminded you of similar instances you have experienced in your daily interactions with people.

The nonverbal mode does make us sit up and take notice. We call some form of the extreme nonverbal behavior into play when all other means of coping with a situation are exhausted. Thus we observe shouting, physical attack, and crying. At another level we see labor strikes and the dropping of a bomb.

We have learned to give subtle nonverbal cues to describe our feelings rather than openly admit what we feel. The receiver of these subtle cues is expected to (1) notice them, (2) interpret them accurately, and (3) respond to them appropriately. This is fertile territory for relationship problems.

Most of us are aware of the power of the nonverbal message. We use it to punish; we use it to get attention; we use it to get out of uncomfortable situations; we use it to communicate affection. It is the how something is said, not what is said, that builds or destroys relationships. A final difference between verbal and nonverbal behavior is in the area of choice. You may be able to choose whether to use words, but your nonverbal messages will be communicated continuously.

2.2 You cannot not behave. Behavior has no opposite.

Many times you may be aware of the fact that you cannot "do nothing." For example, you try to clear your mind and you still find yourself aware of your thoughts, your feelings, your bodily sensations. You may also be aware that you cannot "do nothing" in situations where you are trying to be inconspicuous. For example, in a class when you don't know the answer to a question and are afraid of being called on you will probably scrunch down in your chair and try not to attract attention to yourself in any way. Yet, despite your best efforts you will more than likely feel very, very conspicuous.

On the other hand, when it comes to relationships with people you may have used "doing nothing" as a very convenient cop-out. For example, you are irritated with John. He didn't keep a promise (of course, he may have forgotten) and you decide to punish nonverbally through various cues—perhaps aloofness, clipping your verbal comments, and in general sending double messages. Finally, John gets angry and demands to know what is going on. The coup de grace is the innocent response: "What do you mean, what's going on? Don't look at me. I didn't do anything." In response to this all I can say is "foul." It is interesting to note how so many people in this situation seek to absolve themselves of responsibility for behavior of any kind.

In interpersonal relationships the behavior paradox describes a fundamental rule. In all interpersonal situations you will do some behavior whether or not you intend to. The responsibility implied in this concept lies in the message value of your behavior and its effect on other people. This responsibility will be clarified by Exercises 2.2 and 2.3.

Exercise 2.2

(1) Now, A, would you do absolutely nothing for one minute? Do whatever it is that you consider doing nothing. B, just watch A and keep time. Begin.
(2) Reverse the exercise. For one minute, B, you are to do nothing. A, watch.

What did you see? Were you able to do nothing? Very probably you were breathing, swallowing, looking at the floor, twiddling your thumbs, blinking your eyes, following the second hand on your watch, etc. Did you feel the paradox of doing when you were trying to do nothing?

You have now experienced the reality of the behavior paradox. Despite your efforts you could not do nothing. At the same time you probably felt yourself sending messages (perhaps annoyance at the exercise or the situation it put you in) even when you sought not to do so. As was mentioned in the discussion of verbal and nonverbal behavior, you may feel a choice as to whether or not you _say_ what you are thinking or feeling, but you always communicate nonverbally. You always send messages which express what you are feeling and how you feel about others.

Expressing feelings (verbally and nonverbally) is often equated with weakness or vulnerability and lack of status. In a strange sort of way this makes sense. If everyone else is playing the game, you feel very inadequate not to feel what others seem to feel.

"Are you scared?"
"Of course not. Are you?"
"Oh, no . . . no . . . just thought you might be."
"Well, I'm not!"
("I'm scared, but I shouldn't be. I'd better play games and not show what I really feel.")

Feelings have become a source of embarrassment. To feel is all too often to be different from the way others <u>seem</u> to be—and thus vulnerable. Child-rearing practices seem to build on teaching "game playing." "You don't hate your sister." "You're afraid of a little kitten? Come on, just touch it."

On occasion you may use this paradox to your advantage. Have you ever feigned sleep expecting others to interpret your behavior as "Do not disturb"? Have you ever punished someone by "not communicating"? Gamesmanship prevails and relationship problems build.

Your nonverbal behavior is precise in communicating feelings but is open to a wide variety of interpretations. What was the message you interpreted when a friend did the behavior of "not writing" or "not calling"? "Is he sick?" "Is he angry with me?" Anger is a feeling that is readily recognized, but the interpretation of anger can vary. "Is he angry at himself, at me, at his job, or what?" Does this cause problems? Indeed it does! If your nonverbal signals and your verbal messages are not in agreement ("I'm not angry!"), relationship problems may result. You are responsible for giving clear, concise, unambiguous messages. If you want a good close relationship, you must accept the reality of the behavior paradox and accept this responsibility.

Now experience the paradox in another way. Do Exercise 2.3.

Exercise 2.3

(1) A, for the next minute communicate in no way to B (without leaving the room). B, just watch A and keep time. Begin.
(2) Reverse the exercise. For one minute, B, communicate in no way to A. A, just watch B and keep time.

The minute seemed long, didn't it? Each of you tell your partner (1) how you felt as observer and as doer of the exercise, (2) what you saw your partner do, and (3) what you interpreted this to mean.

As observer in Exercise 2.3 you probably saw your partner as a person who was trying very hard not to communicate but who was trapped by an impossible task. You are a message sender by your nonverbal behavior. You are a message receiver and interpreter by your observations. As a message sender you are responsible for sending clear concise messages. But whether or not your messages are clear and concise, you are responsible for the effects of your behavior on others. They may confront you and request clarification. As a receiver of a message, you are responsible for understanding the message that was intended.

2.4 At any moment each person's perception of the world
is valid and correct for that person.

How an individual views the world and the other people in the world
is determined greatly by how he views himself. One's self-concept
includes all the values, attitudes, and beliefs he holds regarding himself in relation to his environment. It includes how a person sees himself physically and psychologically. It includes what the person would
like to become (his ideal self) and how he perceives others seeing him.
One's self-concept is largely learned. It is probably a combination of
genetic endowment, past learning history, and present physical and
social environment. As each person's learning experiences are different, so his self-concept will be different. As his self-concept is different, the way he views the world will be different.

From this perspective it is legitimate for people to see things differently. It is not legitimate for us to expect others to see what we see,
just as we would not want them to expect us to see the world as they see
it. As a result of learning, our perceptions may become more similar,
but they will never be identical.

This concept does not imply that anyone perceives reality; rather,
at a given moment a person cannot help but perceive as he does. To
deride or to criticize a person for relating what he sees produces
strained relationships, a lowered self-concept, and interferes with the
person's willingness to share his perceptions. And yet, how frequently
we do this to others. "How can you possibly like that loud music?"
"How can you like Chevrolets?" "Are you putting catsup on your cereal?"
"How can you be frightened of a kitten?" The chances are good you have
experienced the nonverbal demand to conform to others' perceptions in
similar statements or questions. The chances are good that you have
done this very thing with many people.

How did you feel when statements like those above were made to you?
Embarrassed? A big angry? Resolved to do your thing no matter what?
Righteously indignant? Such a large part of the beauty in people is that
we do see things differently. However, if each person's perceptions are
not respected, the differences can cause problems. Different perceptions mean learning opportunities for you, a chance to expand your range
of experiences. Try Exercise 2.4.

Exercise 2.4

If there is another person in your immediate environment, both of you
observe him or her for one minute. If there is no one else, look at a
photograph of a person or (perhaps better) an abstract painting. Observe
for one minute. Begin.

> Tell each other (1) what you actually observed and (2) how you interpreted what you observed.

Very probably each of you perceived something different, interpreted somewhat differently. You were both right at that moment. But as you heard the other person you probably acquired new learning—other possible perceptions and interpretations. You may not agree with what you heard, and indeed you need not agree. To insist on agreement may damage the relationship. Your perceptions are fallible. <u>You are responsible to respect the perceptions of others and to acknowledge the limitation of your own perceptions.</u>

This concept will be especially meaningful in Chapter 5 where the focus is on feelings. If you feel angry, at that moment you are not right or wrong; you simply feel as you do. Different people feel anger at different times. If your past learning had been different, you might not feel angry in a given circumstance. Correspondingly, as you obtain information or have new experiences, you can learn not to become angry in the same situation (or you can learn that your anger is appropriate).

2.5   There is no pure cause and effect in interpersonal relationships.

For most people the basic way to resolve conflict is to play the blame game. "I'm angry because of what you did." "You started it!" "It's your fault." A basic assumption of this blame game is that at a precise moment behavior or interpretation can be isolated for fixing the responsibility for conflict. "Everything was okay until you shouted." "I would not have done this if you had done that."

This blame game behavior comes from the "layman's" psychology which tends to view human interaction as sequences of sending and receiving. "I sent, you received; now it's your turn to send and I will receive." A diagram of this is shown below.

etc.

This way of viewing interaction ignores the behavior paradox. While at the moment your partner may be the one who is saying the words (sender) and you are the one who is receiving the verbal message (receiver), you are also a sender of nonverbal messages. If your partner notices, your nonverbal messages will affect what he is saying and how he is saying it. The communication sequence is more accurately diagrammed below. (The dotted line refers to nonverbal signals and the unbroken line refers to the verbal message.)

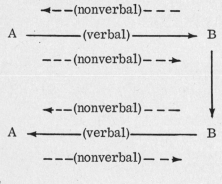

etc.

                                                      etc.

In other words, when you are a sender you are also a receiver; when you are a receiver you are also a sender.

The implication of this concept for interpersonal relationships is the idea of "shared" responsibility as opposed to "projected" responsibility. Projected responsibility is evident in the blame game.

> "Why didn't you tell me my boss called?"
> "I didn't tell you because you looked angry, and I didn't want to bother you."
> "Yes, I was irritated. Every night you start nagging me about everything that went wrong and things I should do before I even get my coat off. I get angry thinking about it before I get home."
> "Well if you'd get some of these things done, I wouldn't have to 'nag' as you put i'. Do you think I enjoy telling you? Besides, I don't nag."
> "You always nag. You're just like your mother."
> "My mother! What about your father? He's as sloppy and procrastinating as you are."

And so it goes. Who is to blame? Both! This concept will be especially important in the chapter on conflict resolution. But let's experience this concept. Do Exercise 2.5.

Exercise 2.5

Both A and B look away from each other until A claps his hands. Immediately, both of you look back at each other. Begin.

> Discuss the reaction you had when you faced each other again.
> Other than for the clap of the hands, who was responsible for the
> reaction of each to the other?

In Exercise 2.5 each of you gave the other a simultaneous message (though the clap of hands did confound this a bit). Relationships and communication sequences are much like this—dynamic ongoing transactions between people. Each person simultaneously affects the other and is affected by the other. When a problem occurs in a relationship it is usually a shared responsibility. It could have been your behavior and/or your partner's perception of your behavior and/or the behavior of both of you and/or the perceptions of both of you. Your behavior and your perceptions are not perfect. Both persons are responsible for their imperfections.

The question "Who started it?" may start a fruitless search that could hurt the relationship more than help if the point of the search is to affix blame. Exploration of what transpired with the goal of identifying what both persons might do differently right now is more likely to lead to an improved relationship.

2.6 Communication is a mutually influencing process.

For many people the desire to learn to communicate effectively stems from a desire to influence people. "I just can't reach him (her)." "There is no way to get through to him (her)." "Why can't he (she) see what I am saying?" Too often this is the basic problem. We seek to "reach," "to get through to," "to get to understand"—without reciprocally "being reached," "being gotten through to," "understanding." From this position there is no way to communicate effectively. This person will always have communication problems.

In the next few chapters you will be learning skills that may help you communicate more effectively and build better relationships with people. But influence is not a one-way street. The concepts presented in this chapter illustrate the reciprocal responsibility that belongs to each person in a relationship. You are responsible for the effect of your behavior on others. Correspondingly, if you would influence people you must be open to the possibility of being influenced. The way you view the world is certainly correct for you (at that moment), but it is not the only way to view the world. Others' views are equally valid for them.

As you learn to communicate more effectively you will find you can influence relative to your own willingness to be influenced. You will be expanding your world of experience as others share their experience. Further, as you change the game-playing norm of communication, you will feel a freedom in your relationship that the existing norm of communication doesn't allow.

SUMMARY

While the verbal mode of communication is important, the nonverbal mode is the power component in building or destroying relationships. Although we may feel a choice in sending verbal messages, we have no choice but to send nonverbal messages. Since we must behave in some way, others will be influenced by our behavior as they perceive us. The way others perceive us is their interpretation, their perception of the meaning of our behavior. Their perception is valid for them at that moment. They have learned to respond in specific ways to the behavior of others. How they respond to our behavior will influence the subsequent messages they will send to us. For example, as our behavior is interpreted as a signal for legitimate anger by others, their response to the felt anger comes back to us. Once a cycle of behave, interpret, respond, behave, interpret, etc., is established, it serves no purpose to analyze the cycle if the purpose is to affix blame. If the purpose is to identify what both persons might do differently right now, analysis may lead to improved relationships. This may mean that the behavior and/or the perceptions of either or both parties may change. The desire to influence must be accompanied by a willingness to be influenced.

Summarizing Exercise

Now, B and A, alternately respond to each of the following statements. As you respond include (1) the concepts you may have learned, (2) the meaning of these concepts for you personally, and (3) the implications of these concepts for you in your relationship with your partner and others. The other person should listen carefully and when the speaker has finished should add what he remembers and the personal meanings and implications for him.

B. Give examples and explanations of the purposes and effects of verbal and nonverbal communication.

A. Give an example and an explanation of the responsibility implied in the behavior paradox.

B. Give an explanation of the responsibility implied in the concept of perceptual validity for both the sender and receiver of a message.
A. Explain the dynamics of ongoing relationships including the fixing of responsibility for relationship problems.
B. Give an explanation of communication as a mutually influencing process.

FOR FURTHER REFERENCE

References are grouped by subject on pages 208-215. For further reading on the concepts covered in this chapter, see references under these headings:

Behavior-Communication Paradox and Values
Communication Theory: Norms, Roles, Expectations, Interaction
Idealized Relationships: Respect, Dignity, Values
Nonverbal Communication
Responsibility in Relationships

CHECK POINT ONE

At this time discuss your learning experience with each other. Specifically share (1) how you felt as you worked through the exercises in this chapter, (2) how you feel about your partner, and (3) how you feel about continuing the task. As your partner is talking, just listen carefully and understand. Whether or not you continue must be a mutual decision.

CHAPTER THREE
Attention for Better Relationships

You will need approximately 90 minutes to get the maximum learning from this chapter.

INTRODUCTION TO SKILL LEARNING

Building and maintaining relationships is hard work. It demands more than good will and good intentions; it demands <u>doing</u>. Some of the new skills may not "fit" at first, and you may feel awkward and self-conscious until they begin to feel natural. But if you settle for awareness without practicing the skills, your situation probably will remain unchanged. If you follow the book—explanations, exercises, plans for transfer of learning—exactly as presented, you should communicate more effectively.

In this and the chapters that follow, you will be doing various exercises that illustrate specific "ineffective" and "effective" skills. Before we get into the actual skill exercises, I would like to have you experience what you may feel in your initial attempts with the skills. Try Exercise 3.1.

Exercise 3.1a

Both of you get a pencil and a sheet of paper. Now each of you write your name three times. Do this very quickly. When you have finished, turn to the next page.

Exercise 3. 1b

Now I ask you to write your name three times once again. Only this time do it with your opposite hand.

    You probably had a reaction like "Oh, no!" when you read the instructions. You may feel similarly when you read the instructions to some of the exercises that follow.

    Let's focus for a minute on how you may have felt as you wrote your name with your opposite hand. Very possibly you felt uncomfortable, not sure how to grasp the pencil, conspicuous, foolish, unnatural. You probably had to think about how to form the letters. "How is the script a formed?" Perhaps the second part of the exercise contrasts with the first part where you probably wrote your name quite easily, automatically, habitually, without thinking about it.

    In the last part of the exercise you were doing a new skill, the beginning of a new habit. It is possible that when you wrote your name with your opposite hand for the third time, you did so with greater facility and with less discomfort than on your initial attempt. Did you notice that your partner's reaction was quite similar to yours? Take a few minutes to discuss how you felt. Would you feel similarly and would you need to think about the skill as much after three weeks of practice? Learning the human relations skills is much like this. With practice you will soon begin to make the skills a part of the "new you."

    As you work through the exercises in the book, you will be role-playing various ineffective and effective behaviors. As I attempted to illustrate in Exercise 3. 1, you may find some of the experiences somewhat artificial. This is very likely since both of you will know the role the other is playing. Despite these circumstances, try to "perform" as genuinely as possible in order to capture the full effect of the exercise. Understanding is not sufficient. Experiencing the "obvious" will make the concepts more meaningful.

ATTENTION FOR BETTER RELATIONSHIPS

We often employ double standards to attention as we do with many other behaviors. Perhaps you have experienced the person who is physically present with you but does not seem to be interested in what you are saying. You take this very personally as well you should. There may even be a tendency to want to get even. Correspondingly, each person in your world takes the attention you give very personally. Perhaps you intend to attend, but you may do so less well than you could. If you behave in a way that says to others "I'm not interested" or "I am not understanding," then for that person at that moment you are not attentive.

There are some very practical reasons for attending well to others. When you attend well you are observing the effects of your behavior on others. You attend beyond the words to the nonverbal commentary about the verbal message and about your relationship. By attending well you can better head off relationship problems before they get unmanageable, while they are still small irritations.

By attending well you can better share in the experiences of others—joys, frustrations, sadness, anger—expanding your own limited range of experiences. Maybe you do this vicariously as you watch TV or attend plays or movies. You can do this in the daily relationships you have with people. You might say, "But the people in my world are dull." Perhaps, but perhaps you have not attended to them to tap their full resource. Attending well is a first step toward the goal of "understanding" and all the benefits that come from that goal.

But let's get on with the task. First, I would like you to experience some behaviors that are probably ineffective in building relationships. The test for each behavior is whether it produces in others the feelings of being attended to and understood (and the feelings of trust and closeness that follow this understanding).

Exercise 3.2

Recall that one of you is A and the other is B.

(1) A, talk about any topic you want—business, politics, cars, clothes, hobbies, etc. B, pay no attention to A in any way. Doodle, look around the room, thumb through a magazine, but do not look at A in any way. A, continue talking until you become uncomfortable, then say "Stop!" Begin.
(2) Reverse the procedure. B will talk. A, give B a dose of his own medicine. Say "Stop!" when you have had enough.

---

(1) Discuss how each of you felt when you were the speaker.
(2) Take a few minutes to discuss what implications this kind of inattention may have on relationships with your partner and other people.

As speaker you probably felt as though your partner could care less. You may have changed subjects a few times in an attempt to gain his attention. Perhaps you felt a need to "get even." Clearly, inattention as listener doesn't do much for a relationship. Perhaps you were reminded of people who do this to you regularly. Maybe you don't enjoy these relationships as much as you could. Perhaps you feel reluctant to share something personally meaningful with the person who is an inattentive listener. Have you or your partner ever given this kind of attention (inattention)?

Let's experience another form of attention that also has an effect on relationships.

Exercise 3.3

(1) Okay, this time you go first, B. Again talk about any topic you wish, but as you talk under no circumstances look at A. A, be as attentive as you can as B is talking. When either of you has had enough, say "Stop!"
(2) Reverse. A, you talk without looking at B. B, attend as best you can. Say "Stop!" when you have had enough.

> (1) When you were the listener, how did you feel? What were you thinking when the speaker did not look at you?
> (2) Take two minutes to discuss the effects the behavior "not attending as speaker" has on relationships.

Now you have experienced the behavior of not attending as a speaker. Perhaps you have met many people who do this. Have you or your partner ever done this type of behavior?

How did you feel? As listener you may have thought that the speaker felt what he was saying was not very important, or that he was wasting his time telling his important thoughts to unimportant you. You probably felt a strong urge to shout, "Look at me!" Okay, inattention as speaker and as listener doesn't do much for a relationship. Can things get worse? Yes, indeed. Sometimes people can be pseudo-attentive.

Exercise 3.4

(1) Okay, your turn to begin, A. A, talk again about any topic you wish. B, as A is talking, look at him for a few seconds, then glance away, look at your watch, tie a shoe, look back at A for a few seconds and away again, say "I'm listening," etc. When you have had enough, A, say "Stop!"
(2) Reverse. Okay, B, now you talk. A, return the favor that B previously bestowed upon you. When you have had enough, B, say "Stop!"

> (1) As speaker how did you feel with the pseudo-attention that your partner gave to you?
> (2) Take a couple of minutes to discuss the implications of this kind of attention on relationships.

How did you feel as speaker? You probably felt frustrated. You may have gotten a bit irritated and had the urge to say, "If you don't want to listen, say so" or "At least have the courtesy of not attending at all." This can be particularly aggravating if, in the process of pseudo-attending, the listener says, "Go on, I'm listening." The inclination is to say "The hell you are!"

Again we see that like beauty, the effect of behavior is in the eyes of the beholder. Does this remind you of people you know? Your partner? You?

Yes, that was bad. It was almost punishing. Can it get worse? Possibly. Attention can be punishing.

Exercise 3.5

(1) Okay, B, you're up. Again, B, talk about any topic you wish. A, this time look at B but with a poker face, the face of the stern father or school principal. No words, no facial expression beyond the stern, punishing "show me" look. B, when you have had enough, say "Stop!"

(2) Front and center, A, your turn. Chatter away. B, have your retribution.

> (1) When you were the speaker, how did you feel when you received punishing attention?
> (2) Take a couple of minutes to discuss the implications of this kind of attention on relationships.

When you were speaker you probably felt like you were being punished on the spot. You may have felt put down and somewhat powerless to do anything except retreat or attack.

In the language of psychology you experienced an aversive stimulus, a stimulus that it felt good to get away from. There seemed to be no way to get out of the situation. Perhaps you kept talking faster and faster, finding yourself getting in deeper and deeper. When trapped like this, silent withdrawal often seems to be the only way out. This is one type of person you might want to avoid in the future. Were you reminded of someone you know? Your partner? You?

There certainly is not much here that would build close relationships. Let's see what alternative and constructive behaviors are possible.

Exercise 3.6

(1) Back to you now, A. Talk to B about something that is meaningful to you, makes you happy, sad, or moves you in some way. B, look directly at A as he is talking. As you look, listen carefully to what A is saying, but most important, listen to what A is feeling about the situation he is describing. In your face try to capture the feelings that A is sharing with you. If A is showing sadness try to express that very emotion with a frown or a down-turned mouth; if happiness, try to capture the happiness with a smile; if anger, try to capture anger with set lips, squinting eyes. Work hard at this. Use no words.

(2) Now to you, B. You share something meaningful as did A. A, try to capture in your face the feelings that B is sharing.

---

(1) How did you feel when you were the speaker? Did you feel understood? Did you feel the listener cared about you, about what you were saying?

(2) Take a few minutes to discuss with your partner what implications this behavior has for your relationship. If you really care, does this behavior show caring?

Most of us genuinely care about people who are significant to us. We are concerned about them and like to share in their happiness, sadness, anger, and frustrations. All too often we assume that the other person knows we care. Yet, ironically, no one likes to be taken for granted. If you care, express this concern and interest in a way that will show the other person that you care.

In Exercise 3.6 you showed and experienced nonverbal empathy. Nonverbal empathy is one way to show interest and care. Without your saying a word it is very probable that the speaker experiences the interest you feel. Recall that your nonverbal expression has much power to build relationships. Nonverbal empathy captures the feelings the listener perceives or those he hears described.

We do not share widely the things that we feel are important to us. We share verbally only with someone who communicates he understands. Let's try another dimension of attention that may convey the caring, concern, and interest that you feel—active listening.

Exercise 3.7

(1) Back to you again, B. Once again, talk about something that is significant to you, something interesting and meaningful. A, look at B as
he is talking and again capture what B is feeling (nonverbal empathy)
in your facial expression. But this time accent and punctuate your
attention by using a few words such as "yes," "I see," "okay," "uh-
huh." Seek clarification when you don't understand; ask for elaboration.

(2) Now reverse. A, talk about a significant something in your life. B,
as listener your instructions are the same as those above.

---

(1) When you were the speaker did you feel that your partner
was interested in what you had to say, seemed to understand
what you said? Each of you tell your partner how you felt.

(2) Take a few minutes to discuss the implications that this
dimension has for building and maintaining relationships.

Perhaps you have met a few people (probably too few) who communicate interest and understanding in what you are saying, what you are feeling. Perhaps one of these persons is your partner; perhaps it is you,
though probably less often than you might wish.

In your relationship, use these effective behaviors and help each other
to do them. When you do these behaviors you are not being phony or un-
real (although for awhile you may feel that way). You are expressing your
real care and concern, but in a way that makes the care and concern obvious to the other. If you don't care about your relationship, then don't
do these behaviors that demonstrate caring.

There are times you may want to show attention but you cannot. And
there are times when you may feel the other person needs or demands
attention that you are too busy to give. Can you genuinely show caring
when your own needs are interfering? The attention you might give in
these situations is likely to be what we called pseudo-attention or half-
attention. In these situations it is better not to give the attention. Let's
look at a way to handle situations where you may not be able to give attention.

Exercise 3.8

(1) Once again, A. This time start to talk as you did before about something meaningful to you. B, this time you have a problem that is
significant to you and is interfering with your being able to give the
full attention that A deserves. (You have a problem at work or you

are on your way to a meeting.) When A starts talking, B, you are to interrupt A with these words: "Excuse me, A. I sense that what you are telling me is very important to you, but I'm just not listening as fully as I'd like. I'm a bit involved with a personal problem now. Could you tell me later when I can listen fully? Perhaps we could talk right after dinner this evening?"

(2) Reverse. B, talk to A, and A, interrupt in a similar way.

---

(1) How did you feel when your partner said he could not attend as well as he would like? Share this with each other.

(2) How did you feel when you interrupted to say that you were not able to attend as well as you would like? Share these feelings.

(3) Take two minutes to discuss the implications doing this behavior has for your relationship.

Perhaps you felt a bit guilty for not attending as you would have liked, and perhaps you felt guilty for interrupting. But this behavior says "I care" more than any pseudo-attention you might give under these circumstances. Further, you affirmed your desire to hear and requested a definite time for doing so.

There is another not so obvious implication here. As speaker you could demand attention in a situation like this. If you do and the attention you get is pseudo-attention, remember that it just may be the best the person can do in his present circumstances.

Another implication is the possibility for changing the focal person. When your partner says, "Excuse me, A, but I'm not attending as fully as I would like . . ." your partner may well have a concern or some preoccupation that he'd like to share. In response you could say, "I sense that you have something bothering you. Would you like to talk about it?" Your partner may not wish to do so; accept this but leave the offer open. "Okay. If you would like to talk, just let me know." This way you show you care by setting aside your needs and giving attention to your partner. This is first-class caring which builds and strengthens relationships.

The situation described in Exercise 3.8 happens in different forms. You are on your way to a meeting and have only a few minutes. You are late for the theatre. You get a phone call that interrupts. The general method would fit each of these situations. "Gee, I'm on my way to a meeting. I want to listen to you but I can't right now." Or "I've only got five minutes. Can we do it in that time or do we need more?" But there must be a follow-up: "When could we talk?" Establish a definite time and place when you can give attention.

There are times when nonverbal empathy and active listening can do more harm in the relationship than good. When? When you are not interested in the topic or when you have another problem with the person and this interferes with attending well. These situations are described more fully in Chapter 6.

SUMMARY

Attention is a seemingly insignificant part of behavior, yet it is very powerful. Inattention as speaker or listener, pseudo-attention, or punishing attention all hurt relationships and have the effect of moving people away from you. Empathetic attention, active listening, and open communication when you are unable to fully attend build closeness and trust in relationships.

You and your partner have a choice as to which attention you will show with each other and in your relationships with other persons. Discuss this at length with each other. Will you help each other? Will you be patient with each other as you learn together? Do you care enough to show you care? Do you care enough to feel uncomfortable in learning to do a new set of behaviors? If your answer is yes, then I suggest you use the procedure called Systematic Behavior Change which starts on page 29.

Summarizing Exercise

Okay, A and B, alternately respond to each of the following statements. As you respond include (1) the concepts you may have learned, (2) the meaning of these concepts for you personally, and (3) the implications of these concepts for you in your relationship with your partner and others. The other person should listen carefully and when the speaker has finished should add what he remembers and the personal meanings and implications for him.

Give an explanation of the probable effects of each of the following:

A. on a speaker when one is inattentive as a listener
B. on a listener when one is inattentive as a speaker
A. on a speaker when one gives polite attention as a listener
B. on a speaker when the attention one gives is punishing
A. on a speaker when the listener gives empathetic, nonverbal attention
B. on a speaker when one adds active listening to nonverbal empathetic attention
A. of deferring attention if one indicates why he cannot listen, indicates interest, and sets up a time when he can listen

FOR FURTHER READING

References are grouped by subject on pages 208-215. For further reading on the concepts covered in this chapter, see references under these headings:

Attitude, Behavior, and Social Change
Nonverbal Communication
Relationship Building Skills: Attending, Listening, Understanding
Role-playing

CHECK POINT TWO

In Chapter 3 you had your first opportunity to experience behaviors that you might want to change. Hopefully you will feel a need to do the effective behaviors more frequently and the ineffective behaviors less frequently. This task will require effort on your part, an effort that may be extremely beneficial in your relationship with your partner and others. Tell your partner how you feel (1) about what has happened thus far, (2) about him (her), and (3) about continuing. Just listen and understand. Whether or not you continue must be a mutual decision.

SYSTEMATIC BEHAVIOR CHANGE I

Hopefully, you will attend well more frequently in the future than you have in the past. If you are like most people (including me), you intend to do more than you do. Unfortunately, we often get so wrapped up in daily activities that old habits return and we make excuses for not following through. Procrastination with good intention doesn't change very much, nor does it help your relationships. I suggest a method that may help you increase your frequency of effective attending behavior—systematic observation by your partner. I suggest that you record the frequency that your partner does the following four behaviors that were the focus of your learning in Chapter 3.

Empathetic attention as listener: When I am listening to someone speak I shall behave in a manner apparently consistent with the person's mood. I will mirror or reflect on my face and through my gestures the feelings that I observe in the person's behavior or that I hear the person expressing.

Active listening: When someone is speaking to me I will look directly at the person, observe his posture, facial expression, and tone of voice, and I will indicate by words that I understand what he is saying and seek clarification when necessary.

Attention as speaker: When I am speaking to a person(s) I will look directly at the person(s). I shall observe his posture, facial expression, and the effect of my message and the manner of delivery of my message on the person(s).

Deferring attention: When someone starts to speak to me and I am not able to attend as well as I would like, I will explain my circumstance to the person, affirm my interest in hearing what he has to say (if I am interested), and arrange a time when I can attend more fully.

On pages 33 and 35 are two observation schedules which you will use to observe the frequency your partner does each of the four behaviors. Each time you have a conversation with your partner, each of you will have several opportunities to function as speaker and listener. You may also observe each other in conversations with others. Keep the observation schedule with you during these conversations. Each time you observe the behavior enter a tally in the space opposite the behavior for that day. If you and your partner have frequent conversations during the day, you might defer making your tallies until after your conversation is finished. At the end of each day record on the progress chart the total frequency of effective behaviors you observed or the total frequency of conversations in which the behavior was observed. An example is presented on the next page.

TALLY CHART

Behavior \ Day	1	2	3	4	5	6	7
Empathetic attention as listener	卌	卌 卌	卌 卌	卌 卌	卌 卌 卌	卌 卌 卌 卌 |||	卌 卌 卌 卌
Active listening	卌|	卌		卌		卌		卌 ||	卌 卌	卌 || 卌
Attention as speaker	||||	卌 卌	||| 卌	卌 卌 卌	卌 卌 ||||	卌 卌 ||	卌 ||| 卌 卌
Deferring attention			||				||			|||

PROGRESS CHARTS

Empathetic attention as listener

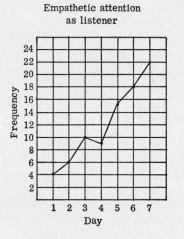

Active listening

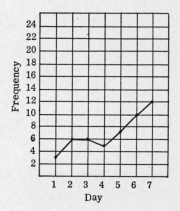

Attention as speaker

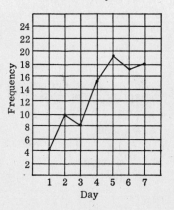

Deferring attention

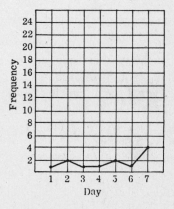

This will take a lot of effort and attention on your part, but the result is well worth the effort. Remove the next two pages from the book (or reproduce facsimiles) and keep records consistently and accurately. It would be most helpful if you and your partner would get together at the end of each day to share observations, to encourage and give moral support.

Two other activities might be very useful to you. Besides keeping a check on your partner, you could keep records on your own behavior as you interact with other people. You might also observe the behavior of others more closely. The tally sheets and progress charts can be readily adapted to both these purposes.

TALLY CHART

Behavior \ Day	1	2	3	4	5	6	7
Empathetic attention as listener							
Active listening							
Attention as speaker							
Deferring attention							

PROGRESS CHARTS

Empathetic attention
as listener

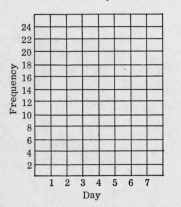

Active listening

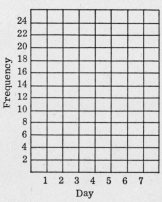

Attention as speaker

Deferring attention

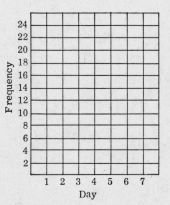

TALLY CHART

Behavior \ Day	1	2	3	4	5	6	7
Empathetic attention as listener							
Active listening							
Attention as speaker							
Deferring attention							

PROGRESS CHARTS

Empathetic attention as listener

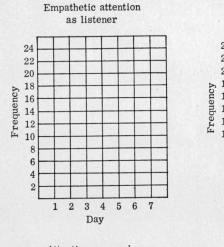

Active listening

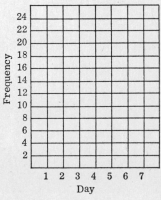

Attention as speaker

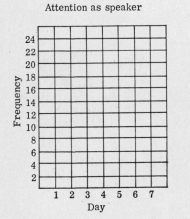

Deferring attention

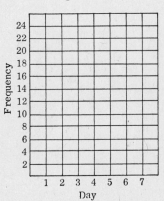

CHAPTER FOUR
Understanding Verbal Messages

You will need approximately $2\frac{1}{2}$ hours to get the maximum
learning from this chapter.

"I know you believe you understand what you think I said,
but I am not sure you realize that what you heard is not
what I meant."

When was the last time you felt that someone really heard what you had to
say? Perhaps you are very fortunate and have many people who listen
well and understand your thoughts and feelings. If you have one or two
such people, you are indeed fortunate.

Ironically, many of us often listen more carefully to the messages
that are unimportant (to the speaker) than to his important messages.
We listen well to gossip and humorous stories but few of us listen well
when the speaker discusses his relationship with us. We quickly ready
ourselves for defense in case the information is negative. Similarly, we
are usually embarrassed if the statement about the relationship is com-
plimentary.

Let's examine other kinds of habits people have developed that interfere with understanding verbal messages. We have learned to listen
rather defensively—listening with the intent of protecting our own positions. "I'll listen, but my mind is made up. The way I see the world is
reality. Don't confound my 'facts' with your opinions." These words
are seldom spoken, but they are often implicit in nonverbal behavior that
one observes when talking to another person. Two people who use this
set of rules will have communication problems. Generation gaps, for
example, result from defensive listening between parent and child. Both
persons in such a relationship are dissatisfied. Both feel misunderstood.
Both feel "I just can't get through!" Implicit in this kind of rule system
is wanting to influence without being influenced. If you have improved
your attending behaviors you may notice this more than you did previously.
You may find it difficult to share your thoughts when the listener does not
understand what you say.

These habits appear nonverbally in different forms. The listener may shake his head in disagreement before you finish speaking. Often the speaker interrupts before you finish. Some "listeners" will let you finish and then respond as though your comment had not been made. If you have been on the receiving end of any of these behaviors, you probably were pretty well turned-off and kept the conversation as brief as possible. Each of these behaviors communicates "I'm not interested" or "I didn't hear what you said."

One effect of these behaviors is the projection of responsibility for being understood to the person who is sending the verbal message. If the listener starts shaking his head in disagreement before you have finished your comment, you may find your attention diverted from what you were saying. You may speed up your comment, becoming less precise in sending your message as you anticipate the interruption that will occur. If you find your message was not understood, you may begin shaking your head when this becomes evident and sooner or later you will interrupt to clarify (or defend yourself). It is most frustrating to be put on the defensive when you are trying to communicate something important or when you most need help.

The more a listener does these behaviors, the less people are inclined to communicate with this person—except when a crisis has been reached. And then his response is often "Why didn't you tell me this before?" again projecting responsibility. The response to this question (usually unspoken except when emotions run high) might appropriately be "Because you don't seem to listen when I tell you anything. You know it all. When I tell you something that I feel is important, I am punished. You make my ideas seem trivial and my efforts unrewarded!"

Within a social system (business, school, family, club) if one individual does these behaviors, others will do similarly, at least with that person. If this person is in an authority position, even more persons will do as he does. The result is that less information flows to the top of the hierarchy where decisions are made. Without critical information from others in a social system, these decisions are far less effective than they could be.

Understanding verbal messages will be the focus for your learning in this chapter. We will again proceed through a series of exercises. In several of these you will experience the norm of communication that we encounter daily. In other exercises, we will take you through a series of steps to help you learn to understand verbal messages, to have your verbal messages understood, and to reward persons for communicating with you.

Let's begin by experiencing a bit of the real world as it now exists. On to Exercise 4.1.

Exercise 4.1

B, this time we will start with you. Talk about any topic you wish. A
few related statements will probably suffice.

A, listen empathetically and actively, but at some point when B is
talking, start shaking your head in disagreement. After a few seconds
interrupt B with "Yes, but . . ." and take issue with B.

B, when A starts to take issue with your statement, listen empathetically and actively, but at some point start shaking your head in disagreement. After a few seconds interrupt A with "Yes, but . . ." and offer
counter argument.

Let this sequence continue for a few rounds.

---

(1) Each of you tell your partner how you felt and thought when
     you observed the head shaking in disagreement.
(2) Both of you tell your partner how you felt when you began
     shaking your head and when you interrupted.

Did that seem familiar? Unfortunately, it is too familiar in too many
relationships. Very possibly, the shaking of the head was pretty easy to
do and interrupting may have been most threatening the first time around.
If you continued for a few rounds, you probably got into the swing of
things and fell very easily into the competitive norm of put-down—refuting
your partner's perception and having yours refuted. If this were real
world interaction as opposed to role-playing, you might even have gotten
angry, begun shouting, and/or withdrawn from the conversation. But
since you were role-playing, it may have seemed entertaining. Sometimes, however, role-playing can strike very close to home and "playing"
can give way to very real combat when the role-playing taps sore points
in your relationship.

If messages like those illustrated in Exercise 4.1 are "heard," very
probably the result will be a gradual increase in competitive, put-down,
emotional overtones. It is likely that there will be a reluctance to communicate further with the person; it certainly is not very rewarding to do
so. But when you cannot avoid communicating with this person, you probably will enter the situation on the defensive, watching closely for little
signals from the previous "conversation," immediately ready to counter-
attack.

This does not imply that you must agree. But it is important to take
the time to understand the other's position fully to see whether or not you
really do disagree. If you do, then is the time to discuss. You will have
opportunities later to do just that.

In Exercise 4. 1 you experienced not being heard and not hearing in a competitive situation. However undesirable this is, however devastating it can be to a relationship, at least there was some response. The person heard enough to disagree with you. There is another kind of conversation one encounters that makes you wonder if the other person knows you are present. Not only do you feel not heard and not rewarded for talking, but the emotional tone is one of indifference. Let's call this an <u>irrelevant</u> <u>conversation</u>. A sample of an irrelevant conversation is presented below. The conversation is such that each person's comments are completely unrelated to what the other person has said. Read these examples aloud.

A. "Where do you think we should go on our vacation?"
B. "Have you heard about Mary Jones' accident?"
A. "I thought it would be nice if we went on a cruise in the Caribbean. "
B. "She's in the hospital now. Probably will be there for a couple of weeks. Would you believe three broken legs?"

B. "I think George has a good idea about re-assigning sales territories. "
A. "Whatever became of Henry Ascot? He was a real good salesman. "
B. "If we re-assign territories, we may open up potential sales in the accounts that current salesmen have not been able to get. "
A. "We need more salesmen like Henry—charisma, drive, purpose. "
B. "Of course, we might lose a few accounts. Some of our salespersons have some well established personal loyalties. "
A. "These young salespeople we are getting now just don't have a tiger in their tank. "

The irrelevant communication pattern may be quite clear to you from these examples. But understanding is not sufficient. Experience it, recall what it feels like. Try Exercise 4. 2.

Exercise 4. 2

Conduct a conversation about any topic that the two of you can agree on. The only rules you have are:

(1) You must talk about the assigned topic.
(2) What you say must be unrelated to what the previous speaker said. It is as though you did not hear him.

B, you begin. If either person makes a relevant comment, remind him that his comment should be irrelevant.

Take a few minutes to discuss the experience. How did each of
you feel? Have you been in situations where conversations like
this occurred? What happens to participation when conversations are irrelevant?

You have now experienced an irrelevant conversation. You may have
felt a bit irritated at first, but probably you got into the swing of things,
joined the norm so to speak. An irrelevant response to a verbal message
despite empathetic and active listening refutes any sincerity that is
intended. You probably found your conversation tailing-off with longer
and longer pauses between statements. No one was rewarded for speaking. You may have found it very difficult to attend well. An irrelevant
response can also be quite punishing, especially if you feel that your
comment is important.

"Dad, I hit two home runs today!"
"Would you pass the butter?"

The long-term effect is reduced participation in conversations with those
whose responses are irrelevant.

There is another kind of conversation that is even more prevalent
than the irrelevant conversation. Most people have learned to be polite
or tactful. They may acknowledge the comment of the previous speaker,
but use it to turn the conversation in a direction they choose. Let's call
this a pseudo-relevant conversation. Here is an example of a pseudo-
relevant conversation.

"Well, the team won today."
"Speaking about today, you know what I did today? I bought
a new car."
"You bought a new car. Great. I'm glad you brought up cars.
I'm having trouble with my car."
"Speaking of trouble, our local congressional representative
is having trouble in his re-election campaign."
"Speaking of campaigns, I've been reading about World War
II and the North African campaign seems to have been the turn-
ing point in the war."
"Turning points. Have you noticed what they are doing at the
intersection of Highway 40 and Smith Road? That is going to be
a real improvement."

And so it goes. We acknowledge the speaker's comment and then select
a small "pseudo-relevant" part of what the speaker said to introduce our
own topic. Perhaps you understand the concept of a pseudo-relevant conversation, but this is not sufficient. Experience it. Do Exercise 4.3.

Exercise 4.3

Continue your conversation about the topic from Exercise 4.2. (If you wish choose a different topic.) Converse for about five minutes. This time you are to listen to what your partner says, but take some small part of what he says and use it to turn the conversation to what would be more interesting to you. In other words, acknowledge his statement but use it only as a polite way of introducing your own ideas into the conversation. To increase the effect begin your statement with a phrase like "Speaking of . . ." or "I know what you mean . . . and I'm glad you brought that up, but . . . ." A, this time you start.

> Take a few minutes to discuss the experience. How did each of you feel? Have you been in situations where conversations like this occurred? What happens to participation in conversations that are pseudo-relevant?

You have now experienced a pseudo-relevant conversation. Chances are good it was quite familiar to you and after you got over the artificiality of role-playing, it became pretty easy to do. Too easy perhaps. It is prevalent in so many interpersonal situations that you may not notice it until it is used inappropriately. Sometimes this kind of conversation may be appropriate and fun in moderation—at an informal social gathering or a cocktail party. In these situations do and enjoy. Pseudo-relevant conversations are particularly destructive when the other person has something important to say—perhaps about personal sadness, happiness, or frustration. In all interpersonal situations we must attend well and learn to recognize the subtle nonverbal signals that communicate "this is important to the speaker."

There are situations where pseudo-relevant conversations begin as fun but turn into competitive, status-seeking conversations.

"I'm going to Montreal for my vacation this year."

"Montreal, that's nice. I went there five years ago, as part of a tour across Canada."

"Canadian tours are fun. But my trip to South America was really different."

"You have been to South America. That's nice. We are planning to go to South America and Africa next year."

"Wonderful. You know I've been to every country in Europe."

"Every country. Excellent. But almost everyone goes to Europe nowadays."

"Yes, isn't that the truth. You know, I have inquired into making one of the first flights to the moon."

Even the competition isn't so bad as long as it stays in the realm of verbal combat. If it is recognized as such and not taken seriously as a prescription for action, little harm is done in "showing up the other person" (though neither person is thinking for himself). But this kind of competition is especially unfortunate when it affects others—our children, for example.

> "Little Johnny has three teeth now."
> "Three teeth. You know, our Mary was walking at nine months."
> "Walking at nine months. That is good. Johnny was saying complete sentences at a year and a half."

Perhaps this is fun to some people, but when it translates into "Come on, kid, walk!" it can become devastating.

At this point, let's change direction a bit. You are now aware of the kind of behavior that does not communicate interest despite empathetic attention and active listening. Let's begin to focus on what you need to do to replace the old habits, beginning first with an examination of the special problems involved in understanding verbal messages.

As the last few exercises illustrated, certain behaviors in a listener make people reluctant to risk sending verbal messages. The remaining exercises in this chapter will help you develop skill in being an effective receiver of verbal messages. Let's look at certain properties of words that make understanding verbal messages difficult.

First we must remember that a word is a label that we assign to an object or idea. A word is not the object or idea itself. Consider the word "chair." We could assign the symbol "x" or "007" to substitute for the word "chair." An old but very meaningful expression to illustrate this point is "A rose by any other name would smell as sweet." Calling a rose whatever you want to will not change the rose's fundamental characteristics.

In common usage the words "car" and "automobile" describe a four-wheeled, self-propelled vehicle designed to transport a few passengers. But suppose the object called "car" does not start on several very cold mornings. It is quite possible that it might acquire a new label—"that stubborn monstrosity." This principle is also illustrated by the assignment of nicknames. John Jones becomes Egghead; psychiatrist becomes shrink; etc.

As times, circumstances, and people change, new words are created for objects that previously did not exist (for example, astronaut, jet, movie, wankel). Over time different words may be used to describe an object or idea previously known by a different label. For example, certain characteristics perceived in a "young man" may lead to his being labeled "square," "hippie," "cat," or "buck." The question "Do you have a car?" can give way to "Do you have wheels?" A quick glance at

any dictionary will illustrate the many different meanings that are
ascribed to specific words and a look at a thesaurus will show the many
words that can have similar meanings.

The difficulty is confounded when one tries to communicate across
cultures and across generations. One culture may have labels to describe objects that do not exist in another culture. For example, certain African wearing apparel not found (until recently) in other cultures
necessitated special words—dashiki and caftan. Similarly, objects or
characteristics may be labeled in one culture but not in others. One
American Indian tribe, for instance, has no label for the color "orange."
It serves no functional purpose to discriminate and label an object
"orange."

The whole point of this discussion is that words do not have meanings. People give meanings to words. The meaning that you assign to
a word is no better or worse than the meaning anyone else assigns to a
word. You can never fully understand the meaning(s) that another person assigns to a word. You can only interpret what the word or sentence
means to you. As a receiver of a verbal message our task is not to
superimpose our own meaning on a message, but to understand as best
we can the message being sent. We should try to approximate the meaning the sender intended.

Let's experience the differences in shades of meaning specific words
can have. On to Exercise 4.4.

Exercise 4.4

Listed below are words that are in relatively common use in our daily
interactions. B, your first job is to say each word aloud. Pause for
a few seconds. Then beginning with A, both of you describe in some
detail the mental picture(s) or the meaning(s) that the word has for you.

table	freedom
father	cool
love	high
entertainment	tall
everybody	slow
fear	square

Take a few minutes to discuss the similarities and differences
you observed in the meanings of the words. What do similarities and differences in meaning imply for effective communication?

You have heard your partner describe the meanings these words had for him. Perhaps a given word had several meanings for each of you. This would not be unusual. If you know each other well, there probably was a certain degree of similarity in the meanings assigned to the words. The danger lies in assuming a greater degree of similarity (understanding) than really exists. Around every word, there is a connotative range relative to the meaning of the word to the persons involved. How fast is fast? How tall is tall? The word "mother" means the organism who physically gives birth (denotation). But it could also describe a warm, caring person—or a cold, authoritarian person (connotation).

Unfortunately, many people assume a certain righteous attitude regarding the meanings of words. Their connotation of a word becomes (to them) a denotation. This can be a tremendous source of conflict in relationships.

> "Hey, Dad, Pete got a new rod."
> "I didn't know he likes to fish."
> "Who said anything about fishing? He got a new set of wheels."
> "Wheels? Oh, you mean car. Why don't you call it what it should be called?"

If the listener had sought clarification, the meaning would have been clearer and the conflict possibly avoided. On the other hand the speaker could have chosen words that would fit the connotative range of the listener. Again, we see the shared responsibility required for effective communication.

A new organization (business, church, profession, club, family) will create new labels. This is not always an attempt to be different for the sake of being different. Sometimes this is a way of developing an identity separate from other groups. Also, this group may see real differences and label objects and people differently for very practical reasons. Their developmental experiences necessitate their interpreting the world differently. Yet within every group of individuals or social system, there are probably more differences than similarities in the way the members of the group originally experienced and labeled their experiences. Over time, the degree of similarity increases if their experiences are similar. But they will never be identical.

Let us return to the task—learning skills to understand the verbal messages we receive. Let's assess the formidable task at hand from another perspective. Try Exercise 4.5.

Exercise 4.5

Okay, A, let's begin with you. Make a statement to B about any topic you wish (interpersonal relations, sex, politics, sports, cars, fashions). Try to keep the statement reasonably short (15-20 words).

B, respond by saying, "What I think you mean is . . ." and then say what you think A meant. Do not try to speculate about why he thinks that or about why A might be saying that. Simply tell A exactly what you think A meant by the statement.

A, do not correct or verify B's interpretation. Say nothing in response but make a mental note of the accuracy of the interpretation. A, make a second statement. B, respond with "What I think you mean is . . . ." A, make a third statement. B, respond as before.

Reverse the process. B, make three statements to A and after each A will respond with "What I think you mean is . . . ." After each person has interpreted three statements, tell your partner how accurate he was.

> Discuss the experience with each other. How did you feel?
> What are the implications for different interpretations of what
> was intended?

Did your partner interpret the statements you made with precision? We have become accustomed to settling for less than precision. "Well, that's close enough." We are not always satisfied with others' understanding of our verbal messages, but we have not pursued it. "I just don't want to bother. It isn't worth the hassle." I ask that you insist on precision as you work through the remaining exercises in this chapter. Don't settle for less precision than you can get. Be patient with yourself and your partner.

Exercise 4.6 is designed to illustrate a means of obtaining clarification of words that are unclear to you or that may have many possible meanings to you. Set aside the embarrassment at seeking clarification that often occurs when we say to ourselves, "I had better not show my ignorance. I should know what he means." You are not showing ignorance. You are showing you care!

The following example illustrates what you will be doing in Exercise 4.6. Read the example aloud.

A.   "This has been a miserable day."

B.   "A miserable day?*"   (Pause)

A.   "Yes. It was hot. I had car trouble. My boss was impossible."

B.   "Impossible?"   (Pause)

A.   "You wouldn't believe what he had me do."

Exercise 4.6

Okay, B, this time we will start with you. Talk about yourself, your partner, or your relationship with your partner. Try not to make bland statements. Say something about which you have some feelings and which can have real meaning for both of you.

A, listen empathetically and actively. This time, however, select words or phrases from what your partner says which are unclear to you or ambiguous in meaning to you. These are most likely to be the more abstract words, words unfamiliar to you, words used differently, or the words about which your partner shows some feeling. Repeat the exact words or phrases that your partner has used. Raise your voice in a question after you have repeated the word or phrase. Then pause momentarily. Interrupt your partner to do this.

Reverse the process. A, talk to B about yourself, about B, or your relationship with B. B, seek clarification of words or phrases that are unclear or ambiguous in meaning to you.

---

(1)   Each of you tell your partner how you felt as speaker and as listener. What did you learn about yourself?

(2)   Each of you give feedback to your partner about how well he sought clarification. Do not expect perfection, but give feedback with the understanding that this was a first attempt.

What happened when you mirrored the words that you felt needed clarification in the manner described? You probably found that your partner expanded or gave more detail. Perhaps you apologized for interrupting. If you did, in the future don't. There is no need to apologize for caring enough to really understand what the speaker is saying. If anything, you should apologize for not seeking clarification when you should. Chances are good that the elaboration gave you a different perspective from your first impression.

---

*The underlined question mark is a means of stressing intonation.

Mirroring words is a simple way to obtain elaboration for clarification. You could also say, "I'm not sure what you mean by 'miserable'" or "Could you clarify what you mean by 'miserable'?"

Exercise 4. 7 further elaborates on mirroring for clarification. It will also help you learn to identify key words in a statement. You will mirror several words to the speaker, seeking not clarification of a specific word (although this may happen), but elaboration of the entire statement. Consider the following example.

"This has been a miserable, frustrating day. I have never been so dissatisfied with my job. Nothing seemed to go right."

There are several key words you might mirror for clarification: "A miserable, frustrating day. Dissatisfied with your job. Nothing seemed to go right." Or simple "Miserable. Frustrating. Dissatisfied."

Exercise 4. 7

Now, A, we will have you begin. Once again talk about yourself, your partner, or your relationship with your partner. As before, try not to make bland statements, but say something about which you have some feelings and which can have real meaning for both of you.

B, listen empathetically and actively. As before interrupt to seek clarification by repeating the exact words and phrases. This time when A has finished, you will repeat the key or most meaningful (to you) words or phrases in the approximate sequence they occurred in A's statements. Use A's exact words, not your substitutes. Thus you might say, "Work, frustrating, boring, just not satisfying." Use none of your own words, just A's words. Again, finish with the tone and inflection of a question, followed by a pause.

Reverse the process. B, talk to A about yourself, about A, or your relationship with A. Use the same rules as described above.

---

(1) Each of you tell your partner how you felt as speaker and as listener. What did you learn about yourself?

(2) Each of you give feedback to your partner about how well he chose the key words and how he mirrored these words back to you. Do not expect perfection, but give feedback with the understanding that this was a first attempt.

As you may have noticed, mirroring gives you a great deal of control over the content of the speaker's message. Mirroring "boss" will probably bring about a clarification of that word. Mirroring "good time" will probably bring about an elaboration of what was meant by that phrase. More than any other exercise the mirroring process illustrates the potential ability you will have to influence people. Sooner or later you will recognize the increased ability to influence that you will have as you use these skills. I can only trust that you will use this influence to help the other person or the relationship. Mirror to seek clarification and to help the person discuss his situation in depth. We will discuss this more fully later in the book.

There is another way to bring about clarification and deeper discussion. If you give empathetic attention and wait patiently and silently the speaker may elaborate without any verbal intervention on your part. Exercise 4.8 allows you to experience this process of showing care by allowing the speaker to experience freedom in whether to elaborate or not.

Exercise 4.8

A, we will have you begin. This time talk about something that happened to you that was happy, sad, or frustrating in some way. B, you will use no words. But you will attend empathetically with all the skill you have acquired. Nod understanding. Do not agree or disagree. When A pauses, no words; just communicate nonverbally that you understand, that you are willing to listen when A wishes to continue. If A becomes very uncomfortable, you may wish to say a few words in support.

Reverse the process. Use the directions given above.

---

(1) Each of you tell your partner how you felt as speaker and as listener. What did you learn about yourself?
(2) Each of you tell your partner about how well he communicated understanding and interest nonverbally. Again, do not expect perfection, but give feedback with the understanding that this was a first attempt.

Very possibly as listener you were pretty uncomfortable with the silence. That's not unusual. Most of us have learned to jump in to escape the silence, to rescue the person ("You poor kid.") or meet our own needs ("What's wrong this time?"). As speaker you may have expected to be rescued or to have the listener change the focus of the conversation to meet his own needs.

In a warm, accepting atmosphere, silence allows the speaker to experience freedom. But silence keeps the focus of responsibility on the speaker. Very possibly as speaker you felt a greater responsibility than you did as listener. On the other hand, if your usual style is rescuing, you may have been more uncomfortable with the silence as the listener.

In the last exercise the instructions were to empathize nonverbally to communicate understanding, not agreeing or disagreeing, not accepting responsibility, but allowing silence to keep the focus on the person with the problem. The speaker can learn to clarify his own thoughts only if he feels the responsibility to do so. This feeling of responsibility will accrue when he experiences freedom.

· · ·

Since this is a long chapter, this is a good place to take a break if you feel the need. The next part of the chapter is very important. Refresh yourself before continuing. Before you break, establish a definite time when you will resume the task.

· · ·

Now on to other skills. The next focus is on a process called paraphrase. While mirroring helps you identify the key words in statements and elicit elaboration by the speaker, paraphrase provides understanding in greater depth and communicates greater depth of understanding to the speaker. Further, the speaker hears his message in another's words and thus gains a new perspective on his situation.

Paraphrase is best described as telling the speaker what his message means to you. Recall that words do not have meanings; people assign meanings to words. Similarly, sentences, intonations, voice inflections, and physical gestures have no meanings in themselves. They only have the meanings you assign them. As you listen to the speaker you might say to yourself, "What do his words mean to me?" To do this you may need to project yourself into a situation that approximates what the speaker is describing. This is not always possible, but most people have experienced enough similar situations to allow some common understanding.

A verbal message in paraphrase may communicate an idea, a feeling, or both. The distinction is very important. In Western culture we have learned to get on with the job quickly. Thus we quickly focus on the thought, the idea, or the description of the situation. Seldom do we focus on the feelings. Somehow expression of feelings is viewed as effeminate in full chauvinist tradition. The typical manner feelings are handled is something akin to putting a hand over the mouth. "There, there, don't cry." "Hey, cool it. Don't get so excited." This response to expressed feelings denies the principle of perceptual validity. Given a particular environmental stimulus, each person with his own genetic background and past learning history can react, can interpret, can see, can feel, can hear only as he does.

This elaboration is important as a prelude to discriminating paraphrase of ideas from paraphrase of feelings. The focus on feelings must always take precedence over the focus on thoughts, ideas, or descriptions of situations, because a person who is in a highly emotional state is in no position to attend to a task rationally. Yes, you can focus first on the task after hushing up the feelings, but the chances are good that the feelings will reappear, necessitating a fresh start. "Oh, don't start crying again."

You must accept and remember that it is okay to feel—and to show that you feel. It is your task as listener to communicate that it's okay. As listener you must allow the speaker to experience freedom to choose when the focus can be moved from feeling to task. Consistent with their training, some people do not share feelings easily. Given this background, they take a real risk in sharing feelings. If you can communicate understanding and acceptance of these feelings, you will help your relationship with other people tremendously.

In the next two exercises, you will be paraphrasing statements made by your partner. In Exercise 4.9 the content of the statements will be ideas or descriptions as much as possible. As feelings are expressed include these in the paraphrase. As you paraphrase try to capture the meaning of the statements in the approximate sequence in which ideas are presented. If feelings are communicated, begin your paraphrase with the feelings you heard expressed or observed. This will require very careful listening on your part. Seek elaboration as you feel necessary by mirroring, allowing silence, or questioning.

In the exercises that follow, the instructions suggest that you use one of several phrases to introduce your paraphrase. These phrases serve to qualify the paraphrase as your interpretation, what you understand the speaker to have said. They work well because they leave room to disagree and help prevent a defensive response from the speaker. They may also, however, communicate use of a technique and may turn off some people. You could begin your paraphrase without these introductory phrases; if you feel more comfortable, do so. Paraphrasing without the introductory phrase will be no problem if you somehow communicate in your own style that this is what you heard the person say and that it is okay to disagree. Only the speaker can tell you what he means. Only the speaker can verify your interpretation. Like all people, both of you are less than perfect senders of messages and interpreters of messages. Your goal is to approach a meeting of the minds. Two ways you might begin your paraphrase are illustrated on page 52. The key words you would include in both are underlined.

With Introductory Phrase

"I hear you saying you are angry and frustrated and feel like walking out."

or

"I understand you to say you are excited about the opportunities available in your new job."

Without Introductory Phrase

"You are angry and frustrated and feel like walking out."

.or

"You are excited about the opportunities available in your new job."

There is no right way. Choose that which fits you and your relationships. Now try Exercise 4.9.

Exercise 4.9

B, your turn to begin. Make a statement about a topic that is of interest to you (sports, politics, literature, hobbies). Try to keep your statement reasonably short (15-20 words).

A, listen empathetically and actively. Seek clarification as you deem appropriate. When B has finished his statement respond by saying a phrase like one of the following that qualifies your interpretation.

> "What I think you mean is . . . ."
> "I understand you to say . . . ."
> "Are you saying . . . ."
> "I hear you saying . . . ."
> "Let me see if I understand what you are saying. You . . . ."

Use your words to communicate what you understand B to say. Do not try to psychoanalyze or speculate about why B thinks or feels that. Simply tell B exactly what you think B meant by the statement. Do not try to embellish or go beyond the original meaning. You will probably be accurate if you focus on the key words in the statement and ask yourself, "What does B's statement mean to me?"

A, when you have finished your interpretation, pause and allow B to verify or modify your interpretation of B's meaning. You may well interpret incorrectly at first. Remember the goal is to understand. After B qualifies, paraphrase once more. Pause. Allow B to verify or modify again. Paraphrase. Pause. Continue this procedure until B says, "That is exactly what I meant," and shows in his face the satisfaction at having been understood.

B, make a second statement. A, paraphrase, using the same instructions. B, make a third statement, A, paraphrase to understanding.

Paraphrase the instructions. Check with your partner to be sure he understands as you do. Then begin.

Reverse the process. A, make three statements to B. B, paraphrase using the rules set forth above.

---

(1) Each of you tell your partner how you felt both as speaker and as listener. What did you learn about yourself? About your partner?

(2) Each of you tell your partner about how well he interpreted the accuracy of your statements. Do not expect perfection, but give feedback with the understanding that this was a first attempt. As your partner gives you this feedback, paraphrase to understand what he said. No defense. No apology. No embarrassment. Just understand.

How did you feel? As listener you probably felt the responsibility to listen more carefully than usual. This is appropriate. You do have a responsibility to hear what the speaker says. Listening carefully may have been particularly difficult if you disagreed with some part of your partner's statement. The old habit of listening until we disagree interferes with hearing and paraphrasing well. Yet, this old habit must be fought and pushed aside. This does not imply that you must agree, but you must understand fully just what it is you are disagreeing with. The habit of listening until you disagree and then interrupting serves to exaggerate differences beyond the differences that really exist. If you do this, the other person will also follow this pattern. Together you will successfully obscure any common understanding you may have.

The process of paraphrasing will help you break this old habit. By including in your paraphrase all of the ideas that the speaker has presented, you will include areas of agreement as well as areas of disagreement. The pause after you paraphrase serves as a stimulus for elaboration—more detail, more data for possible agreement. Finally and most importantly, by paraphrasing in a manner that communicates acceptance of the other person and his ideas, you will be able to maintain a relationship despite disagreement on specific issues.

One other aspect of paraphrasing needs further discussion. When people first present an idea or a situation, they tend to do so very abstractly (i.e., they tend to present the idea in very general terms). Perhaps it is a way of protecting oneself. A listener can be helpful if in paraphrasing he moves the focus toward specifics and concrete details. In this way the focus of the idea becomes clearer—both to the speaker and the listener. Consider the following example. Read it aloud.

A. "Boy, I'm mad! Nothing seems to go right!"

B. "I hear you saying that you are really upset. The whole day was a mess. Everything you did went wrong?"

A. "It sure did. I overslept. I missed my bus. By then I had a headache. When I came to work, the first person I saw was my supervisor and right away he began to chew me out. It didn't matter to him that I worked overtime last night to help him out."

B. "You are really furious. From the beginning your day went badly. You really hurried to get to work on time. And even though you were late you expected a little consideration from your supervisor, but it didn't seem to matter to him that you had stayed late to help him."

A. "Yes. But I know better than to get consideration from him. He always expects people to be perfect, to bend over backwards to help him, but in no way does he try to understand other people. He's terrible, right? Don't you think he could show consideration?"

In this example, although the first statement is very general, the real problem centers very specifically on the relationship with the supervisor. Classically, the speaker is projecting all responsibility for his feelings to the other person. The air is one of righteous indignation which is very common when feelings run high like this. The rule of shared responsibility for relationship problems becomes obscured by the need to protect oneself. Notice the last two sentences in the example; the speaker is reaching out for support to justify feelings and thoughts about the situation. The most helpful response to this? Paraphrase!

B. "You really don't expect him to be considerate, yet it bothers you that he maintains a double standard—demanding without understanding. You feel justified in being angry and you want me to agree with you?"

A. "Yes. I don't think what I did was so bad. He could have just asked 'What happened?' What do you think?"

B. "I'm not sure I can judge what would have been appropriate. You were there and you seem to feel that it would have been helpful to you if he had just asked if anything was wrong."

Again we see an attempt to enlist support for a position on data that comes only from one perspective. If you really want to help the person and allow him to experience working through his own interpersonal problems, don't rescue or oversupport, don't agree or disagree. Try to accept and under-

stand how he feels. When we get upset, we often project responsibility
to the other person and obscure our share in the responsibility. As we
have seen, relationship problems involve a shared responsibility.

If you belittle feelings ("Oh, don't worry about it.") the other person
probably won't come to you again. If you take sides ("You are right, he's
a mean old person.") the person will continue to project responsibility
and not take action to help himself. If you take the other side ("You probably had it coming.") the other person may no longer share his concerns
with you.

Paraphrasing is one of the most useful tools you will encounter in this
book. As you use it appropriately you will attain great precision in understanding ideas and feelings. Through paraphrase you promote the experience of responsibility. As the other person experiences responsibility
he learns to help himself, to take responsibility for his feelings and ideas,
to avoid building dependency.

Read the following examples aloud. Contrast the paraphrased feelings
to the other possible responses that may be less than helpful.

"Darn it. Peter got sick again. I guess we'll have to postpone
the trip."

This: "You are really disappointed. You were so counting on
           this trip."
Not this: "Oh well, there will be another time."
           "Why don't you worry about others for once?"

"That teacher is going to make us do two hours homework
each night."

This: "You are feeling like that's a mighty long time."
           "You are pretty angry with the teacher right now."
           "You are concerned that you will need to sacrifice some
           things you enjoy doing."
Not this: "It'll be good for you."
           "That's a shame. The teacher must be mean."

"This is the fourth time I've rewritten this report. It just
doesn't come out the way I would like. That deadline is approach-
ing rapidly."

This: "You're frustrated. You have really worked hard on
           this report. Each time you rewrite it you discover new
           problems. You are concerned that you will not meet
           the deadline."
Not this: "Oh, I'm not worried. You will get it done."

"I'm pretty irritated right now. When I come to the desk to do my work, I find it cluttered with papers, crumbs, coffee stains. I have to clean these up before I can go to work."

This: "You are really upset to find the desk all messy and cluttered. When you have to clean it before you can work, you don't really feel like working."

Not this: "You aren't so damned neat yourself."
"Don't worry about it. You just get more upset."
"That is a pity. Some people are so inconsiderate. My kids do this all the time. I've told them and told them. I don't know what the younger generation is coming to."

"I really appreciate your willingness to take the time to work through this book with me."

This: "You feel real good about my efforts to improve our relationship."

Not this: "It's nothing."
"What did you expect me to do?"

The focus of Exercise 4.10 is on paraphrase of feelings. Try this now.

Exercise 4.10

B, this time we will begin with you. Make a statement about yourself, your partner, or your relationship with your partner. As before, try not to make bland statements, but say something about which you have some feelings and which can have real meaning for both of you.

A, listen empathetically and actively. As before, seek clarification by repeating the exact words and phrases. When B has finished his statement respond by saying something like one of the following phrases.

"What I think you mean is . . . ."
"I understand you to say you feel . . . ."
"I hear you saying you feel . . . ."
"What you are saying means to me that you feel . . . ."

This time use your own words to communicate what you understood B to say. Do not try to psychoanalyze or speculate about why B thinks or feels that. Simply tell B exactly what you think B meant by the statement. Do not try to embellish or go beyond the original meaning. You will probably be very accurate if you focus on the key words in the statement and if your thoughts are "What do B's statements mean to me?"

A, when you have finished your interpretation, pause and allow B to verify or modify your interpretation of his meaning. This is likely to happen if you end your interpretative statement with the inflection and intonation of a question.

After B modifies his original statement, begin again with the phrase "I think you mean . . ." followed by a pause. Repeat this procedure until B can say, "That is exactly what I mean," and shows in his face the satisfaction and excitement at having been understood.

B, make a second statement. A, you respond with "What I think you mean is . . . ." B, make a third statement. A, respond as before.

Paraphrase the instructions to be sure you understand. Check with your partner to be sure he understands as you do. Then begin.

Reverse the process. A, make three statements to B. B, respond using the rules set forth above.

---

(1) Each of you tell your partner how you felt as speaker and as listener.

(2) Each of you tell your partner about how well he interpreted the accuracy of your statements. Do not expect perfection but give feedback with the understanding that this was a first attempt.

In this exercise it may have been particularly tough to paraphrase because the content of the statements was very personal. If your partner made a statement about you, you may have been inclined to defend yourself, to apologize, or to show embarrassment. Maybe you had to stop yourself and really work to hear all that was said and to paraphrase for understanding. We have learned that when someone compliments us (gives us positive feedback) we tend to be embarrassed. When we get negative feedback, we usually defend ourselves. Understanding becomes obscured. Throughout the book we will focus on changing these old habits. For now, let me urge you to hear and understand.

However effective paraphrasing can be in helping speaker and listener understand, another tool can be even more effective—if properly used. This tool is called self-disclosure. It is a tough skill to learn to use well, but with practice it can be remarkably effective. The goals are the same —seeking to understand and to help the speaker feel understood. It adds one dimension that paraphrase does not provide; it shows the speaker he is not the only person to feel as he does. When people are experiencing difficulties in their lives, they so easily feel that everybody else is okay except them. Let's see what self-disclosure looks like. Read the example on the next page aloud.

Johnny: "This darned old math. I'll just never understand it. I study so hard and I never get higher than a C."

Teacher: "I hear you saying that you are really upset about not doing better in your math. You try so hard and just don't do as well as you would like. You are really disgusted."

Johnny: "I sure am. I mean what is the use of trying so hard if I don't get better grades. Mary hardly studies and she gets A's."

Teacher: "You know, Johnny, I think I know what you mean. I think something similar happened to me. Let me tell you about it and see if my situation is similar to yours. I failed math when I was in the second grade. I cried so hard. I felt so dumb. I felt like it wasn't fair. I really worked hard. Is that what you are feeling?"

Johnny: "Boy, it sure is. I feel like quitting school and running away. Did you feel that way, too?"

Teacher: "I sure did. It was just too embarrassing to face the kids after I failed. Is that what you are feeling?"

Johnny: "Yeah, they kind of poke fun at me. It sure feels good to know I'm not alone. You must have found a way to learn. You are a teacher."

Teacher: "They kind of pick on you and tease you a bit. None of this sounds very pleasant. I wonder what you could do about it."

In this interaction, notice that the teacher's first response is to paraphrase. The teacher realized that Johnny had to work through his feelings before he could consider trying again. By the end of Johnny's second statement (this may occur much later), the teacher felt reasonably sure that he had a similar experience. This he shared with Johnny, but then <u>returned</u> the responsibility to Johnny. Johnny elaborated further. The teacher self-disclosed once more and again returned the responsibility to Johnny. Johnny may be amazed that the teacher failed and yet succeeded; there is hope for Johnny. The content of the last statement may occur much later, but the focus ultimately will need to be returned to Johnny to decide what he wants to do about it. If the teacher had prescribed something for Johnny to do at this time, the teacher would have been assuming the responsibility.

There are many components to the effective use of self-disclosure. The situation you disclose must be reasonably close to that which the speaker is sharing. (For example, a middle-class white person who has never lived in a black ghetto probably cannot identify with the black experience in that setting.) You will need to listen extensively to be sure. At the end of the self-disclosure you <u>must</u> return the focus to the speaker.

Many people use somebody else's problem to talk about themselves.

"When I was a boy, I milked ten cows morning and evening and walked six miles to school. . . ." Here the intent may be good ("You are not as bad off as you think.") but at best it is an irrelevant response. Then there is another familiar one that is well-intended but disastrous. "Well, I'm not surprised. I had trouble with math when I was in school." This response gives Johnny the perfect excuse for not even trying. After all, what can he do? It runs in the family. Given a few responses like these, Johnny will continue to fail and will give up communicating his feelings.

You don't self-disclose to talk about yourself. You self-disclose as a check to see whether you can identify with the other person's situation. If you can, let him experience being understood in depth and let him feel he is not alone. Your experience will communicate "I survived—so will you" without your saying so.

Seeking clarification, paraphrasing, and self-disclosure are effective skills to understand another person and to communicate that understanding. They also serve to help us become better senders of messages. Often the messages we send are incomplete or ambiguous, especially when emotions run high. As you paraphrase and are paraphrased in return, you will learn to make your statements more complete and less ambiguous. By speaking more specifically at the outset, you will reduce the need for clarification. Thus, while these skills are practical skills for receiving messages, they also help you become a more effective sender of verbal messages. If people notice that you seek background information and/or specifics regarding a situation, they will slowly but surely provide this information in their initial efforts. Correspondingly, as you paraphrase several statements into a shorter sentence, the speaker will more frequently send concise, shorter messages.

Understanding and feeling understood are so very important in building a good relationship. However, understanding what another is saying is not sufficient. As you paraphrase and self-disclose to seek understanding, you must communicate that you accept the person as he is at that moment. Thus, even if you cannot understand the thoughts or feelings that he is communicating, you still allow him to think or feel as he does. "I really do not understand what you are feeling. Yet, I see that this is significant to you. Even though I don't understand, I will allow you to be the person you are at this moment. I'm with you." Seldom are these words communicated explicitly. Acceptance may be communicated nonverbally through respectful silence and empathetic attention. This is the "You're okay" said to a friend who has done something that is embarrassing for him. It is that quality that transcends the specific behavior to the potential and worth that is each person. There is a nonjudgmental quality to acceptance. We always make judgments, but it is important to remember that judgments are made from a frame of reference that may not fit the circumstances of the other person. You should not put down another's feelings—by disagreeing, agreeing, or oversupporting.

So now you are becoming a better listener. "What about me? I want to be heard, too." Indeed you do, and so you shall. If you use the paraphrase and other skills often enough over a long period of time, others with whom you use the skills will use them more frequently, too. This is probably the basic way you can change the norm of communication between you and the other people in your world. But you can expedite the process. The simplest and most direct way is to help others learn as you have learned. Perhaps you can work through this book with them.

Some of the upcoming exercises will teach you how to help others use the skills with you. The next exercise illustrates a specific process that will help others learn to paraphrase and better understand what you are saying. This will be especially useful with those who have not learned these skills for effective communication. (Hopefully you and your partner will paraphrase each other's comments without the reminder. If you both wait to be reminded, neither of you is accepting responsibility and your situation will remain unchanged.)

Let's call this process <u>requesting</u> <u>paraphrase.</u> This process can counteract irrelevant, pseudo-relevant, and listen-until-you-disagree-and-then-interrupt conversations. By requesting paraphrase you seek a closer agreement between the message you intended and the message the listener interpreted. Recall that there is a shared responsibility here. You may have sent your message with less precision than desirable, the listener may have no appropriate frame of reference to understand your message, and/or the listener may be reading his own needs into your message.

The most common way people request paraphrase is to project responsibility. A statement is made and the request for paraphrase is expressed. "Do you understand?" "Are you understanding what I am saying?" "I'm not sure you are listening. What are you hearing me say?" Any of these questions may be perceived as a test and may provoke defensiveness. If your request projects responsibility for understanding to the listener, his reaction might be an indignant "Of course I understand." Whether the original message was understood or not is irrelevant, for the listener is now busily trying to save face. If this happens, you have another task—to work through the relationship problem that developed by the listener's response to the way you made your request. We will discuss this in Chapter 6.

To avoid this possible problem, express the request for paraphrase by accepting the responsibility for possibly sending an ambiguous message. "I'm not sure I have made myself clear. It would help me if you would tell me what you heard me say." In this example, the responsibility for possible misunderstanding is accepted by the speaker. The listener can paraphrase comfortably. But the speaker must follow through. "That helps. Thank you. I didn't make myself clear. Let me state it another way." Or "Yes, that is exactly what I meant. Thank you."

The difference between the two approaches is important. Let's experience the difference by doing Exercise 4.11.

Exercise 4.11

In this exercise you will experience the difference between requesting paraphrase while accepting responsibility and requesting paraphrase while projecting responsibility.

(1) A, we will begin with you. Make a statement about any topic you wish (15-20 words). After the statement, say "Do you understand?" or "I'm not sure you understand what I am saying." B, respond in any way that seems appropriate to the request. Trust your feelings. Paraphrase the instructions. Check with your partner to be sure he understands as you do. Begin.

(2) A, repeat the same statement. After the statement say "I'm not sure I have made myself clear. Could you help me and tell me what you heard me say?"

(3) Reverse the process. B, make a statement to A. A, respond in the same manner as described above.

Each of you tell your partner how you felt with each of the two approaches. What implications does your reaction have for your behavior? What did you learn about yourself?

In Exercise 4.11, the role-playing may have confounded the "natural" response a bit, but the chances are good that the request for paraphrase while accepting responsibility was less threatening than the request which projected responsibility. Why the difference? Very possibly the key lies in our learned norm of communication. We must not show weakness or feelings. We must not admit publicly that we don't understand. ("I might look foolish.") A person who requests paraphrase "to be sure you understand" is requesting a public display of the listener's possible inadequacy. But if the speaker requests a public display to help him make himself clear, it's okay. This difference illustrates very vividly the defensive norm of communication so prevalent in our society.

With this process (as with others) the task is formidable. Remember that these shades of differences are important in developing an effective norm of communication. With the exception of your partner, don't expect others to help you very much; they have not learned. You have.

Sometimes you may become impatient, but hopefully you will persist. At times you will try to short-cut the process. For example, you might say, "Do you understand?" or "Have I made myself clear?" The answer may well be "Certainly."

The "thank you" is important. When a listener complies with your request to paraphrase he takes a risk of exposing misinterpretation. "Thank you" or "I appreciated that" lowers the degree of risk felt. In time the person may develop greater confidence and take greater risks.

When should you paraphrase? Do you always have to paraphrase and request paraphrase? These are excellent questions. For the next few weeks exaggerate the use of paraphrase to the point of absurdity. You have a new habit to learn. As you paraphrase and request paraphrase you will become more proficient and you will learn to discriminate when you must paraphrase and when it is unnecessary. Your individual situation is unique, but the guidelines below may help you. Perhaps the best guide lies in assessing when to request paraphrase. Sometimes you send messages that are very important to you. Sometimes you send messages that are not particularly important and you can settle for less than the best understanding. As a speaker, if your message is important, you will be very sensitive to misinterpretations (or to no interpretation at all!). At other times—when your message is not important—you won't be too shook about misinterpretations. Trust your feelings. When you are bothered, however slightly, at not being interpreted or at being misinterpreted, request paraphrase. If you are not bothered, don't. Experiment a bit. Begin by requesting paraphrase in all situations and then selectively omit it in some situations. You will soon learn to discriminate. Here the responsibility is yours. You know how; others may not. Be selfish, insist upon being understood. In a sense, that means insist upon making yourself clear.

Your feelings are also your best guide as you learn when to paraphrase. In the latter case, however, your feelings are responses to the nonverbal behavior of the speaker, the little signals that communicate to you "This is important" or "Please hear me." What are these signals? Often they are changes in voice tone, inflections, sentence punctuation. They are accelerated speech (as though the person fears not being allowed to finish). They are furtive and self-conscious glances to the listener(s) seemingly in search of support. When you observe these signals, paraphrase. Get outside yourself and observe the speaker. The expression on his face, the smile or the "Yeah!" accompanying being understood will be very evident. This is your reward in addition to satisfaction in understanding. Your best cues for discriminating when to paraphrase lie in developing your attending skills. These skills you must use all the time.

There are times when the paraphrase is absurd. Some statements or questions deserve direct answers.

A. "Excuse me. Could you tell me where the restroom is?"

B. "You are sorry for having bothered me, but you wish to know the location of the restroom."

A. "Yes, I don't want to bother you, but it is imperative that I know where to find a bathroom."

B. "You really didn't want to interrupt me, but you felt it was appropriate since you needed to find a bathroom."

In this situation, give a response. Soon.

As you paraphrase, you may feel very conspicuous; so seldom does one encounter this in society. People may say, "Are you using some technique with me?" First, paraphrase to be sure you understand the question. Your best response: "Yes, I am. I have not listened to and understood people as well as I would like in the past, but I sincerely want to. I am learning how. I want to be very sure I understand you. Could you bear with me and help me?" Again, if you sincerely desire to understand, you will not need to apologize for your efforts.

Whether or not you paraphrase, it is important that you acknowledge the speaker's message in some way. You could do this nonverbally, but it is preferable to acknowledge it verbally. Recall your experiences with the irrelevant conversations. If you decide that you understand the message and there is no need to paraphrase, you could reply with a short statement. "I understand." "I hear what you are saying." "Yes." "Okay." However, these words will probably not be sufficient if the speaker's nonverbal message indicates the message is important to him.

Thus far we have been concerned with paraphrasing single statements. Sometimes, however, you will get several statements at one time—either from one individual or from several individuals at once. In the latter situation, it is ideal to paraphrase the comments of each individual, but sometimes they occur so rapidly that this becomes virtually impossible. Even when you can paraphrase the comments of each individual it is useful to paraphrase the comments of several individuals that center around a specific topic. Consider the following example. Read it aloud.

"I want to take a field trip to the museum. I like all the art and old stuff."

"I want to go to the zoo. I really enjoy seeing the animals, especially the snakes."

"I want to visit a factory. I just like to watch all the machines. Hey, can we go to the automobile plant?"

"It seems like each of you likes different things and would like to go to different places. Mary, you enjoy museums. Beth, you would like to see the animals. John, you would enjoy seeing the automobiles assembled. We have a problem. What can we do about it?"

When there are several individuals involved, it is useful to offer a summary paraphrase to point up similarities and differences. Notice that the last statement kept the focus of responsibility on the people making suggestions.

In group interaction like this, each individual should learn to respect the opinions of others. A group leader has tremendous influence to establish the norm of respect for each person. Read the following example aloud.

> "I want to take a field trip to the museum. I like all the art and old stuff."
>
> "Oh, who wants to go to the old museum. Some people have dumb ideas. I want to go to the zoo."

At this point it is important to intervene to promote a cooperative norm respecting each individual, rather than the competitive norm that may result.

> "Beth, let's just hear each other's ideas. Each of your ideas is important. Let's see. Mary, you enjoy museums. Beth, you would like to see the animals. Both ideas are fine. But we haven't heard from John yet. John, could you tell us what you would like to do. Let's hear from John and then we'll see how we can work out our differences."

Notice, Beth was not punished or lectured in any way. You stopped her. But you quickly moved the focus back to the task, defining it in the process as sharing and hearing, not evaluating. Mary feels heard. Beth is not put down. John can share his ideas without getting ready to protect himself. You've laid the ground-work for understanding before evaluating.

Try Exercise 4.12 to practice giving summary paraphrases of several statements.

Exercise 4.12

A, this time we will begin with you. Make several statements (related) about your partner, yourself, or your relationship. As before, try not to make bland statements, but say something about which you have some feelings and which can have real meaning for both of you.

B, listen empathetically and actively. As before, seek clarification by mirroring exact words and phrases. Do not paraphrase after each statement. Wait until A makes several statements. Then paraphrase beginning with "What I think you mean is . . . ." Try to capture the essence of the meaning that A's comments had for you in the approximate sequence in which they occurred. Do not try to psychoanalyze or speculate about why A thinks or feels that. Do not try to embellish or go beyond the original meaning. Simply tell A exactly what you think A meant by his statements.

B, when you have finished your interpretation, pause and allow A to verify or modify your interpretation of A's meaning. After A modifies your interpretation, paraphrase again beginning with the phrase "I think you mean . . ." followed by a pause. Repeat this procedure until A says, "That is exactly what I mean."

Reverse the process. B, talk to A. Use the same rules as set forth in the instructions above.

---

(1) Each of you tell your partner how you felt as speaker and as as listener. What did you learn about yourself? Your part-ner?

(2) Each of you tell your partner how well he interpreted the meaning of your statements.

You had to listen very carefully here, as always. Your partner prob-ably had to give additional clarification after your paraphrase. This is just fine. You seek to be sure you understand, not to demonstrate how well you interpret. Be pleased with yourself if your paraphrase is accu-rate. But don't paraphrase with "looking good" as your motive. You probably won't be as accurate.

One familiar story fits the context very well.

Johnny: "Daddy, where did I come from?"

Dad: (Says to himself, "Well, the time has come. We were told not to give the information until the child asks. He's asking, so I guess now is the time.") "John, let me tell you about it. You have seen birds and you have seen bees. Well, it is this way . . . ." (A couple of hours later) "Do you understand what I am saying, Johnny? Does this help you?"

Johnny: "I guess so. I was just curious. My friends Pete and Mary came from New York. I was just wondering where I came from."

Sometimes we can save a lot of work if we take the time to understand the question!

SUMMARY

Every person deserves to have his verbal messages understood. Irrelevant, pseudo-relevant, and listen-until-you-disagree responses neither promote understanding nor make the speaker feel understood. These behaviors restrict the contributions a member of any social group is willing to make.

Understanding verbal messages is particularly difficult by the very nature of words. Words in themselves do not have meanings. The meaning of any word depends partly on the individuals who use the word. No word means exactly the same thing to any two individuals. We should aim for approximation of agreement on meaning, particularly when words describe abstractions or general ideas.

Several skills can help you assure a closer approximation between the meaning intended by the sender and the meaning understood by the receiver. If certain words are not clear in meaning to you, you can mirror the word or phrase that you wish to have explained in greater detail. You can say, "I'm not sure I understand what you mean by the word 'excitement.'" You can be silent, letting the sender experience freedom to elaborate.

Paraphrase is another basic tool to assure understanding of verbal messages. Paraphrase is best defined as a process of reflecting to the sender. "This is what your comment means to me." "This is what I understand you to be saying." Paraphrasing does not mean evaluating or judging, agreement or disagreement. It is important to understand feelings as well as thoughts and ideas. Paraphrase feelings and thoughts as they occur in sequence. The goal is to understand as precisely as possible and to allow the sender to experience being understood.

Remember that most people have not learned to work for precision of understanding. They must learn. One way to help them learn is to paraphrase their messages. In this way you will serve as a model, and in time they will reciprocate and begin to paraphrase your comments. You can also request paraphrase, assuming the responsibility for sending an unclear message. If you reward persons for paraphrasing your comments ("Thank you." "I appreciate that." "Yes, that is exactly what I meant.") they will feel sufficiently rewarded to continue.

It is not always necessary to paraphrase, but it is important to paraphrase and request paraphrase when the message is important to you or the speaker. Trust your feelings about the importance of your own messages and request paraphrase. Trust your feelings as you observe the nonverbal behavior of others and paraphrase their comments. If the relationship with the other person is important to you, it may be necessary to set your needs aside for a short time and really hear the other person.

Summarizing Exercise

A and B, alternately respond to each of the following statements. As you respond include (1) the concepts you may have learned, (2) the meaning of these concepts for you, and (3) the implications of the concepts and the behaviors for you in your relationship with your partner and others. The other person should listen carefully using the attending, clarifying, and paraphrasing skills you have learned. He should add what he remembers and the personal meaning and implications for him.

B. Explain the probable effects on a speaker when someone listens until he disagrees and then interrupts.

A. Explain the probable effects on a speaker when someone gives an irrelevant response to the speaker's comments.

B. Explain the probable effects on a speaker when someone gives a pseudo-relevant response to the speaker's comments.

A. Explain the probable effects on a speaker when someone mirrors specific words or phrases for clarification.

B. Explain the probable effects on a speaker when someone responds to comments with empathetic, understanding, respectful silence.

A. Explain the probable effects on a speaker when someone responds to comments with paraphrase.

B. Explain the probable effects on a speaker when someone uses each of two different ways to request paraphrase.

A. Explain the probable effects on a speaker when his efforts at paraphrasing are acknowledged and rewarded.

B. Give an explanation of the special difficulties entailed in understanding verbal messages. Address yourself specifically to the nature of words.

A. Distinguish between paraphrase of content and paraphrase of feelings. Discuss which is most important when both occur in a statement or sequence of statements.

B. Give an explanation of the times it is most necessary and most unnecessary to paraphrase and request paraphrase.

FOR FURTHER REFERENCE

References are grouped by subject on pages 208-215. For further reading on the concepts covered in this chapter, see references under these
headings:

    Acceptance and Understanding
    Idealized Relationships: Respect, Dignity, Values
    Modeling and Reinforcement
    Perceptions of Self and Others
    Problems in Understanding Words
    Relationship Building Skills: Attending, Listening, Understanding
    Responsibility in Relationships
    Self-Disclosure

CHECK POINT THREE

You have been exposed to many concepts and many exercises that may
have implications for possible changes in your behavior. If you can make
changes so that the more effective behavior occurs more frequently, you
should feel the benefit of better relationships. Take a few minutes and
tell your partner how you feel (1) about what has happened thus far, (2)
about her (him), and (3) about continuing the task. As your partner
expresses his feelings, just listen and paraphrase to understand. Whether
or not you continue must be a mutual decision.

SYSTEMATIC BEHAVIOR CHANGE II

Listed below are the behaviors that were the focus of your learning in Chapter 4. For seven days record the frequency that your partner does each of the behaviors with you or with others. Two observation schedules are presented on the following pages for your use. Enter your totals on the progress chart at the end of each day. Discuss your progress with each other each day.

Seeking clarification: When I am listening to someone speak, I will mirror those words or phrases that are not clear in meaning to me.

Showing respect through silence: When I am listening to someone speak I will respect his choice as to whether he wants to discuss his situation in greater depth. I will allow him to experience freedom to elaborate by showing nonverbal empathy and understanding but will use no words.

Paraphrase of feelings and thoughts: When I am listening to someone speak and I observe that the message is important to the speaker, I will paraphrase the thoughts and feelings he has expressed in the sequence in which he has presented them. As I paraphrase I shall not agree or disagree, explore motivation, or evaluate. My sole goal is to understand and help the speaker feel understood. Understanding of feelings shall take precedence over understanding the thoughts or ideas.

Requesting paraphrase: When I am talking about something important to me, I will ask for a paraphrase of my message to be sure I have made myself clear.

Rewarding effective behavior: When another person is doing an effective communication behavior, I shall thank or otherwise show appreciation for his having done the behavior.

Summary paraphrase: When I am listening to several people speaking, I will paraphrase the comments of each individually or paraphrase in summary as seems appropriate for the situation.

Acknowledge message received: When I do not paraphrase, I shall verbally communicate to the speaker that his message has been heard.

TALLY CHART

Behavior \ Day	1	2	3	4	5	6	7
Seeking clarification							
Showing respect through silence							
Paraphrase of feelings & thoughts							
Requesting paraphrase							
Rewarding effective behavior							
Summary paraphrase							

PROGRESS CHARTS

Seeking clarification

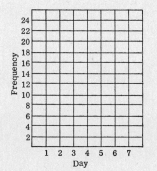

Showing respect through silence

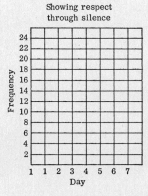

Paraphrase of feelings and thoughts

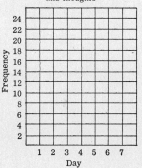

Requesting paraphrase

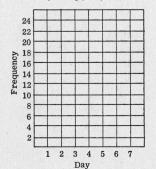

Rewarding effective behavior

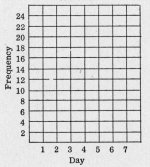

Summary paraphrase

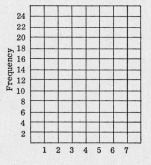

TALLY CHART

Behavior \ Day	1	2	3	4	5	6	7
Seeking clarification							
Showing respect through silence							
Paraphrase of feelings & thoughts							
Requesting paraphrase							
Rewarding effective behavior							
Summary paraphrase							

PROGRESS CHARTS

Seeking clarification

Showing respect through silence

Paraphrase of feelings and thoughts

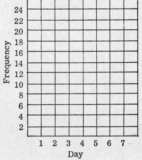

Requesting paraphrase

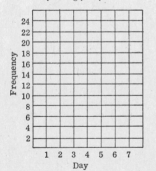

Rewarding effective behavior

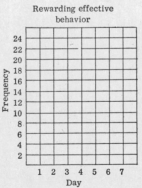

Summary paraphrase

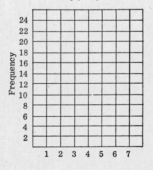

CHAPTER FIVE
Expressing Feelings Effectively

You will need approximately $1\frac{1}{2}$ hours to get the maximum learning from this chapter.

In this chapter you will learn effective ways to express your feelings. Expressing your feelings effectively and paraphrasing feelings are the basic skills you will need to resolve conflicts in your relationships with others. Let's begin with a review of what we know about our feelings.

In the beginning there was the child. The child responded to his world openly, honestly, and spontaneously. The child laughed when he was happy. The child cried when he was sad. The child struck out when he was angry. The child explored when he was curious. The child stared when he was fascinated. But the child learned:

"You don't hate your sister!"

"Big boys don't cry."

"Now shake hands with each other and apologize."

"Johnny, are you playing house?"

"Why don't you go in the house and help your mother like little girls should."

"Little girls should be seen and not heard."

"Of course not. You're not afraid of Grandpa, are you?"

"Don't be so curious."

"Quit playing with yourself."

"Don't stare at that man."

And the child wondered, "When I follow my feelings, I am punished or ridiculed. I feel and yet I must not. I try not to feel, but the feelings persist. I feel guilty when I have feelings. Nobody else seems to feel like I do. What's wrong with me?"

The child "matured." He learned to blame others for making him feel. The child learned, "Though I'm not supposed to feel, when I do feel, I must not show my feelings openly. I must be ready to deny my feelings lest I be punished. I know of no other way to deal with them. I cannot sort out my feelings anymore. They are all mixed. I have difficulty talking about my feelings. I don't know how to label them. I have feelings about myself when I attempt to talk about them."

Thus many of us were reared. We were short-changed in the one area that is so important in deriving satisfaction or dissatisfaction in our relationships with people—our ability to deal with our own feelings and those of others. The norm of communication we learned warned us to repress our feelings. A basic assumption of this norm is that the perfectly "rational" person is desirable and possible—if feelings are repressed. By some mysterious process feelings will go away. Like so many things, this too is incompatible with reality. The idea of repressing feelings and feeling guilty if we cannot repress them is the ultimate in paradox. By this dictum we should feel guilty for feeling guilty! In action it translates into "Don't express your feelings directly." It is okay if you do so indirectly. Your expression of feelings should be sufficiently ambiguous to keep others guessing. Since we are not supposed to feel we must punish others for provoking feelings in us. Of course, they will reciprocate since we have provoked feelings in them.

We have very good reasons for not wanting to express our feelings. "I don't want to hurt his feelings. His friendship is so important to me. I don't want to lose it." And so the perfect martyr is born. Over days, weeks, years the relationship that is so important gradually becomes worse. The feelings show up indirectly, but neither person calls it to the attention of the other. "I might hurt his feelings." Indeed, you might hurt his feelings. It might be more accura·e to say "I'm not sure I can handle his reaction" rather than "I'm afraid i might hurt his feelings." It seems more likely that felt inadequacies in dealing with feelings are projected to others who become "less capable." Inside each of us there are those little voices that might sound like the following:

"I'm upset with Mary, but I'm afraid that if I tell her she will become angry. If she becomes angry then I will become angry. That's the only way I know to defend myself." (This is probably an honest voice.)

"But Mary is so sensitive. She gets so upset. She just can't handle it. I guess I won't tell her directly, I will just hide my feelings. I will protect her." (Rationalization and projection begins.)

The second inner voice begins to project the responsibility, but there is a certain reality in the rationalization. Many of us have not learned (1) to accept our feelings, (2) to express our feelings directly, or (3) to deal with feelings expressed by others. These are the learning goals for this chapter. The task will not be easy, but if you wish more satisfying relationships, it may be worth the price. Nothing expresses the care you might feel about a relationship more than caring enough to express your feelings and to create an environment in which the other person feels free to express his feelings.

Exercise 5.1 will help you recall how if feels to feel. This exercise seems fairly easy, but it may make you uncomfortable. Just remember, your feelings are legitimate; they're okay. Enjoy getting in touch with your feelings. Do Exercise 5.1.

Exercise 5.1

Turn your chairs so that you face each other directly. Using no words, observe each other for one minute. Decide which of you will keep time. During this minute just respond to each other, paying particular attention to your feelings. At the end of this minute, each of you will tell your partner (1) what feeling or feelings you experienced during the minute and (2) how you felt about your feelings.

A, begin. Talk only about yourself and your feelings. No exceptions. Begin with "I felt . . . ."

As your partner expresses his feelings, seek clarification as you feel the need or allow your partner to elaborate by allowing respectful silence. Paraphrase his feelings, not agreeing or disagreeing, just understanding and helping him feel understood.

Paraphrase the instructions. Check with your partner to be sure he understands as you do.

> Each of you tell your partner how you felt during the experience. What did you learn about yourself? About your partner? Paraphrase each other's feelings and thoughts.

That minute sure was long. You probably felt uncomfortable at the "trap" imposed by the structure of the exercise—no words, just respond to each other. You may have felt the urge to say something. When you could not do this, you probably changed your nonverbal behavior several times. You may also have had feelings about the feelings you were having! Whatever your feelings were, they were okay. You should have felt what you did. Your feelings are very important. They are a large part of what makes you a human being—feeling and awareness of feelings.

You may have had difficulty expressing your feelings. We have learned not to talk about them. Expressing your feelings was probably easier if your partner paraphrased in a way that communicated it was okay to feel, that he accepted your feelings.

Now that you are in touch with your feelings, the next step is to learn to express your feelings in ways that are clear messages easily received by the listener. Basically there are four ways you can express your feelings: directly, indirectly, directly with metaphor, and physically.

Indirect expression of feelings is characterized by not fully accepting the feeling, communicating the feeling ambiguously (leaving it open to several interpretations), and projecting responsibility to the listener. Indirect expression of feelings is a favorite form of punishment when there is a relationship problem. Positive feelings can be expressed indirectly as well. Some examples of indirect expression of feelings are exemplified below:

> "Can't you even get home on time?"

> "That was a wonderful evening."

> "Will you stop that!"

> "Whenever there is nobody else to kick around, there is always me."

In each of these statements, one can infer that the speaker was feeling something, but the feeling state must be inferred by the listener. Responsibility is projected to the listener. Thus the speaker can easily protect himself and punish further by another indirect expression of feelings. Read the following exchange aloud.

A. "Whenever there is nobody else to kick around, there is always me."
B. "What's bugging you?"
A. "Who me? Why nothing. What makes you think that?"

Pity the poor listener. The words and the nonverbal messages just do not match. As we have seen, the power to build or destroy relationships is in nonverbal behavior. Clearly, there is a relationship problem here now if there was not initially. But the listener, having been punished, will wait his turn and perhaps express his feelings indirectly, too. He could choose to express his feelings physically, another indirect form. He could frown, raise and roll his eyes, give the silent treatment, shake his head, etc. Here, too, the responsibility is projected to the observer. If asked "What's bugging you?" he might respond with "Who me? Why nothing. What makes you think that something is bugging me?"

The intent of both indirect and physical expression of feelings is not always to punish, but that is often the effect. These may be the best ways a person knows to express his feelings. (Recall he has been taught that he is not supposed to feel.) But even if the intention is not to punish and produce tensions in relationships, the effect of not directly communicating remains the same.

There are two alternatives available to us. We can express our feelings directly or we can express them in metaphor. Several characteristics make these more effective. The responsibility for feeling is accepted by the speaker. The message is clear; there is no inconsistency between the words and the nonverbal behavior. Consider some examples:

Direct Expression

"I'm angry."
"I feel lonely."
"I'm frightened."
"I'm confused."
"I feel rejected."

Expression in Metaphor

"I feel like something the dog dragged in."
"I feel like the walls are coming in on me."
"I feel like a child in a room full of adults."
"I feel like I'm in the middle of a four-lane highway at five o'clock."

Both of these "acceptable" forms begin with the pronoun "I." Compare the direct expressions with these:

"You make me angry."   "He makes me angry."
"You scare me."   "He scares me."

The speaker of these statements projects the responsibility for the feeling to another person. This is an important difference. By accepting or owning your own feelings with the pronoun "I," you make your statements more receivable. Further, "I" statements describe more accurately the true state of events. All you know is that you feel. You can infer that the behavior of the other person influenced your feeling, but you may have misinterpreted or overreacted to his behavior.

Both of these "acceptable" forms include some description of the feelings. This should be a label that is fairly clear in meaning—love, anger, attraction, boredom, curiosity, fear, frustration, hope, hurt, joy, rejection, relief, embarrassment, trust, vulnerability, etc. Sometimes the metaphor can be better or equally effective. The critical aspects are narrowing the range of possible meanings to approximate a "meeting of the feelings" and accepting the feeling as yours.

Let's learn to discriminate between direct expression of feelings, direct expression with metaphor, and indirect expression. On to Exercise 5. 2.

Exercise 5. 2

Listed below are statements that one might hear in different interpersonal contexts. Read each statement aloud trying to capture the feelings implied in the statement. Then discuss the statement and decide whether you feel the statement expresses (1) feeling in metaphor, (2) direct expression of feeling, or (3) indirect expression of feeling. As you discuss each statement, attend to each other, seek clarification, and paraphrase each other's comments. (Yes, paraphrase; no exceptions. You learn a new habit by practice.) Do this for each statement. Come to a mutual agreement, a decision that both of you can be comfortable with. If there is disagreement, seek greater elaboration from your partner. Mark "FM" (feeling metaphor), "FD" (feeling direct), or "FI" (feeling indirect) in the space to the left of the item.

Before you begin, one of you paraphrase the instructions to be sure you understand. From this point, I will no longer designate which of you should begin. This you will need to decide between you. I trust that you will be honest and express your discontent with your partner if you feel that you are beginning too often. No simple rule like "ladies first. " This must be a conscious decision-making experience. Further, I admonish you not to let one person make the decision, nor to use anything so devoid of responsibility as flipping a coin.

_____(a) "Man, that's cool!"

_____(b) "Where are we going to get the money?"

_____(c) "I feel rejected by what you just did!"

_____(d) "Oh, what's the use. "

_____(e) "I'm really discouraged by what happened today. "

_____(f) "I like it very much, but you shouldn't have spent the money. "

_____(g) "I feel like I'm walking on a cloud. "

_____(h) "I feel like I've got an albatross around my neck. "

_____(i) "When I see it, I believe it. "

_____(j) "I'm very frightened at what he might do. "

_____(k) "The whole situation is frightening. "

> (1) Each of you tell your partner how you felt as you used the process set forth in the instructions. Did you feel like disagreeing, interrupting, and perhaps arguing?
>
> (2) Each of you tell your partner how well he followed the instructions and used the skills you have learned to date. By this time, you can expect a bit more perfection, so be as candid and helpful as you can. Express your feelings directly.

My interpretation of the statements in Exercise 5. 2 is as follows:

(a) Clearly an indirect expression of feelings. The "I" component and the direct labeling of inner state are missing. Feelings are in evidence, but the object is labeled.

(b) Again, indirect expression of feelings. No feeling is labeled. The feeling is not owned by the speaker.

(c) Direct expression of feelings. "I feel rejected." All components present.

(d) Indirect expression of feelings. Feeling is not owned, nor directly labeled. Take special note of this one. This is a real sympathy elicitor; all hope is gone.

(e) Direct expression. All components are present. Contrast this with (d). Discouragement without despair.

(f) Indirect expression of feelings. You may well take issue with me here. It just seems that the label "like" is directed more to the object than to the inner state. The latter part is clearly an indirect expression, not particularly effective since it rather dampens the giver's satisfaction.

(g) Expresses feelings via metaphor.

(h) Expresses feelings via metaphor.

(i) Indirect expression of feelings. A feeling (probably distrust) is not directly expressed.

(j) Direct expression of feelings. This stands in contrast to (k).

(k) Indirect expression of feelings. Here the feeling is not owned but assigned to the object or situation.

Direct expression of feelings is preferred. Hopefully, the next exercise will help you understand this through experience as well as logic. It is not easy to express feelings directly. We have not learned to do so and we risk becoming vulnerable through removal of the mask that accompanies either the indirect or the physical expression of feelings. With direct expression of feelings you present your inner state for examination.

A relationship problem may be the result of (1) the effects of your behavior, (2) the other person's behavior, (3) your perception, and/or

(4) the other person's perception. Relationship problems are impossible to resolve effectively unless each person is willing to acknowledge the fallibility of his perception and behavior. This responsibility is met by direct expression of feelings. As you acknowledge your responsibility, you increase the probability that the other person will do likewise. In most relationships, the best you can expect is indirect expression of feelings. As you express your feelings directly you can help others do the same.

Is the direct expression of feelings more effective? Experience the contrast for yourself. Do Exercise 5.3.

Exercise 5.3

In this exercise you will experience the effect of direct and indirect expression of feelings. Listed below are pairs of statements. One statement expresses feelings directly. The other expresses feelings indirectly. Alternately read each pair of statements.

Decide which of you will begin. (A mutual decision-making process, what else?). Whoever begins, read the first statement of the pair, trying to capture the feelings implied in the statement. Pause. Listener, do not respond to the statement, but just notice how you felt. Share this feeling with your partner. Paraphrase your partner's feelings as he shares them. Then read the second statement of the pair.

One of you paraphrase the instructions before you begin.

(a) "You are a fun person to be with."
(b) "I really enjoy talking with you."

(a) "I'm angry because you just interrupted me."
(b) "You are very rude."

(a) "I'm disappointed and angry that you have to work again tonight, John."
(b) "Don't worry about me. What does it matter that you have to work every night and leave me home with the children?"

(a) "I don't know how fast we are going, but I'm scared right now."
(b) "How fast are we going?"

(a) No words, just frown and look puzzled.
(b) "I'm confused. I don't understand that concept."

(1) Each of you tell your partner how you felt during the exercise. What did you learn about yourself? About your partner?

(2) Each of you tell your partner how well he attended, sought clarification, and paraphrased your feelings.

(3) Each of you tell your partner how well he expressed his feelings in reaction to the statements. Were all reactions direct expression of feelings?

I can but speculate about your reactions to each statement, but hopefully you experienced the benefits that accompany the direct expression of feelings. In your relationship with each other, I hope that each of you will make direct expression of feelings the rule rather than the exception.

The direct expression of feelings in itself is not sufficient. Two additional ingredients must be present to make the direct expression of feelings most effective in working through relationship problems. First, it is important that you accompany the direct expression of your feelings with a description of the situation that you feel influenced you to feel the way you do. Second, you should include a prescription of what the other person could do differently to help your relationship with him.

Direct Expression

"Mary, I'm irritated."

Plus Behavioral Description

"Mary, I'm irritated. You began to speak before I finished."

Plus Behavioral Prescription

"Mary, I'm irritated. You began to speak before I finished. It would help me if you could wait until I finish and maybe ask if I'm finished before you respond."

In the first situation, the direct expression of feelings assumes some responsibility but still projects most of it. "It's up to you to find out what I'm angry about and what you can do about it." The second accepts a bit more responsibility but still projects some. "You know how I feel and what was involved in my feeling, but it is up to you to discover what would help the situation." The third assumes most of the responsibility and reduces ambiguity a bit more.

One component is still missing—the opening for negotiation. "While this is the way I felt, perhaps I was overly sensitive. I may have given the impression that I was finished speaking. As a result you probably felt it was okay to begin speaking." This component is critical. It acknowledges the possibility that your feelings may have resulted from a misperception of the situation. Most of us have some unlearning to do in this area. At any moment your feelings are legitimate. In later discussion you might find that you overreacted after misinterpreting the behavior. In similar circumstances in the future you may feel differently. Hopefully you can learn from each negotiation.

Many people have developed heightened "sensitivity." This is a learned response to a norm of interaction in which feelings are usually expressed indirectly. Because they have had little experience in open discussion of feelings, many people read "intent to hurt" into the behavior of another person who may not have the intention to interfere. They overreact.

Similarly, when many people get upset with the behavior of others they project their anger when legitimately they have no right to do so. For example, it is legitimate to be angry with Johnny when he does not come in until after midnight if before Johnny went out the expectation that he would be in before midnight was explicitly expressed and agreed upon. Anger directed at Johnny in this circumstance is inappropriate and may lead to legitimate anger and resentment on his part. It would be fairer to be angry with yourself for not having discussed when you expected Johnny to return.

Sometimes people spread their feelings around rather freely. They arrive at meetings, school, office, or home obviously upset and subject the people there to anger that does not involve them. If you find yourself in a situation like this, communicate that the anger does not involve the people who happen to be near you. "If I seem a bit abrupt and insensitive today, try to understand. I had a bad night. I'm not angry at you. Try to be patient with me."

Let's move on to another important aspect of expressing feelings. While it is important that feelings be expressed in a form that is receivable, the nonverbal behavior that accompanies your words should fit the depth of emotion that you feel. The degree of emotional expression should fit the situation. If you respond with the same depth of emotion when Johnny spills milk as when he hits his sister, he will not learn to discriminate more important from less important. And since he will get the same reaction regardless of what he does, he might as well do something that fits what he will get.

Exercise 5.4 allows you to experience varying degrees of emotional content in the expression of feelings. You want to communicate the full depth of emotion you feel and yet you have a responsibility to the listener to make it receivable—so it isn't likely to provoke a defensive response. Do Exercise 5.4.

Exercise 5.4

In this exercise you will learn to make your expression of feelings receivable and believable. Your nonverbal behavior should fit the words you use to describe what you are feeling. Listed below are statements that could occur in a variety of interpersonal situations. There are three statements in each of two sets. One set is for A. The other set is for B. Negotiate which person gets which set and who goes first.

Whoever goes first will say the first statement in a rather bland tone of voice, with rather bland mannerisms. Repeat this statement again, only this time put in the nonverbal tone that you feel appropriately fits the statement. The listener will observe carefully and indicate only (1) receivable and believable, (2) receivable but not believable, (3) believable but not receivable, or (4) not believable or receivable. Continue expressing the statement until your partner indicates believable and receivable. Go on to the second and third statements and do likewise.

Reverse speaker and listener. Work through the second set of three statements using the instructions above. One of you paraphrase the instructions and check with your partner for confirmation before beginning.

(a) "I'm angry! That really bugs me!"
(b) "I really enjoyed this evening. I don't know when I have had more fun."
(c) "I'm discouraged! After two weeks of work now I must start all over again."

(a) "I like you!"
(b) "I'm excited! Wow, he made that shot from forty feet to win the game!"
(c) "I'm disappointed and confused. You told me that you would clean out the garage tonight. I don't understand why you said you would if you didn't mean it."

> Each of you tell your partner how you felt during the exercise. What did you learn about yourself? About your partner?

Hopefully, you really showed nonverbally the feelings that you were expressing in words. In your relationship with your partner, you should experience the freedom to express the full depth of your feelings. It usually feels good. Hopefully, you will learn to value your partner's expression of his full depth of feelings. With others you may need to make some judgments as to the degree of emotion you should express.

You want to express your feelings in a manner that is receivable and that fits the context.

There is always an accommodation factor in relationships. To be a constant is to demand that all persons "fit" you. No way of relating to people is that universally perfect. You will need to make some judgments about how you will express your feelings directly, not whether to express your feelings directly. Here is where your attending skills come into play. "Is the listener receiving your message?" "Is the listener beginning to get defensive?" "Is he withdrawing?" This will be discussed in more detail in Chapter 6.

You do not express your feelings to punish another person. If you feel like punishing him, that is the feeling you should express. "I feel like punishing you." You express your feelings to offer an opening to discuss a relationship problem. If you tend to express your feelings with a heavy load of emotion, you probably are waiting too long—until you begin to boil.

Let's summarize a bit. It is important that you express your feelings directly or in metaphor. The expression of your feelings should include a description of the behavior or situation that you feel influenced your feeling. It is helpful to provide a behavioral prescription of what the person could do or how the situation might be changed to help you. The communication should also involve a direct expression that your reaction may be inappropriate.

Let's move our attention to the description of the situation that you feel influenced your feelings and the prescription of what the person could do to help you in your relationship with him. Most people have some learning to do in this area. While labeling is useful in expressing feelings, it is not particularly effective in describing situations. There you need to describe the behavior. Consider the following examples. One uses labels. The other gives descriptions of behavior. Read them aloud.

A. "You are rude and thoughtless! You don't care what happens to me!"

B. "I'm angry. You began to speak before I finished. You didn't call me to let me know when you would be home from work. You didn't ask me about my day."

The effect of the first example is punishment. It is very likely to provoke a defensive response. The intent is apparently to put the other person down rather than to give information that would resolve the conflict constructively. This may, however, be the best that person can do at the moment. In the second example we see feelings expressed directly, followed by an exact behavioral description of what the speaker feels influenced the feelings.   Consider the two statements presented below.

Labeling	Describing
"You are rude . . .	"You began to speak before I finished."
. . . and thoughtless!"	"You didn't call to let me know when you would be home from work."
"You don't care what happens to me!"	"You didn't ask me about my day."

Unless your intent is to punish, the behavioral descriptions are much more helpful, receivable, and more likely to produce changes should the negotiation so indicate.

Most people prefer specific feedback, whether positive or negative. Did you ever say, "Johnny is a good boy" only to have Johnny disprove you in a few moments by doing something disruptive?   Johnny knows he is not always a good boy and the expectation carried with the label is too much for him to handle.   On the other hand, Johnny can accept "You did a good job picking up your clothes" or "John, you washed that car very well." Similarly, admonishments to "Behave" or "Knock it off" are not particularly functional in changing behavior, except perhaps momentarily.

One more example and then we will move on to a practice exercise. See if you can get a picture of the individual described below.

John leaned back in his chair and extended his legs. He put his hands behind his head and pulled his head toward his chest. He yawned, rubbed his eyes, and then wet his lips with his tongue. He moved his legs back toward the chair and twisted his torso back in the chair. He then leaned forward and looked directly into my eyes. He smiled, blinked, and moved his eyes to look down at the floor. He coughed, looked up at me, opened his mouth, and said, "I feel very conspicuous right now."

Try to approximate this description as you do Exercise 5.5.

Exercise 5.5

In this exercise the focus of your attention must be on behavior. Avoid interpreting the behavior through labels as much as possible. Find a third person to observe. If you are alone, you might turn on the television for a couple minutes and observe a performer. Observe this person for two minutes. Ignore his words. Focus your attention instead on the nonverbal behavior of the person. Do not keep notes. At the end of the two minutes, return to your original position and turn off the television. Each of you tell your partner the behavior you observed in the sequence in which it occurred. Use a mutual decision-making process to determine which person will begin.

As you listen to your partner describe the behavior he observed, attend well and clarify if necessary. In addition, it is critical that you help your partner give behavioral descriptions and not use labels. If he uses a label, remind him that the word he used is a label and help him describe the behavior. If he uses "rude" you might mirror this word ("rude . . . ?") and allow him to elaborate. Help your partner learn to describe behavior. Let your partner help you.

Paraphrase the instructions before you begin and check with your partner to be sure he interpreted as you did. Begin.

> Each of you tell your partner how you felt during the exercise. What did you learn about yourself? About your partner?

How did your first attempt at describing behavior go? Many people call themselves "people watchers." Unfortunately, most tend to watch interpretively rather than descriptively; they tend to label as a short-hand interpretation of what they observe. It is not particularly "wrong" to do this, but it is not very precise in communicating for clear understanding. While behavior may have one meaning for you and certain labels may fit this meaning, these labels may have very different meanings for your partner. It would be more helpful to describe the behavior and to allow your partner to put his own labels on it. More important for your relationship, descriptions of behavior are critical for effective conflict resolution, as you will see in Chapter 6.

It is fairly safe to observe a third party. The task becomes much more difficult when you must observe and feel observed at the same time—when you are intimately involved in the relationship. In the next two exercises, the "risk level" will be increased to approximate what you will experience in the reality of daily living. Try Exercise 5.6.

Exercise 5.6

In this exercise, one of you will be the observer and the other the obser-vee. Decide who will be who in the first round.

Observer, you are to observe your partner for one minute. Observer, you keep time. Under no circumstances are either of you to say any words. Seat yourselves facing each other. At the end of this minute, observer, you will tell your partner (1) what behavior you saw him do and the sequence in which it occurred, and (2) what you interpreted this behavior to mean. "I saw you look away from me, glance at your watch, wind your watch. I interpret this to mean that you were uncomfortable or embarrassed, and impatient for the minute to end."

Observee, just respond to the situation the best you can and do whatever moves you except to get up from your chair or to interfere with the observer in his task. After the observer has described the behavior you did and told you what it meant to him, paraphrase what he said. If his interpretation does not fit what you were feeling, clarify. Observer, if the observee amends your interpretations, interpret.

After you have finished, both of you share how you felt. Again, paraphrase. Paraphrase to be sure you understand the instructions and check with your partner. Okay, begin.

Reverse the process. Follow the instructions set forth above.

---

(1) Each of you tell your partner how you felt during the experience. How did you feel as observer? As observee? What did you learn about yourself?

(2) Tell your partner how well he gave precise behavioral descriptions and interpretations. Tell your partner how well he paraphrased your descriptions and interpretations.

Very possibly, you were most uncomfortable as the observee. As observer, you were somewhat removed from the pressure during the (very long) minute. However useful this exercise may have been to help you learn to describe behavior, it lacked the shared responsibility that is the reality in all relationships. In Exercise 5.7 we will add this component. Try this now.

Exercise 5.7

This exercise is similar to Exercise 5.6, but with additional components. In this exercise each of you will be the observer and the observee simultaneously. Turn your chairs so that you face each other directly. Using no words, observe each other for one minute. Decide which of you will keep time. During this minute just respond to the nonverbal signals of the other person.

At the end of this minute each of you will tell your partner (1) what you saw the other person do (behavioral description), (2) what you thought this person was feeling (your interpretation), (3) what you observed yourself doing (self behavioral description), and (4) what you were feeling. "I saw you become red in the face. This made me think you were embarrassed. This made me think that I was looking at you too intently and so I smiled. I felt better when you smiled back."

After you and your partner have related your observations, interpretations, and feelings, paraphrase to be sure you both understand what the other was saying.

Paraphrase the instructions to be sure you understand. Check with your partner. Begin.

---

(1) Each of you tell your partner how you felt during the exercise. What did you learn about yourself? Your partner?

(2) Tell your partner how well he gave precise behavioral descriptions and interpretations. Tell your partner how well he paraphrased your descriptions and interpretations.

You may have found that being observed in silence made you uncomfortable. On the other hand, you may be accustomed to the silence by now. Your feelings may have been similar to situations where you were speaking to a large group of people. Possibly you were less proficient in describing behaviors objectively since you were being observed simultaneously. So much of our attention is inner-directed in interpersonal situations. We have learned to be very sensitive about how we are coming across, but our ability to observe and respond to others is reduced.

Your long-term task is to learn to attend simultaneously to both your feelings and your behavior. Another part of your task is getting outside yourself (putting your own needs aside for the moment) to attend to the needs of others. Recall from Chapter 3 our discussion of offering to listen to the other person when his concern interferes with attending to us. You also probably need to learn to accept positive feedback without belittling the sender with "It was nothing." This means expressing your feelings directly, knowing that you do this to help the other person or your relationship, taking the risk that the problem may be your behavior and/or your interpretation rather than the other person's behavior.

The task is not easy, but if you are successful the payoff is great. You will need to devote less energy to game-playing and waiting for the other person to pick up on your feelings. You will act directly to influence your world instead of responding passively to your environment. Your feelings will not control you.

At this time let's pause for a moment to reflect on the quality of your relationship with your partner. If you have been doing all of the exercises you should be feeling the benefit of greater openness in your relationship—perhaps more closeness, a bit more trust, and an increased willingness to take risks. Take a few minutes to discuss how you feel about each other. Do this now!

In your relationship with your partner, the direct expression of feelings should be no problem. If your partner expresses his feelings directly or indirectly, your task is clear. Hear him! Paraphrase! Understand his feelings in depth. If the emotions are high, the components of description, prescription, and shared responsibility may be obscured for the moment. But if you continue to paraphrase for understanding, these components will gradually fall into place. You may need to say, "It would help me if you could describe what I did." If your partner is unwilling to do so, you have not heard his feelings in sufficient depth. Listen! Hear! Request a bit later. Your patience will need to be your forte in times like these.

Similarly, you may need to make requests. "It would help me if you would tell me what I could do differently." Again, your partner may be unwilling or unable to comply. Once again, paraphrase. Listen! Hear! Request help a bit later. A respectful silence may be the most helpful response. When emotions run high, the old habit of projecting responsibility to others may come back. Over time, this will occur less frequently. Heightened emotional states in interpersonal conflicts do not maintain themselves unless you respond with similar emotion.

Sometimes your partner (or others you communicate with) will be unable to describe the situation that precipitated his feelings. This is understandable. Accept this, but make a request. "Would you tell me if I do the behavior again? It would help me. Thank you."

If you are a good listener you can help develop a prescription with a variation in the paraphrase. As you paraphrase you seek to understand the other person's thoughts and feelings. By using the appropriate qualification ("I think you mean . . .") you describe what his words mean to you. You begin by understanding what he is feeling and the situation he is describing. Let's take a look at an example we used earlier. Read it aloud.

A. "I'm angry. You are rude and thoughtless. You don't care what happens to me."

B. "I hear you saying you are pretty angry right now. Really upset with me. Ready to slug me."

A. "I sure am. You would be too if I did the stunts that you pulled."

B. "If you pulled the stunts that I pulled."

A. "Yes. How would you feel if I kept interrupting you, if I didn't call you to let you know when I was going to be home, and to top it off, if I never asked you about your day?"

In this last statement we have enough data to infer the prescription for behavior change. You could stay with the negative content as you paraphrase, or if your partner's emotions have come down and he feels heard, you could flip your paraphrase from the negative to the positive to understand the prescription for change. For example:

B. "You would feel much better about me and our relationship
if I would wait until you are finished before I speak, if I
would call you to let you know when I will be home, and if I
would spend time listening to you share your daily activities?"

Although not checked out yet, based on the data this is a good inference.
You are no longer wallowing in negative feelings. Rather, you and your
partner are beginning to formulate a prescription for change.

One point needs a bit more emphasis. You have been learning rather
ideal ways to deal with feelings. Only with time, effort, and practice can
you approximate the ideal. The old habits will recur periodically. But
learn to value the expression of feelings, the attempts at paraphrase, the
attempts at seeking clarification, the attempts at describing behavior and
making prescriptions in whatever form they occur. Show that you value
the willingness of others to take risks. "Thank you for telling me." "I
appreciate that." Share your feelings directly as you do so. "I feel
threatened, but I appreciate your telling me." By so doing, people will
continue to express their feelings to you rather than behind your back.
Receive well and appreciatively. Do so immediately, after each behavior.
If someone says, "You're stupid," you have every right to express your
feelings in response. "I feel hurt." "I'm angry." "I feel threatened."
He (the accuser) may then respond defensively or with guilt, but these
are feelings he must own. Correspondingly, you must own the anger or
guilt that you may feel. The response, "You're not so damned bright
yourself" may be the best you can do at that moment. Hopefully, the
heightened, legitimate expression of feelings on both your parts will
eventually give way to more effective sending and receiving. Although
you did not intend to do something "stupid" you may have done something
less effectively than possible. Your social system needs this information. Similarly, as a member of the social system the other person
needs to learn a better way to give feedback.

When the feelings expressed involve you, you may feel irritated,
defensive, and self-protective. At that moment it is most important to
express your feelings and try to paraphrase for understanding. As you
will see in the next chapter, a defensive response rather than paraphrasing usually precipitates an argument.

While you have been urged to express your feelings directly, I am
uncomfortably aware that the focus has been on negative feelings. You
also have positive feelings about your partner and other people in your
environment. Too often we hear "I never hear anything until I foul up."
This is unfortunate from several perspectives. Despite the modesty that
we have learned we should show, it still feels good to have your efforts
acknowledged. Further (and much more pragmatically for you and your
relationships), the more frequently you acknowledge and reward the

things people do that you like, the more frequently they will do the rewarded behavior. Given so much time in a day, this often translates into a decrease in the frequency of behavior that you dislike. How long does it take to say a thank you? "You really listen to me." "I appreciate your efforts to really understand what I am saying." "Thanks for clarifying what I meant." "I really like the way you expressed your feelings so directly."

This carries over into all aspects of life. "Thanks for picking up your toys. I appreciate that." "I'm pleased. It was helpful of you to remind me that we were going to read a story after recess." "I like the way you and Johnny helped each other with your arithmetic problems." "I really like the way you edited the manuscript."

If all we do is share negative feelings, the other person must learn what is appropriate through trial and error. Do you recall many situations like the following?

> "Johnny, don't touch the lamp. Stay away from the coffee
> table. Quit playing in the water. Leave the television alone."

Johnny sure knows what he shouldn't do, though he may not know what he <u>should</u> do. What makes it even worse for Johnny and for you is that he will probably continue to do these things. Even though it is not pleasant, it seems to be the only way he can get your attention. You must also give him attention when he does things you approve of.

When should you express your feelings directly? Depending on the context, it is best to express them when they occur. If you have noticed, almost all examples of direct expression of feelings were stated in the present tense. "I'm angry." "I'm bored." "I'm excited." "You are frowning." "You are smiling." These are "here and now" statements. These stand in contrast to "then and there" statements. "I was angry at you." "I was bored." "I was excited."

If you do not express your feelings while you are experiencing them, you may repress them, only to have them surface in the form of nonverbal behavior at a later time. The one exception is the context. Problems should not be brought up when there is not sufficient time to work things through. Often the social setting is not appropriate (church, business meeting, or a party). It takes but a minute to express the fact that a problem exists and to negotiate a time when it can be discussed. "I have a problem that I would like to talk over with you. I guess it'll take about a half hour. When can we talk?" You may need to make some judgments here as well. A statement like that above may affect the person's enjoyment or work effectiveness. This may precipitate a problem worse than the one that initiated the statement.

SUMMARY

It is important for you to express your feelings directly:

> to provide behavioral descriptions and prescriptions;

> to qualify your feelings as responses which may be inappropriate;

> to paraphrase for understanding when your partner expresses his feelings;

> to express your feelings in a manner accepting responsibility;

> to make your expression of feelings believable and receivable;

> to express your feelings when they are felt given sufficient time and an appropriate context.

You now have some skill in expressing your feelings directly. In the next chapter we will focus on applying these skills in resolving conflicts that occur in relationships. If it is at all possible, move on to the next chapter immediately. If this is not possible, arrange a time in the immediate future while the learning in this chapter is still fresh. This has been a long, tough chapter. There is much to remember. Thanks for a good effort.

Summarizing Exercise

Once again alternately respond to each of the following statements. Include (1) the concepts you may have learned, (2) the meaning of those concepts for you, and (3) the implications of the concepts and the behaviors for you in your relationship with your partner and others. The listener should use attending, clarifying, paraphrasing, and direct expression of feelings.

(1) Give an explanation of why the valued "rational" person is not possible.
(2) Give an explanation of the paradox implied in the statement "We should feel guilty for feeling."
(3) Demonstrate and explain the probable effect on the listener of expressing feelings (a) physically, (b) indirectly, (c) directly, and (d) with metaphor.
(4) When your feelings concern your relationship with another person there are three additional components necessary for expressing your feelings effectively. Name these, demonstrate each, and explain the probable effect of each on a listener.

(5) Give an explanation of the probable effects on a listener if the only feelings expressed are negative feelings. Further, explain the effect on a listener if positive feelings are expressed.

(6) While it is preferable that feelings be expressed when they occur, there are several qualifications to this general rule. Explain these.

FOR FURTHER READING

References are grouped by subject on pages 208-215. For further reading on the concepts covered in this chapter, see references under these headings:

Communication Theory: Norms, Roles, Expectations, Interaction
Human Development and Normalcy
Interaction Analysis
Interpersonal Problem Solving: Feelings, Feedback, and Conflict Resolution
Modeling and Reinforcement
Nonverbal Communication
Openness, Authenticity, and Trust in Relationships
Perceptions of Self and Others
Responsibility in Relationships
Self-Disclosure

CHECK POINT FOUR

Well, you are on your way now. Only three more chapters remain. Tell your partner how you feel about what has happened so far (1) to you personally and (2) to your relationship with your partner. Tell your partner how you feel about continuing the task. Just listen and understand each other. Hopefully you are feeling some benefits from your efforts and will decide to continue the task. But the decision to continue must be mutual.

CHAPTER SIX

Conflict Resolution, Feedback, and Negotiation in Relationships

All of us experience conflict in our relationships at some time or other. For some it may seem to be constant. However frequently we experience conflict, it is an inevitable consequence of the relationship between two unique people. Conflict is closely tied to our capacity to feel relative to our past learning. As we have seen, feelings will be experienced despite our attempts to repress them. We have no choice but to manifest our feelings in some kind of behavior at some time. We have a choice in how we deal with our feelings of conflict. We can deal with them directly or indirectly. We can deal with them overtly or covertly. We can deal with them fairly, recognizing the imperfection of both our perception and behavior, or unfairly, projecting responsibility for the conflict we feel to the behavior or perception of others.

As used in this book, conflict has a broad meaning. A distinction is made between "conflict" and "conflict resolution." The word "conflict" commonly refers to wars or arguments. Here we will call these not "conflicts" but attempts at conflict resolution. For our purposes, let's define conflict as the state that exists prior to attempts at resolution. Conflict resolution refers to the behavior we use to deal with our feelings —how our feelings manifest themselves in behavior. Conflict, then, describes the feelings that we experience when the behavior of another person interferes with what we would like to do or what we probably would have done if the person had behaved differently.

The following analogy may put this definition of conflict in a useful perspective. Read it aloud.

> Let's take a fantasy trip for a moment. Imagine you are at a movie. It is an excellent movie. It moves you to tears and laughter appropriately. The photography is excellent. The acting is superb. Of course, it is full color with all the three-dimensional perspective of cinerama. Sound good? It is good.
>
> Suddenly, however, something happens. A fly lands on the lens of the projector. Its image is projected onto the screen. The scene is spoiled. The acting distorted. You try to ignore

it and enjoy what you can, but this is less than desirable. You have to choose between living with the fly, getting rid of the fly, and leaving the theater.

Let's translate this story into the realm of interpersonal relationships. Read the following example aloud with feeling.

It was a good day. The weather was perfect. The bus was on time. The boss met me at the door and commended me for a job that I had done well. He invited me to lunch with other people at the office. I liked them all and the lunch was excellent. The conversation was interesting and entertaining. Buoyed by this experience, the afternoon went beautifully. Inside I am just bursting with the joy and the beauty of the day. I rush home. I just can't wait to share my experience. I run up the stairs, open the door, and call out a cheery "Hi!"

The response: "I found another pair of socks with holes. When are you going to quit working and take care of the place like you should?"

Conflict? A fly on the projector? Very likely. In fact there are two people with conflict in this example. The man who found the hole in his socks experienced a feeling of resentment that his wife was working and not taking care of holes in socks. He resolved the conflict he felt by projecting responsibility and attacking her. On the other hand, the joy the wife experienced was immediately displaced with a feeling of conflict—perhaps approach-avoidance, anger, frustration, resentment, projection. You decide; you may have been there. An argument might begin. This is a possibility. However, both have a choice in how the conflict is dealt with. The choice is between dealing with conflict constructively (to possibly enhance the quality of the relationship) or destructively (to produce greater tensions and conflicts in the relationship).

The skills you have learned in previous chapters are the basic tools you need to resolve conflict constructively. In fact, as you learned these skills you were dealing with conflict. When you felt "unsure" about the meaning of a word, you learned to seek clarification. When you felt "in a bind" between wanting to attend to a person and being pressed for time or bothered by another problem, you learned to defer attention. You learned to request clarification when you felt that you had not made yourself clear. In previous chapters you also learned to prevent conflict. You learned to attend empathetically, thereby helping another person feel support rather than conflict. You learned to paraphrase and to help another person feel understood. You learned to express your feelings directly, thereby reducing the degree of conflict the other person might feel.

In this chapter we will help you apply these skills you have already learned to specific situations that may produce conflict for you. The situations range from mildly irritating conflicts to conflicts experienced in an argument. When you are resolving conflicts you feel, you are giving feedback and entering into negotiations with your partner. This will be discussed extensively. Finally, we will explore various means of resolving conflict when an impasse is reached in negotiations.

This chapter is very important for your relationship with your partner and for any social system of which you are a part. If anyone in a social system does behaviors that produce conflict in others, that social system will function less productively than it could. As feelings of conflict increase, competition rather than cooperation among members may become evident. Each member of a social system is a potential resource for accomplishing the goals of the system, but those who do behavior that produces conflict may unknowingly reduce the efficiency of the system substantially.

Let's begin by reviewing some behaviors that may produce conflict in us and/or in others. They take many forms.

(1) You may experience conflict when another person expresses feelings indirectly. These can be expressed in statements like the following:

> "What a crummy job!"
> "Nobody cares what happens to me."
> "You are rude."
> "Is this bridge safe?"
> "When are you going to come over?"

Or they can be nonverbally expressed—the frown, the raised eyebrow, the smile that does not seem to fit the context, the firm setting of lips, the intense stare, the shaking head.

(2) You may experience conflict when the message sent does not provide enough information.

> "Why did he do it?" (Why did who do what?)
> "You are a terrible person." (Is he serious? Teasing?)

(3) You may experience conflict when the sender puts words in your mouth and limits your freedom to respond.

> "Isn't that right?"
> "You agree, don't you?"
> "Right?"
> "I know you agree with me."

(4) You may experience conflict when another person speaks for you without prior arrangement to do so.

"We all feel that way."
"Everybody feels that way.
"The group feels that we should go."

These are familiar to many of us. That's the problem; they are too familiar. Unfortunately, many of us are equally guilty of sending messages in ways that produce conflict in relationships. Add the learned component of not expressing our feelings directly and we find ourselves trapped in a cycle of reacting to conflict by producing conflict in others who in turn produce conflict in us, etc., etc., etc.

Let's review the basic approach you will use in dealing with the conflicts you experience. The direct expression of feelings (including the components of description, prescription, and negotiation) plus the skill to paraphrase feelings are fundamental to constructive conflict resolution. Further, you must have the attitude that the feeling of conflict is yours. It is _your_ problem. _You_ are experiencing the conflict. Consider the following example.

> You and two other people are having a discussion. Your companions take different sides on an issue and in the heat of the discussion both are talking at one time. Literally they are talking by each other. From your perspective you experience conflict. Perhaps you want to hear both, but when both speak at once, you can hear neither. This is your problem. They may enjoy arguing. Perhaps you become impatient with them as they attempt to reconcile their differences. They may not be impatient. It is your problem.

Others may experience conflict, too, but for you the prescription is clear. Since it is your feeling, it is your responsibility to deal with the conflict you feel.

When you assess that the conflict you feel was precipitated by another person expressing his feelings indirectly, treat that assessment as a hypothesis, not as a truth that the other person is experiencing conflict. If the person _is_ experiencing conflict, it may be important for your relationship to have him express his feelings directly, so you intervene to this end. Given the perspective that it is your problem, you begin by accepting your feelings and expressing them directly, rather than assuming the other person is experiencing conflict. Read these aloud.

> "I've got a problem. You are frowning. It would help me if you would tell me what your frown means."

> "I'm uncomfortable. You are shaking your head. If you disagree, it would help me if you would share your ideas with me."

"I'm really out in left field. You said you enjoyed the ride, but the way you said it makes me think that it was not particularly enjoyable. It would help me if you could clarify for me."

The speaker in each of the above examples does not assume the other person has a problem. Rather, he assumes responsibility, expresses his feelings, and offers the hypothesis that a problem exists. Direct expression of feelings, behavioral description, and behavioral prescription are all present. The tone communicates that there is room for negotiation. It may be your misperception.

Many people may express their feelings directly when the opportunity is extended in the manner exemplified above. They may express their feelings directly when they are given reasonable assurance that they will be heard or when others express their feelings directly. And they will be reinforced when they experience their feelings and ideas as understood or when their efforts are rewarded with a tangible thank you. Others may express their feelings directly when you do not demand that they share their feelings but rather allow them to experience the choice to open up or not. They may do so if you can accept them not despite their feelings but because they feel.

The manner of dealing with conflict that we usually observe does not meet the above criteria and may lead to defensive reactions and continued indirect expression which may then hurt the relationship. The following examples "request" through indirect expression of feelings.

"You are angry!"
"What's bugging you?"
"You've got something bothering you."

Whether or not these provoke a defensive response or a denial depends on the quality of the relationship and the manner in which the statement is made. These statements assume a feeling exists. If the tone is one of command, hostility, demand, or impatience, a defensive response or denial is very likely. There is little assurance in these statements that the speaker will receive and try to understand should the listener decide to express his feelings directly.

So, direct expression of feelings plus description, prescription, and negotiation is preferable to "requests" through indirect expression of feelings. There are two "shorthand" alternatives to direct expression requests. The first describes the behavior you observe with or without direct expression of your feelings.

"I'm concerned. You are frowning."   or   "You are frowning."

"I'm worried. You are holding your   or   "You are holding your
head in your hands and perspiring."   head in your hands and
                                             perspiring."

Expressing requests through <u>behavioral</u> <u>description</u> (as illustrated on the bottom of page 100) allows the listener to experience freedom. The speaker does not put a feeling inside the listener. He merely describes what he observes. The tone is accepting, not demanding or evaluating.

In the second alternative (see example below) the speaker communicates what he infers the behavior to mean with or without direct expression of feelings.

"I'm concerned. You seem puzzled."   or   "You seem puzzled."

"I'm worried. You appear to be ill."   or   "You appear to be ill."

This is more direct and allows less freedom for the listener, but it does appropriately qualify the speaker's perception (perception checking). There are many variations on this that are acceptable.

"You <u>appear to be</u> . . . ."
"It <u>seems like you</u> . . . ."
"I <u>perceive you to be</u> . . . ."
"<u>You look as though</u> you feel . . . ."

With perception checking and behavioral description add the rest of the statement as necessary.

"It would help me if you could tell me whether you feel ill."

If invited to express feelings directly, most people will respond most of the time. Since it is your problem and since it is your request, you are obligated to understand the person's feelings should he choose to respond. Similarly, you are obligated to respect his right to be silent. If you allow him to experience this freedom, he will more likely help you with your problem in the future.

Receiving the directly expressed feelings of others may be difficult at times. The person you are trying to communicate with may respond defensively. He may even attack you. If the feelings have been smoldering for some time, they may come out with a full head of steam. If you want him to continue expressing his feelings directly you must understand what he is saying and paraphrase to help him experience being understood. This will help him be willing to take the risk to express his feelings again. If you paraphrase his feelings, his heightened emotional state will come down to a point where the situation can be discussed.

When you understand and he feels understood, indicate how you felt, reinforce him for his behavior, and request that he continue to express his feelings with your help.

"I felt very threatened, but I really appreciate your willingness to tell me what you were feeling. It may not be easy to hear, but I want you to continue to share your ideas and feelings even

when I do not notice that you have something to say. Will you help
me and do this?"

When you request that another person continue to share his feelings, it is
useful to obtain a definite yes or no. By requesting a verbal response you
obtain information about how he feels about your request to continue.
Whether he feels free or coerced may come through in his nonverbal
behavior (for example, in the tone of the response). Further, if you get
a verbal response, you have a legitimate basis for confrontation should
he not express his feelings in the future. He shared his feelings only at
your direct request. He may continue to share only when you request.
This keeps him dependent on you and places the responsibility on you.
Neither is desirable if you wish a shared responsibility in your relationship.

It's time for some practice exercises. In Exercise 6.1a you will use
direct expression, behavioral description, and behavioral prescription to
deal with the conflict you may feel when your partner expresses his feelings indirectly.

Exercise 6.1a

Turn your chairs so that you face each other. Using no words, observe
each other and respond to the nonverbal signals of the other person.
Observe each other until one of you notices a nonverbal signal that suggests an unexpressed feeling and which influences a feeling (conflict) in
you. When you observe this behavior, respond with:

(1) what you are feeling in relation to the nonverbal behavior
     ("I'm uncomfortable.")
(2) a description of the behavior you observed ("You're blushing.")
(3) a request that your partner help you with your problem and
     share his feelings with you

When your partner complies with the request:

(1) paraphrase his response so that you understand and he feels
     understood
(2) express appreciation for his sharing his thoughts or feelings
(3) request that he do so in the future without your asking ("It
     would help me if . . . .")
(4) request a verbal response

The instructions above are a bit involved. Paraphrase them in some
detail. Check with your partner. Try to help each other in this task.
Begin.

Reverse the process. The other person attends until a nonverbal
signal is observed. Check it out. Use the same rules as above.

---

(1) Tell your partner how you felt as observer and observee.
     What did you learn about yourself? Your partner?
(2) Tell your partner how well he expressed his request and
     followed through. Be honest, but recognize that this was
     a first attempt.

That was a pretty tough exercise. There was much to remember.
You were asked to do some behaviors that you have been practicing, but
this time the context was different. You may have found some old habits
getting in your way a bit. That's okay. It's expected.

Let's try that exercise once more, only this time with a twist. Your
partner will not respond to your request. Try Exercise 6. 1b.

Exercise 6. 1b

Turn your chairs so that you face each other. Using no words, observe
each other and respond to the nonverbal signals of the other person.
Observe each other until one of you notices a nonverbal signal that suggests an unexpressed feeling and which influences a feeling (conflict) in
you. When you observe the behavior, respond with:

(1) what you are feeling in relation to the nonverbal behavior
     ("I'm uncomfortable. ")
(2) a description of the behavior you observed ("You're blushing. ")
(3) a request that your partner help you with your problem and
     share his feelings with you

Whoever receives the request simply respond with something like "I'd
rather not" or "I'm not comfortable doing that now. "

Paraphrase the denial of your request. Accept this for the moment,
but make the offer to listen should the person wish to express his feelings.

Paraphrase the instructions. Check with your partner. Help each
other in the task.

Reverse the process. The other person attends until a nonverbal
signal is observed. Express your request. Use the same rules as
above.

(1) Tell your partner how you felt as observer and observee.
    What did you learn about yourself when the request was
    denied? What did you learn about your partner?
(2) Tell your partner how well he expressed his request and
    followed through. Tell your partner how well he accepted
    your denial of his request. Be honest, but recognize that
    this is a new skill.

Each person should experience the freedom to respond to requests or
not. Paradoxically, if you can extend this freedom and communicate (in
words or with silence) acceptance of another person's unwillingness to
respond, he is more likely to respond. The same rules apply even when
you don't get a verbal denial. Role-play the following example.

B. Just frown.
A. "I'm concerned. You are frowning. This makes me think
   you have a problem. It would help me if you could tell me
   what your frown means."
B. Say nothing. Just turn away slightly and look down as though
   you were somewhat embarrassed.
A. "I get the impression that you don't want to talk about it.
   Okay. Should you want to discuss it, just let me know."

Let's move on to another exercise. This time you will use one of
the abbreviated forms in expressing your request. You will merely
label the feeling state that you perceive with the appropriate qualification. Try Exercise 6.2.

Exercise 6.2

(1) Decide which of you will be the observer and which the observee.
    Whoever begins select one of the following statements and say it
    aloud, capturing the full depth of feeling as you read the statement.

    (a) "Don't worry about me. What does it matter that I'm home
        alone every night!"
    (b) "Where are we going to get the money?"
    (c) "When I see it, I'll believe it!"
    (d) "Oh, what's the use!"

After your partner has made the statement, respond with a statement
beginning "You seem . . ." and add a label describing a feeling or a
metaphor as you deem appropriate. You might choose "You appear
to be . . ." or "You sound . . . ." Paraphrase the feelings of any

response you get. If you get no response, accept this, but extend the offer to listen.

(2) Reverse roles. The other person selects a statement and says it aloud.
(3) Again reverse roles until all four of the statements have been stated and requests expressed.

---

(1) Tell your partner how you felt as observer and observee. What did you learn about yourself? About your partner?
(2) Tell your partner how well he expressed his request and followed through by paraphrasing. Tell your partner how well he accepted your denial of his request. Be honest, but recognize this is a new skill.

In these last three exercises your request for a direct expression of feelings involved rather low risk for the receiver. The risk was considerably lower than a request like "What's bugging you?" or "You look like you are waiting for someone to call on you. Around here if you want to be heard you will need to fight your way in." You requested a direct expression of feelings and provided an experience of freedom to respond or not in a very accepting manner. When this type of request is used, the atmosphere is relatively nonthreatening and the receiver may become dependent—waiting for you to request again and waiting for assurance that he will not be put down. Under these conditions you bear a disproportionate share of the responsibility. It is helpful for the relationship if both people express their feelings without the request and without the assurance of safety. This is more nearly the reality of day-to-day interaction. This may build a greater confidence to deal with feelings in relationships. To do this you can request that the person initiate direct expression of feelings. "I appreciate you expressing your feelings. It would help me if you could do this in the future without my asking. Could you do this?" This is extremely important for those in authority positions—employers, executives, teachers, parents, and group leaders. Employees, subordinates, children, and students may have a high initial dependency— responding to the authority rather than initiating. If you wish a more interdependent social system, stimulating this initiative is critical.

Some people have learned to enjoy producing conflict in others. They may not intend to punish, but producing conflict may be the only way they feel they can get attention. Most teachers are well aware of these circumstances. These individuals, for whatever reason, just continue to give nonverbal signals that produce conflict for you. They may respond very compliantly to your request for change in their behavior. "Yeah, sure. Anything you say." Or they may not respond

verbally at all. If direct requests are not effective, what do you do?
Probably the most functional solution is a process called <u>extinction</u>.
Since getting a rise out of you seems to keep this behavior going, you
can extinguish or stop this behavior by not letting it get a rise out of
you. When you observe a distracting behavior, act as though you had
not noticed it. This is particularly effective if you can give these
"trouble-makers" the attention they need when they do behavior that
you feel is effective. Observe them closely enough and you will see
much behavior that makes you feel good. Express the positive feelings
immediately after each behavior you like. Ignore each behavior that
you dislike. The frequency of the conflict-producing behavior will
increase at first as they try harder to get your attention. Eventually,
however, it will decrease markedly. Whether or not it decreases and
how fast it decreases depends on how often you refuse to be "bugged"
and how frequently you express your positive feelings.

In Exercise 6.3 you will experience situations that may produce conflict for you. In general, each situation describes somewhat ineffective
interpersonal behavior. With each situation you are asked to role-play
a response that may elicit more effective interpersonal behavior. Under
each situation, a guideline is presented that describes a possible reason
why this behavior is ineffective. Try this now.

Exercise 6.3

In this exercise you will encounter interpersonal behavior that may produce conflict in relationships. Read each situation aloud. Read the
guideline aloud. Alternately role-play a response that may elicit more
effective interpersonal behavior. In general, use the following format
as you develop your responses.

(a) Express your feelings directly.
(b) Describe the behavior you observe.
(c) Ask for help with your problem.
(d) Prescribe with a behavioral description of what would help
    you with your problem.
(e) Reward the person when he complies with or considers your
    request.
(f) Request that he continue to do the behavior in the future.
(g) Obtain a verbal response to your request.

At your discretion use a shorthand version of this format. With either
choice, allow the person to experience freedom and acceptance.

(1)   "I don't know where you get your information. Everybody does it."

Guideline: "Everybody" does not qualify the limited frame of reference that each person has. You are one of everybody. It would help if the person qualified his observations to the limits of his experience: "All the people I have talked to."

Role-play a response.

(2)   "That was a horrible movie."

Guideline: The word "was" makes the characteristic "horrible" an integral part of the movie rather than the perception of the viewer. Without perceptual qualification it is difficult for another person to express his own opinion. It would help if the reaction were qualified as a perception: "I didn't like the movie."

Role-play a response.

(3)   While you are listening, John and Mary are both speaking at the same time.

Guideline: If you observe two people speaking at the same time, you cannot hear well what either is saying. Further, neither is listening if both are speaking. Their behavior is equivalent to an irrelevant conversation. This behavior may lead to an argument or exaggerated differences. It would be helpful if each would listen and respond when the other person is finished.

Role-play a response.

(4)   "I am really excited about this project." (Pause) "I don't think I want to do it."

Guideline: This is an inconsistent message. The person said one thing and then said the opposite. It would be helpful if the person would give consistent messages or give information that justifies the change.

Role-play a response.

(5)   "What do you think about the idea?" (Statement made in a group)

Guideline: To whom is the question addressed? If anyone can respond, this should be so indicated. If the speaker wishes a specific person to respond, he should address that person.

Role-play a response.

(6) "Mary, we have discussed the problem at some length, but we haven't heard from you." Her response: Silence. Nonverbal behavior is eyes closed, head lowered, rubbing forehead with right hand.

Guideline: Silence is often interpreted as assent. Since you have not heard from Mary and you wish to use all resources in making the decision it is important that her ideas be heard. It would be helpful if Mary would give a verbal response. Saying "That's dumb" is better than no response. Further, by remaining silent Mary is reacting to rather than directly influencing her world. You must honor the decision not to respond, but the opportunity should be extended.

Role-play a response.

(7) "We have been planning where we will go on our field day. We are pretty well in agreement that we will go to the zoo tomorrow and we will go to the museum and to a factory later when the weather is colder. What are your feelings about this schedule?" The response: "What time would we leave and when will we return?"

Guideline: The response did not answer the question asked. If the person doesn't want to answer the question, he should so indicate. If there is another question he needs clarified before he responds, he should so state. As it is, the response is equivalent to an irrelevant statement. The original speaker is left hanging. A few such responses and his level of participation may decrease.

Role-play a response.

(8) "I think it would be fun to go hiking on our vacation. We could go to the . . . ." You are interrupted: "Hey, let's go visit a farm."

Guideline: You probably were not heard, at least by the person who interrupted. If your ideas are not heard your level of participation may decrease. You may feel a need to get even and interrupt in competition. It would be helpful if the listener paraphrased for understanding, but at the very least he should wait until you are finished.

Role-play a response.

(9) You observe the following. John states: "I think it would be fun to go hiking on our vacation. We could go to the . . . ." Mary interrupts John: "Hey, let's go visit a farm."

Guideline: John was interrupted, but you were interrupted as you attempted to listen to John. John's participation level may decrease or he may interrupt Mary to get even. Since Mary interrupted you and others who may have been listening to John, her comment may not be heard. Her level of participation may decrease. You saw it. It is your problem. It is also the problem of every person in the group. It would be helpful if John were to intervene to help himself.

Role-play an intervention to help you with your problem and to help John take responsibility for his own problem.

(10) "Okay. Sure. That's okay. Whatever you say is okay with me."

Guideline: There is a basic incongruence between words spoken and the nonverbal behavior. Also, passive compliance is not effective in any social system. In this statement there may be some underlying feelings that would be useful to hear.

Role-play a response.

This group of situations is more representative than exhaustive. Each social environment contains a tremendous range and variety of interpersonal contacts. You will need to observe the behavior of people in your own environment and attempt to apply the skills you have learned. But your first line of responsibility is your own behavior. You must behave effectively, consistent with the norm of communication you would have others learn. The guidelines presented in Exercise 6.3 relate to your behaving effectively. You might review these at this time to formulate effective behavior to use in your relationship with your partner and others.

Let's move to another situation that may produce conflict for you. Questions can be particularly troublesome. Three ways questions can be the source of conflict in relationships are presented below.

(1) A person might ask one question when he really has another question in mind. He may ask "What time is it?" instead of "I'm tired. Would you mind if we went home?" In this situation the listener is expected to be a super-sensitive mind reader. It is helpful if the question adresses the concern directly.

(2) A person might ask a question when he has a feeling he wants to express. He might say "How would you like to go to a ball game?" instead of "I would like to go to a ball game." Again the responsibility for being sensitive is projected to the listener. The listener seems to have a choice. But if his answer is "No," he may provoke anger, pouting withdrawal, or some other form of getting even. It is helpful if a question includes the preference if there is one. It is helpful if "choice" questions are real rather than polite.

(3) A person might ask a question when he already knows the answer. A teacher sees two children fighting and asks, "What are you doing?" A supervisor knows a report has not been prepared and asks, "Did

you prepare that report?" A parent knows that Johnny did not make his bed and asks "Did you make your bed?" These examples illustrate possible attempts to trap someone in a lie. It is helpful if feelings are expressed directly without complicating them with possible anger at a lie. True, the listener should not lie, but we have the obligation to create an atmosphere that makes lying unnecessary.

Of course, one can develop suspicion for all direct questions. If you read dishonesty into every question or if you read every question as a trap, your existence can be pretty miserable. Respond directly to the question if you feel comfortable doing so. If you are uncomfortable responding to a question, you can request clarification or a frame of reference. For example, if someone asks "What are you doing Saturday night?" you may be uncomfortable responding directly. The response "Nothing" may produce "Good, then you can babysit for me." Thus trapped, you may need to get creative. "Oh, I just remembered. I'm going to get a headache." You might just respond honestly. "I'm not doing anything in particular, but I'd rather not babysit."

It is useful to seek clarification to make a question more facilitative (more easily responded to) if you are uncomfortable with the question. "I'm uncomfortable with your question. It would help me if you could tell me why you are asking." This response gives you more freedom and helps the other person become a better sender. If you know the frame of reference, you are more likely to give the response that will answer the question. This serves to deal with your discomfort and help the other person learn to give more information with his questions.

Similarly, if you observe that a person is uncomfortable with your question (perhaps funbling for a response), you might volunteer clarification to make it more receivable (facilitative). You may find that others will become more open in your relationship.

Recall Johnny's question "Dad, where did I come from?" Dad could have asked "Why are you asking?" Or Johnny could have volunteered "Peter and Mary came from New York. Where did I come from?" In both cases much time and energy may have been saved and both may have been more satisfied.

Let's try an exercise that may help you learn to request and offer a frame of reference for your questions. Try Exercise 6.4.

Exercise 6.4

There are two parts to this exercise. In the first part you will have direct questions posed to you. If you are comfortable responding to the direct question, do so. If you are uncomfortable with the question, express your feelings and request that your partner give you a frame of reference to make the question more facilitative.

(1) A, ask B a direct question. Allow B to respond or to request a
frame of reference at his discretion. Provide a frame of reference
in response to the request. If B responds to the direct question,
continue to ask questions until B requests a frame of reference.

B, trust your feelings. If you are comfortable with the question,
respond to it. If you are uncomfortable with the question, request
that your partner make it more facilitative by providing a frame of
reference.

Reverse the process. B, ask A a direct question. A, respond
or request a frame of reference at your discretion.

(2) A, ask B some direct questions. Allow B to respond. Watch B
closely. If you sense that B is uncomfortable responding to your
question, intervene to give B a frame of reference. "You seem
uncomfortable with the question. Let me explain why I am asking."

B, listen to A's questions. Try to respond, but <u>do not request</u>
<u>a frame of reference</u>. Allow B to develop his observation skills to
detect any discomfort you might feel.

Reverse the process. The same rules apply.

---

(1) Tell your partner how you felt during the exercise. Specifically share how you felt when you (a) requested a frame of
reference, (b) complied with the request for a frame of
reference, (c) waited for your partner to detect your discomfort, and (d) responded to the discomfort you observed
and provided a frame of reference.

(2) What did you learn about yourself? Your partner?

On the witness stand you can be directed to answer direct questions,
but in our daily relationships we don't have to answer them. Instead we
can express our feelings directly and request a frame of reference from
the speaker—to make the question facilitative. There is also the reciprocal responsibility to make your questions facilitative when you perceive that the other person is uncomfortable with your question.

Let's focus now on another common conflict-producing situation. A
particularly knotty problem that most people encounter is the discomfort
in feeling a need to attend when they are not particularly interested in the
topic. This is brought about in many forms. It may be the person who
responds to a simple "How are you feeling?" with a blow-by-blow medical history. It may be the proud parent who discusses each of four children in detail complete with pictures in response to "How old are your
children?" I'm sure you can recall numerous other examples. It might
be useful to distinguish between not being interested and not being interested to the degree that the person is assuming. This situation is parti-

cularly tough since we were taught to be polite. Thus, we may give partial attention, make up excuses to get away from the person, avoid asking the same question in the future, and/or simply avoid this person.

Incessant rambling to a captive audience may reflect the lack of effective communication in our society. People become starved for understanding, for recognition, for expressions of appreciation. The more they feel the need to be heard, the more they take advantage of every opportunity to talk. Ironically, this may work against them in the long run, for others may avoid them and thus they become even more deprived. A self-defeating cycle is maintained. The person who speaks incessantly when given attention could get sincere attention if he would become a better listener. Yet he may need attention so badly he cannot get outside himself to reciprocate. If you would like to be heard, you must first hear. If you would like to influence, you must be willing to influence. The concept of mutuality applies here.

In the long run you can help yourself and the other person by helping him become a more effective listener. Whenever he listens to you—however briefly—express appreciation for this. It is probably the relationship that he needs more than to talk about a specific topic. As he begins to listen more effectively, you may begin to feel better about the relationship. You may be surprised at how much interest you may have in a topic when the other person is also interested in topics that are important to you.

You may also try to express your feelings directly rather than listen politely. If someone begins to ramble in response to a simple very direct question, you might simply interject, "Mary, you are giving me more information than I requested." After a few interjections like this Mary may well respect the boundaries of your request.

Remember, a large part of the problem may be yours. You may be expressing your questions without a frame of reference. You may get more information than you need with "How have you been?" than with "I've heard you were ill. Are you feeling better now?" In either case, if you are getting a medical history, you could respond with "I'm sure that was a trying experience. I'm glad you are feeling better now. That is all I needed to know."

If someone is talking about a topic that simply doesn't interest you, you can help yourself and him in a couple different ways. You can interject, "John, I'm uncomfortable. I see that baseball is important to you, but it is something that I'm not interested in. Maybe you have felt like this when someone was talking about a topic in which you had no interest. Perhaps we could find a topic that is of interest to both of us." There are several components to this response: the direct expression of feelings, the description of the interaction process that influenced the feeling, an attempt to help the other person identify with your discomfort, and a prescription for possible solution. In a relatively new relationship this may be pretty easy to do, but if you have been attending politely to discussions of baseball for some time, you have a more difficult problem because you will have to acknowledge that you have not been interested for some time. Also, your friend may feel uncomfortable that he subjected you to the baseball discussions as well as hurt that you did not tell him sooner that baseball bores you.

Of course, you may meet someone who seems so insensitive that your best efforts come back at you like words into the wind. In my experience, these cases are few. Most people will respond to your efforts at confrontation through direct expression of your feelings. Perhaps your own fear of not being able to handle the response you elicit is your biggest handicap.

Another type of person we're all familiar with is the one who may seek your help in resolving their problems with others. The following two rules of thumb may be useful as you seek to help yourself and others with interpersonal problems.

> (1) A problem with Mary cannot be reconciled in conversations with individuals other than Mary.

If John has a problem with Mary, he will need to deal with Mary directly. John bitching about Mary without confronting her is counterproductive. If you listen well to his bitching, you may even reward him for continuing to have the problem with Mary! Further, the longer the problem exists the more difficult it will become for John to deal with. Procrastination tends to build guilt feelings (since John knows he should talk with Mary). But since guilt as a feeling cannot be accepted, the projection of this guilt to Mary will exaggerate the negative feelings that already exist.

Prescriptively this means that your interaction with John should lead to helping him broach the problem with Mary. That is, if the negative feelings communicated increase over several conversations, it is time to confront John. Read the following example aloud.

> "Do you want to do something about it? I am no longer willing to just listen to you complain. If you wish to work on ways of dealing with the problem with Mary, I'll be glad to help you. Otherwise, I would like to drop the subject."
>
> "But you do help. It just feels good to have someone listen. You listen well."
>
> "Thank you. But that is the problem. I listen well and I hear the same things over again. And you feel worse than you did."
>
> "You don't care."
>
> "It may seem like I don't care, but I do. This is my best judgment as to how I can best show I care."

In brief, you want a commitment from John to do something about the problem or you will stop discussing it with him. Too many relationships are irreparably damaged when others listen too well.

(2) The way you present a problem to a third party is probably the way you should present the problem to the person with whom you have the problem.

When you present a problem to a third person, you probably present it in a functional way—expressing your feelings directly, describing the behavior that bothers you, and prescribing what the person could do differently to help.

"Boy, that Mary drives me up the wall. She really makes me angry. I barely get started on one task when she comes over and gives me another. A few minutes later she asks whether I have the first task done. Neither job gets done well. I want to do a good job. If she would just have some realistic expectations. If another job has a higher priority, great, but I can't do both jobs at the same time. It would sure help if she could do this."

Let's revise this statement a bit. Read it again, substituting "you" for "Mary" and "she." It sounds pretty receivable. If John would present his problem to Mary in this manner, he would make a good beginning. Your task is to help John learn to handle the many possible ways he and you think Mary could respond. "How will you respond if she . . . ?" As you listen to possible responses, try to put yourself in Mary's shoes. "If I were Mary after hearing the above, I would respond . . . ." As you help John shape his responses to fit the guidelines for giving and receiving feedback (see page 119), you may teach some of the skills you've learned here: how to paraphrase, how to listen without agreeing or disagreeing, how to express feelings directly, etc. As you rehearse the probable responses, you are increasing the chances for success and lowering the felt risk.

To further lower the felt risk, help the person choose the earliest possible time to follow through on the task. The longer the task is put off, the greater the felt anxiety and the probability for success is reduced. "How much time will you need?" You end with a verbal commitment to take action. "So you will contact Mary at her office at 2:00 this afternoon. You have planned for an hour with her at that time and you feel that would be sufficient. Good. I would like to know how it comes out. Could you stop by at 3:00 and let me know?"

Your task is similar as you attempt to deal with your own problems. If you are alone and you don't know how to handle the problem, you might tell your problem to a real or imaginary third person (your partner?). Again, the way you present it then is probably the way you should present it to the person with whom you have the problem.

Let's try a real situation. In Exercise 6.5 you will help your partner develop a strategy to deal with a problem your partner has with a third person. Try this now.

Exercise 6.5

In this exercise each of you will help your partner deal with an interpersonal problem he has with a third person. Before you read further, reread the last two pages. Decide which of you will present a problem first. Whoever begins should identify a person whose behavior in some way interferes with your behavior. Do not select the most difficult problem you have. Since this is a first attempt, you probably should not choose a person who occupies an authority position.

Helper, listen carefully to your partner. Seek clarification and paraphrase his feelings in depth. You must understand the problem and how your partner feels about the problem. Spend several minutes just listening, seeking clarification, and paraphrasing feelings. When you feel you understand and when you perceive that your partner feels understood, ask whether he would like to do something about his problem. He probably will feel some reluctance to deal with the problem directly. Paraphrase these feelings. When you have a commitment:

(1) prepare your partner to approach the person
(2) anticipate possible reactions from the person
(3) develop responses to deal with reactions using skills learned in this book
(4) help your partner establish a definite time and place to deal with his problem
(5) arrange a meeting with your partner as soon as possible after the meeting

Do not give advice. Do not assume responsibility for the decision to deal with the problem. Assess the appropriateness of any approach by asking:

(1) Is the problem presented honestly and directly?
(2) Are the skills learned here used in the approach?
(3) Is the approach receivable as you respond to role-played responses?

Reverse roles and repeat the exercise using the same rules as given above.

(1) Tell your partner how you felt as helper and helpee.
(2) Tell your partner how well he used the skills. Did he fall into the old habit of giving advice? Did he help you see how you might use the skills in dealing with the problem? Did you feel understood?
(3) Tell your partner how you feel about the approach the two of you developed. This exercise was for real. Discuss your feelings about following through on the commitment.
(4) Be sure to finish working through Chapter 6 before you actually deal with your problem.

One aspect of our past learning makes it difficult to resolve some of the smaller conflicts we feel. Many of us have been taught to ignore the little things that bother us. "Although I don't really like you putting your elbows on the table, it is so small, so petty, I will ignore it." Wearing curlers to bed, calling mother every day, visiting relatives every vacation, playing golf every Sunday, not mowing the lawn, going beyond the budget are all "such small things, I'll ignore them." But, try as you may, you probably find that you can't ignore them. You still feel discomfort; you just don't express it directly. Instead you send nonverbal signals and the feeling remains submerged until the inevitable "big blow-up." Then the pie-throwing contest begins.

"You think my table is not as it was. Well, you don't help by putting your elbows on the table."

"You and your curlers. Sleeping with you is like sleeping with a robot with antennae."

"Then there is you and your mother. Everyday you must call her. When are you going to grow up?"

"Grow up! You're the one who has to go to visit the relatives every vacation."

"You have your vacation every Sunday on the golf course."

Suddenly we see that all these "little" things are not so little after all. Over time they accumulate to form a force so devastating they can destroy a relationship. So it probably is not too effective to let little things build-up. Express your feelings when you feel them. The skills in this chapter will help you express feelings over little things as well as big. Then the "little" things will not become big.

. . .

This is a long chapter. You have worked hard and it is time for a break. The material that follows is very important. Be refreshed before you resume. Arrange a definite time to resume the task before you break.

. . .

As you express your feelings to resolve the conflicts you feel, you are giving feedback. You are explicitly expressing how the behavior of another person affects you. As you describe and as you prescribe you are requesting that someone else change to accommodate you. The receiver of your feedback has a decision to make—to change or not to change. And as you receive feedback from others you too must make the same decision. In any relationship there must be room for negotiation. Let's explore the problem.

Feedback is a constant in life, whether or not it is expressed. A mirror gives us feedback every morning. (It shows us the reality which at any given moment may fit our ideal image of ourselves.) The store window that reflects our image (which we glance at surreptitiously) similarly gives us feedback. We obtain feedback by assessing the way people respond to us with their nonverbal behavior. If they listen attentively to our comments we often interpret this to mean that they think what we have to say is important. When their responses to our comments are irrelevant we often interpret this to mean that we are not important to them. We compare ourselves to others in the office, in the classroom, even in our own families. As we observe others and experience their reactions to us we form and change self-concepts.

Relying on the interpretation of others' reactions for feedback is complicated when different people respond to us in different ways. Trying to sort out an identity from among many various reactions can lead to a rather schizophrenic existence. As a result we may learn to discount some individuals' reactions in favor of others. All too frequently our own individuality can become lost amid attempts to accommodate many individuals who respond differently to us. A similar problem occurs when we attempt to accommodate the many and varied moods of the same individual.

At the other extreme are those who maintain themselves as constants. They seem to discount the reactions of others totally. They demand total accommodation to their behavior. Perhaps they had difficulty trying to accommodate all and ended by accommodating none. This particular style is also unfortunate. Such people may have difficulty relating to others like themselves. People who can relate to them are those who are willing to be dependent and who lack a unique identity of their own.

The process of feedback and accommodation is continuous. But it has decided shortcomings. Because feedback must often be interpreted from behavior rather than from directly expressed feelings, we are limited by our subjective interpretations of the reactions of others to our behavior. For our relationships to be fully satisfying we need to give and receive feedback through direct expression of feelings. But there is a responsibility that you assume. As you directly express your feelings to deal with your conflicts you maximize the probability that the other person will change his behavior to accommodate you. Suppose you make a request like this.

> "I have a problem. I notice you are frowning. It would help me if you would tell me what your frown means."

The chances are very high that the other person will comply. In effect you are making a value judgment that says "It is important that people express their feelings directly." As you request and reinforce direct expression of feelings the norm of communication will slowly but surely change.

Is this manipulative? Assuredly it is. However, it is overt manipulation. You are openly asking for a behavior change and the other person can comply or not (though the manner of asking is "calculated" so that he's likely to comply). In each interpersonal contact, people influence each other. You cannot not behave. You cannot not communicate. Much of the influence we encounter is incidental, haphazard manipulation. Most of us are guilty of conscious covert manipulation. The approach advocated here describes an open mutual process for changing to a more effective and satisfying behavior style.

Despite the fact that your request is manipulative and will very likely be accommodated, when the other person begins to express his feelings directly you, too, will be asked to accommodate. The norm of mutual expression of feelings provides the equalizer. The norm has been changed from competitive coercion by the indirect expression of feelings to a norm of cooperation through understanding and respect.

As you express your feelings and request change, attend carefully to the nonverbal behavior of the other person. He may be complying, but may not be comfortable with the change. Paraphrase and understand how he feels about the change. And as he requests of you, you must express your feelings about the change.

In a relationship you should experience the freedom to change or not to change. You need your individuality apart from the relationship. You need a sense of basic identity across all relationships. But there should also be a part of you that accommodates others. And you should also extend these same rights and obligations to each person in your world.

A fully mutual relationship can be developed if both parties meet the following obligations in giving and receiving feedback through the direct expression of feelings.

Giving Feedback

(1) You should express your feelings directly when the behavior of your partner interferes with your behavior.
(2) You should describe the behavior that you feel interferes with your behavior, recognizing that your perception of feelings about this behavior may be an overreaction on your part.
(3) If your reaction is conflict rather than positive feelings, you should describe the behavior that you would like your partner to do differently to replace the old behavior.
(4) You should understand your partner's feelings about the feedback he received from you.
(5) Recognizing that in an interpersonal system no individual's behavior exists in isolation from the behavior of the other person, you should accommodate your partner by reciprocal changes in your behavior when necessary and helpful to the other person.
(6) Whether or not the person agrees to change, you should express appreciation for understanding your concern.

Receiving Feedback

(1) You should hear and understand your partner's feelings, description of behavior that he feels interferes with his, and prescriptions for change that would help him.
(2) You should give the feedback serious consideration, weighing the consequences of changing or not changing to accommodate. These thoughts and feelings about the alternatives and your feelings should be expressed to your partner.
(3) You should communicate your decision to your partner.
(4) Whether your decision is to change or not to change, you will need to accept the consequences of your behavior.
(5) You should communicate to your partner changes in his behavior that may need to be made to help you change.
(6) Whether or not you use the feedback, you should express appreciation to your partner for caring enough about the relationship to give you the feedback and request that he continue to do so.

When the negotiation for possible change is concluded, the attitudes of each person should resemble those reflected in the following situations. Read them aloud.

A. "I can make a good try at not interrupting you. I will need your help. I may forget sometimes. Will you remind me or let me know more directly when you are finished?"

B. "Yes, I will remind you for a while, but if I always need to remind you I think that I will be carrying most of the responsibility. I am willing to help for a while, but I do hope I won't need to continue."

A. "You are concerned that I might depend on you to remember. I should learn to check myself?" (Pause)

B. "That is exactly what I mean."

A. "That is fair enough. I will stop interrupting you."

B. "And I will let you know when I am finished more clearly than I have in the past. I will remind you should you forget, but you will learn to think before you speak."

A. "I am really in a bind. I intend to ask about your day. I sure am interested in what happens to you. It is pretty tough. Things have not been going very well at work and I guess I bring the problems home with me although that isn't fair to you."

B. "I hear you saying that you are interested in me, but sometimes you are very preoccupied with the things at work that are not going well. This makes it difficult to get outside yourself to hear me."

A. "Yes. I feel guilty for bringing the problems home, but when I think about them away from work, I often get some useful perspectives on how to handle the problems."

B. "I appreciate your problem. You are in a bind. You want to hear about me, but you need time away from work to think through some of the problems that you face there."

A. "Precisely. Is there some way that we can work this out?"

B. "Maybe we could spend time helping each other. If we could take a half hour before dinner and devote that time to just hearing each other, perhaps both of us would be better off. What do you think?"

A. "As I understand you, you are suggesting that we set aside half an hour to hear each other, preferably before dinner."

B. "Yes. It might make dinner much more satisfying for both of us. I don't know whether talking to me about your problems would help you as much as thinking about them, but I sure would like to give it a try."

A. "I hear you saying that dinner might be better if we could put aside the conflict we have both experienced in the past. You don't know whether talking about the problems would help as much as my thinking them out, but it might be worth a try."

B. "Exactly."

A. "It just might work. I would like to give it a try—say for a week and then see if we are both satisfied with it. Let's see, I get home at 5:45. I would like about fifteen minutes to unwind a bit. How about getting together at 6:00 and just talking and listening until 6:30?"

B. "Let's see if I understand. When you get home at 5:45 you need a few minutes to relax a bit. And other than greeting you, I won't bug you during this time unless the house is on fire. At 6:00 we will sit down and just share what happened to each of us during the day. We will continue until dinner at 6:30. I really like that."

A. "Good. I do, too. When can we begin?"

B. "I see no reason why we can't begin tomorrow night."

A. "Great. Tomorrow it is."

B. "I really enjoyed discussing this with you. You didn't interrupt me once. I really appreciate that."

A. "I almost slipped a couple of times, but I caught myself."

B. "I noticed. Thanks."

There are situations where a request is more like a demand. The behavior change requested may be one you just do not wish to comply with. Stating your feelings and maintaining your position can be extremely difficult in the context of peer pressure. Read the following example aloud.

A. "Hey, I've got some grass. Why don't you light this up?"

B. "No, thanks. I don't smoke."

A. "Why not? What's the matter?"

B. "I just don't use the stuff."

A. "There is nothing the matter with it. I use it all the time. We all do. Don't you like having a good time?"

B. "Sure I like a good time, but I don't need that stuff to get it."

A. "Oh, come on. Everybody else is smoking."

B. "I'm starting to get angry. You made the offer. I refused, but now I feel you're pushing me to do something I don't want to do."

A. "You are out of it. Any people I'm with are with it."

B. "Are you saying that everybody in the group has to do what you do?"

A. "No, you don't have to do what I do, but if you want to be a part of the group, you've got to be willing to go along."

B. "That really bothers me. I like everybody in the group, but I just don't feel that I need to do everything the group does. I should have a choice."

A. "You have a choice—with us or against us. We can't have you sitting by just watching and maybe tell other people what we are doing."

B. "So you are really concerned that I will cop-out and tell if I don't smoke."

A. "Yeah."

B. "I guess you will just have to trust that I won't. I just won't do what I don't want to do. There is no way I'm going to do anything just because everybody else is doing it."

A. "You're just a creep."

B. "I may just be a creep if that means not smoking and not going along with what everybody else is doing. I'll have to live with that if that is the way you feel. But you will need to live with it, too. Okay?"

A. "Creep."

You can negotiate with most people most of the time. Try another one.

B. "I'm angry with you. I had something I wanted to say at the meeting, but you didn't notice and call on me."

A. "You're really upset with me. You feel neglected and irritated that I didn't notice you had something to say."

B. "I sure am. You know how difficult it is for me to come into a conversation uninvited. I rely on you for help."

A. "You are really uncomfortable taking the initiative to enter a conversation. It is much easier for you if I invite your comment."

B. "You could make me feel more comfortable. Will you watch more closely and help me?"

A. "John, I understand how difficult it is for you. I would like to be helpful, but I just don't see how I can be the super-sensitive person you would like me to be. It irritates me that you want me to take that much responsibility. I'm not at all sure that my taking that responsibility will help you. You would just become more dependent on me."

B. "I hear you saying that you would like to help me but you're uncomfortable doing so because all the responsibility would fall to you and I would become more dependent on you."

A. "Exactly. I feel confident that if you would take an initiative once or twice you would develop greater confidence in yourself."

B. "You feel sure that I can handle coming into conversations uninvited if I would just do so once or twice."

A. "Right. If you could do that I would be so pleased with you. I think you might be more pleased with yourself, too."

B. "I really know what you mean. I guess I would like to change. I don't really enjoy having this fear, but it is tough."

A. "You feel afraid to enter the conversation, but you wish you could. You would like yourself a lot better."

B. "I sure would."

A. "I wonder if there is some way we could prepare you for the next meeting. Perhaps we could rehearse and role-play different ways you might come into the conversation."

B. "That might help. You are suggesting that we plan for the next meeting and rehearse how I might ask a question. Hey, there is a question I would like to ask."

A. "Okay! Good! Why don't you write the question exactly as you would like to say it. Then we could see how you might ask the question. How does that sound?"

B. "That sounds okay. I feel like I shouldn't have to write out the question and rehearse, but it may be for the best."

A. "You feel a bit awkward right now. You suspect that writing and rehearsing will make it easier, but you sure wish you didn't need to do that."

B. "Right. Well, let's get on with it."

There will be times when arguments will occur in your relationships. In fact, this is the way most conflicts are resolved. We try to make the other person experience conflict as he made us experience conflict. As he thwarted our behavior, so we shall interfere with his. From his perspective, since you interfered with his behavior, he will interfere with yours. Although the responsibility is shared, the conflict we feel obscures the reality. Literally it is the "Do unto others" in action. Thus we begin to argue and we destroy relationships.

Let's experience one of the unproductive ways we try to resolve our conflicts. Do Exercise 6.6.

Exercise 6.6

In this exercise you will experience an ineffective way people try to resolve conflicts. There are two parts to this exercise. The basic strategy for resolving conflict is identical in each.

(1) A, you are to say only the word "yes." B, you are to say only the word "no." Beginning with you, A, say the word "yes" in a determined, challenging manner. B, respond by saying "no" in a manner slightly more determined and challenging than that used by A. Gradually, each of you is to top the other person. Continue until you are shouting "yes" and "no" at each other. Yes, the neighbors might hear you, but their lives are pretty dull; give them something to talk about. No physical blows may be struck! Paraphrase the instructions, check with your partner, then begin.

(2) We will use the same game plan as above. This time we will use different words. B, you are to say only "You did!" A, you are to say only "I did not!" Same rules as above. B, you begin. Paraphrase the instructions. Check with your partner to be sure he interpreted as you did. Then begin.

> (1) Take a few minutes to discuss whether or not you have ever experienced this before in different settings. Describe how you felt. Paraphrase to be sure you understand the situation and the feelings your partner is sharing.
> (2) Tell your partner how you felt during the exercise. What did you learn about yourself? Your partner? Paraphrase.

What you did and what you felt during Exercise 6.6 may have seemed very familiar to you. Most of us have been involved in situations where the only recourse in resolving a problem was to put down and destroy. You may have tried to "win" a few rounds by this method and then withdrawn. This makes a lot of sense. After you have reached the shouting stage, what is left but physical attack? You may have learned that if you withdraw you "win" because the other person is striking out at air. Of course, those in authority positions can always "win" using this method by calling upon their authority. "It is 'yes' because I say so. I'm the boss." "I say you did and I am the boss."

This means of resolving conflict is an exercise in futility. You may "win," but it may cost you the relationship and the open flow of information that is so necessary to the optimal functioning of any social system. The atmosphere becomes one of "Sure, he says he wants to hear from us. Big deal. Just be sure that you don't disagree with him."

Of course, you may change the rules a bit and not play the other person's game, but the intent is the same—to respond in kind or worse (usually worse). This occurs in many forms—the snide comments at a social gathering, the facetious remark, the quip, the disruption in the back of the classroom that is ambiguous enough to keep the teacher guessing.

When an argument occurs, the pattern of interaction must change. Let's experience how. Do Exercise 6.7.

Exercise 6.7

In this exercise we will repeat a part of what we did in Exercise 6.6. We will add one small twist which is indicative of an alternative strategy for resolving conflict.

(1) As before, A, you are to say only the word "yes." B, you are to say only the word "no." Beginning with you, A, say the word "yes" in a determined, challenging manner. B, respond by saying "no" in a manner slightly more determined than that used by A. Gradually, increase the challenge until you are shouting "yes" and "no" to each other.

Now for the twist. At some point when you approach the height of your attempts at put-down, A, you are to remove the determination and challenge from your tone and say B's word "no" in a manner communicating a willingness to listen. "No?" (Pause)

Paraphrase the instructions before you begin. Check with your partner. Then begin.

Reverse the process. Same rules. This time B will take A's word. "Yes?" (Pause)

(2) Same instructions as in (1) but this time, B, take "You did." A, say "I did not." Again, come down. B, come down to "You didn't?" (Pause) A, come down to "I did?" (Pause) immediately after B comes down.

Each of you tell your partner how you felt during the exercise. How did you feel when you came down and indicated a willingness to listen? Did you want to stay up and keep competing? How did you feel when your partner came down and indicated a willingness to listen? What did you learn about yourself? Your partner? Paraphrase each others' comments.

In Exercise 6.7 you experienced a shift in the pattern of interaction. You literally refused to fight. Your partner was disarmed at the time. There was no one left to fight with. A shift alone is not sufficient. You must either express your feelings and/or begin to do behavior that is more effective in reconciling your differences. Experience these approaches in Exercise 6.8.

Exercise 6.8a

In this exercise you will do an activity similar to that in Exercises 6.6 and 6.7. If you recall, you argued. One of you said "yes" and the other said "no." One of you said "You did" and the other said "I did not." Again there will be a new twist.

A, take a position on a controversial topic. Simply begin by asserting your position in a determined and challenging manner. B, take the opposite side on the topic (even if you can't agree with it). Respond to A in a determined and challenging manner, slightly more so than that which A used. Argue. Gradually accelerate the argument until you are literally shouting at each other. At some point in your argument, A, you are to do the following:

(1) Come down in emotional level and express your feelings directly.
(2) Describe your behavior and the other person's behavior and what you think he might be feeling with the appropriate qualification.
(3) Request help with the problem you feel and request discussion of the way the two of you are trying to resolve differences.

What you seek is a shift from the topic to a discussion of "how." B, respond to A's "shift" in any way that feels appropriate.

Paraphrase the instructions. Check with your partner. Then begin.

Reverse the process. Same rules as above. This time, B, you come down and request the shift from the topic to a discussion of "how" the two of you might reconcile your differences.

---

(1) Tell your partner how you felt in each role in the exercise. What did you learn about yourself? Your partner?
(2) Tell your partner how well he performed the roles according to the instructions.

In Exercise 6.8a you responded to the conflict you felt over the futility of the argument. When you came down in emotion, you expressed your feelings directly, described what you saw happening and what you felt the other person was feeling, and requested a discussion about the relationship. The other person may resist this and attempt to keep the argument going. He can do so only if you play his game.

He may refuse to discuss the relationship. He may even withdraw. These may be his last attempts at "winning." You must hang tough. "I need to talk about what we were doing to each other. Our relationship is more important than the topic at this moment. You may not want to talk about it now, but we will need to talk about it sometime. When can we do this?" The desired end-product of this approach is to promote a discussion of "how" we reconcile our differences.

If he does begin to talk about his behavior, the relationship, or your behavior, no matter how he does it, paraphrase. Model the kind of behavior that each of you needs to do. This will not be easy, for he will be projecting all responsibility to you. You may be pretty upset yourself. You don't have to agree with him, but you must hear, try to understand, and help him feel understood. Under these conditions he may eventually begin to reciprocate.

But there's another effective way to handle this kind of conflict. Do Exercise 6.8b.

Exercise 6.8b

Again, B, take a position on a topic. Assert your position in a determined, challenging manner. A, take the opposite side of the topic.
Respond to B in a manner slightly more determined and challenging
than B used. Gradually accelerate. At some point in the argument,
A, you are to do the following:

(1) Take the last statement that B used and mirror this state-
    ment to B. Come down in emotion to do this.
(2) Paraphrase subsequent statements by B or groups of state-
    ments. Indicate in your manner a willingness to listen.
    Continue until B's affective tone comes down.

Paraphrase the instructions, check with your partner, begin.
     Reverse the process. Same rules as above. B, come down in emo-
tion. Mirror the first statement. Paraphrase subsequent statements.

---

(1) Tell your partner how you felt in each role in the exercise.
    What did you learn about yourself? Your partner?
(2) Tell your partner how well he performed the roles accord-
    ing to the instructions.

In Exercise 6.8b you did not shift to the relationship problem directly;
you did not express your feelings directly. Your behavior shift was not
to change from discussion of topic to discussion of relationship, but from
argument to mirroring and to paraphrasing your partner's position on the
topic. You assumed responsibility, you began to listen carefully, to
understand, and to help the other person feel understood. One person
listening is better than neither listening. With this approach, you eventually will need to discuss the relationship—both your perceptions and
behavior and his. This discussion must conclude with prescriptions for
change by both of you and commitments to follow through on the change.
     Will this discussion of the relationship help to reconcile differences?
Very often the answer is yes. As the atmosphere changes from competition, projection of responsibility, and indirect expression of feelings to
one of acceptance of responsibility, direct expression of feelings, and
understanding of feelings, the chances for cooperatively working through
differences are enhanced. On some issues, however, basic values and
beliefs may be so diametrically opposed as to preclude mutual accommodation toward agreement. It is not always necessary to agree on all
issues in a relationship. This is the romanticized ideal so often depicted
in movies or literature. (We often use this perspective to judge the quality of our relationships.) A very satisfactory relationship can be main-

tained despite differences on some issues. In fact, mutual respect for each other's positions plus freedom of action to pursue these interests independently can enhance a relationship. This is a kind of togetherness through independence.

But before an irreconcilable difference is assumed, there are several other activities that you might use to work through differences. (As you read the following read it from two perspectives: first, as a participant in a disagreement; second, as an observer of a disagreement between two other people.)

A first step might be to enlist the aid of a third party to observe your two-person social system. Despite our perception of ourselves as objective and "fighting fairly," it is impossible to be a part of a social system and perceive it without bias. Select someone who is acceptable to both of you and who has some skill in focusing on "how" you are attempting to reconcile your differences. This third person serves to maximize your use of effective communication skills in your discussion. You are more likely to hear this third party than you are to hear your partner who is, despite the quality of your relationship, your antagonist on this issue. (You might serve as this third party to help others, too.) There will be a tendency to want to enlist the support of this third party on your side of the issue. This is not desirable. If he complies with your request, his power to influence you and your partner and his ability to focus on "how" you fight will be markedly decreased. Of course, this is why you requested it. If this happens, you may "win" the battle but lose the relationship.

The third party may need to get pretty hard-nosed. One of the most effective things he could do is to insist that person A paraphrase B's comment to understanding (to B's satisfaction) before A can respond. "Okay, A, paraphrase." "B, do you feel he understands what you said?" "No? Okay, A, try it again." "No, you can respond when B feels you understand what he said." "Yes, I know you're angry and want to respond. But paraphrase to understanding and you can have your say." "Yes, I'll make sure that B hears you."

This hard approach will very effectively stop the cycle of competing, accelerating emotions. To paraphrase accurately, both people will need to control their feelings to some degree. Further, they now have a common ground—their mutual irritation with the third person. But despite the threat, both people can survive a conflict and the relationship may just be helped and ultimately thrive.

A second alternative is available. You may bring in a third party who is an expert on the particular topic. Again, this should be someone acceptable to both of you. This person should be one who is relatively objective about which side of the issue would be best for your social system. Hopefully he would merely present information that seems relevant and allow the two of you to choose. Your use of him must not be to take sides, but rather to present as much information, facts, and research as he can. This new data may have been information that neither of you had and it may make a difference in the value you place on your position. This may be tough, for you may need to "back down" from the position you held for so long. It takes a trust in the relationship with your partner and a great deal of self-confidence to set aside your feelings and opinions in the face of cold, hard facts or logic. If your partner changes position, remember to give him the understanding and support you would expect in the same situation. A parting "There, I told you so" will undo that which you might have accomplished. On second thought, if a statement like that is made in any form, you probably have not accomplished very much.

A third alternative is a strategy to get each of you to re-evaluate your positions, to examine more closely for accommodation.

(1) State and record a mutually acceptable, concise definition of the problem.

(2) State and record as concisely as possible the areas of disagreement between your two positions. Seek to lower these to the fewest and as distinct from each other as possible.

(3) State and record as concisely as possible the areas of agreement between your two positions. Seek to maximize the number of these and to make them as distinct from each other as possible.

(4) Each of you state and record as concisely as possible the circumstances under which you would alter your position. Exchange these with your partner. This is not to prepare bribes but to understand in greater depth.

(5) Spend an agreed upon period of time away from each other to consider the data. Do not trust to memory.

(6) As each person weighs his values and his alternatives, each should have the freedom to seek further elaboration from the other as necessary. When you go to get information, your purpose is just that. Do not open negotiations at that time. State your request concisely, together with the frame of reference for seeking the information.

(7) Reconvene. Hear each other again. Repeat steps (1), (2), (3) and (4). Repeat steps (5) and (6) as necessary.

The presence of a third party can add to the effectiveness of the process just described. Remember you seek a decision that will be satisfying to both parties. "Winning" or "losing" should not be the goal. Often problems are defined in such a way that "win" or "lose" are either explicitly stated or implied. If you feel the definition of the problem is not fair, ask for a restatement of the problem.

It is often useful to augment the process with a statement or challenge to reconcile differences for the good of the social system. This challenge appeals to the possibility that one or both may be willing to set aside some individual values to benefit his social system. This is a bit of "Ask what you can do for your country."

All the approaches described so far have one fundamental problem. The individual never gets outside his own position to view the problem from the other person's perspective. Perhaps this is never entirely possible. Paraphrasing seeks to approximate this, but does not really put one person in another person's shoes. There is a strategy that comes close to approximating this. This process is called reverse role-playing. As implied by the name, each person assumes and argues the other person's position. Recall for a moment the various exercises you role-played earlier in this book. You may have found yourself becoming involved in the situation to the point where you had to remind yourself that you were role-playing. A similar effect may occur here. This process is most useful if you have completed the preliminary work of problem definition, delineation of differences, maximizing of common ground, and statement of circumstances under which accommodation would be made. In this process the presence of a third person can help to assure fair fighting from opposite positions. Do Exercise 6.8b again. Reverse positions on the topic. Do it now.

As you reversed roles in Exercise 6.8b, initially you may have found it difficult to assume the other person's position. This suggests a bit of discomfort at playing a role, but it also suggests the possible fear that you may be influenced to change your position. This is more likely if the attempts to reconcile differences are prolonged and not conducted fairly. However, if you got into the role, you may have detected the good sound logic the other person evolved to support his fundamental premises, values, and beliefs. The other person may have noticed the logic of your position in support of your values. At the same time, you see your position mirrored. In your attempts to support your new position, you may detect weaknesses in your previous position where the new position has merit. The other person may observe similar things from his new position.

Another strategy that may be effective in resolving differences involves getting away from the task. Stop the debate and engage in an activity that involves cooperative effort. This situation should minimize the chances for disagreement and maximize the need for cooperation to complete the task. This activity allows you and your partner to see each other in a different role than that of antagonist. The expectation is that some of the "feeling good" about the other person in the cooperative enterprise will filter back into efforts at resolving differences. And getting away from the topic may help you look at it more objectively, from "outside."

Which of these activities should you use? You may wish to use any one or various combinations of them. The key in each of the strategies is fighting fairly and utilizing all the skills you have learned thus far in this book. The next time you find yourself involved in a disagreement that seems irreconcilable, you might engage in the cooperative activity of rereading this chapter and/or examining and selecting a strategy that both of you feel would be appropriate.

After this rather long and heavy chapter, you might be feeling the following. "I'm overwhelmed. You presented so much material. There are so many little things to watch for I'm not sure where to begin." I can only respond with "You are absolutely right." I certainly don't expect miracles overnight, and I hope you don't expect this of yourself, your partner, or others in your world. But I do think you can expect a greater awareness as you encounter situations that are similar to those presented. You can go back to specific sections of this book. "What should I do now?" And you can experiment a bit with some of the new behaviors in many different settings. You may be uncomfortable in the process but be willing to take the risk. You can expect to increase the frequency of these behaviors as you experience success. You can expect to increase the frequency of these behaviors as you experience success. You can expect to discuss the situation with your partner to examine "how" you proceeded and to rehearse some particularly difficult situations with your partner. As you work together to help each other in your relationship and in relationships with others, you can expect your own relationship to become more satisfying to both of you.

One of the fundamental errors that most people make when they attempt to use the skills you have learned is to immediately attack their biggest problem with the most difficult person in their world. If you do this, the chances that you will be successful are almost nil. Begin realistically. In your initial efforts, use the skills with people you feel comfortable around. When you have rung-up a string of successes in a variety of settings, then contemplate that "difficult" problem. But before you undertake it rehearse it carefully with your partner. Recall that if you label it as "difficult" you may have a very biased perspective. You may make the situation worse.

Let's put your expectations in perspective a bit. Let's do Exercise 3.1a again. Write your name three times using your usual hand. Do this now! This is the way you think you will feel.

Now do Exercise 3.1b. Write your name three times with your opposite hand. This is the way you will feel.

Begin to use these skills with your partner. Let's conclude this chapter with four special exercises that will set the pace for cooperation, understanding, and openness in your relationship.

Exercise 6.9

Let's call this exercise "As Others See You." It serves to give you feedback indirectly. In this way you can gain a perspective of aspects of your behavior that you might want to change and observe behaviors that you like. It will also serve to increase your attending skills.

A, make a statement to B about yourself, about B, or about your relationship. Try not to make bland statements. Say something about which you have some feelings and that can have real meaning for both of you.

B, repeat the statement back to A exactly as A said it. Use A's exact words, tone, inflections, and gestures. You are to mirror the statement back to A exactly as you perceived it.

A, observe yourself as B mirrors your statement. Describe what you saw. Describe how you feel about what you saw. B, paraphrase A's reaction to your mirroring.

Paraphrase the instructions. Check with your partner. Begin.

Reverse the process. B, make a statement to A. A, mirror. B, react.

---

(1) How did you feel as you did the exercise? What did you learn about yourself? About your partner?

(2) Is there any aspect(s) of your behavior that you would like to change? If so, tell your partner what you will do differently in precise behavioral terms. If your partner wishes to change, paraphrase his commitment and ask how you can help him.

(3) Is there any aspect(s) of your behavior that you particularly liked? Share this with your partner—no false modesty. As listener paraphrase your partner's observation.

Most of us have mirrored others and been mirrored, but much of this reflection is mimicking or mocking. Unfortunately (or fortunately) we have few opportunities to see ourselves mirrored in a setting where we can profit from the experience. Perhaps you have discovered some things about yourself that you like and that you dislike. If you look around, you may see yourself mirrored often. Children use mother and father as their models when they play house. Students use the teacher as a model when they attempt to play school or help others learn. Subordinates may use their superiors as models in interaction with employees.

But whether or not we are directly mirrored, we can learn a great deal about ourselves by watching others and reacting to them. These are opportunities to learn what <u>not</u> to do and they provide information to develop alternative behaviors.

As you have worked through this book, you may have become aware that you do some less than effective behavior. However, you do some things very well. We'll work with these now. Try Exercise 6.10.

Exercise 6.10

In this exercise you will learn to persist in a task despite uncomfortable feelings with the aim of overcoming old habits. Further, you will learn to accept yourself and those things about you that you like.

B, we'll have you begin this time. For a period of two minutes tell your partner those things you feel you do well. No false modesty. No qualifying. No apology for acknowledging your strengths.

A, as B shares his strengths, do not let him qualify, apologize, or in any way show false modesty. He must state his strengths firmly and straightforward. Paraphrase his observations. Do not agree or disagree. Just understand.

Paraphrase the instructions. Check with your partner. Begin. Yes, I know you will be uncomfortable. Do it anyway.

Reverse the process. A, share your strengths with B. B, enforce the guidelines set forth above.

> Tell your partner how you felt as you did this exercise. What did you learn about yourself? About your partner?

That may have been very difficult for you to do. Your past learning probably dictated that you must be "modest." Given this disposition, you may have difficulty seeing your strengths in what seems to be a forest of weaknesses. This continuous focus on weaknesses and shortcomings may serve to motivate you for a while, but there comes a point when you feel "Oh what's the use?" This pattern is very difficult to break, especially when you only receive negative feedback from others. <u>You</u> are the <u>most</u> <u>important</u> <u>person</u> <u>you</u> <u>know</u>. You do most things very well. Others feel this way, too, but they've been taught not to tell you. Let's remedy this situation immediately. Do Exercise 6.11.

Exercise 6.11

You are not the only one who feels you can do things well. Your partner and others feel that way also. In this exercise you will hear them.

A, it is your turn to begin. For two minutes you are to tell B your observations of his strengths—the things you feel he does well, the things you like about him, and the things you think other people like about him.

B, your task is simply to understand. Do not take issue with A's observations. He is entitled to his perceptions. When you receive a piece of feedback, respond with "What I think you mean is . . ." and then very immodestly acknowledge it with a "Thank you."

Paraphrase the instructions. Check with your partner. Begin.

Reverse the process. B, tell A the things you like about him and the things you think he does well. A, just understand and receive following the instructions above.

---

(1) Tell your partner how you felt during the exercise. What did you learn about yourself? Your partner?

(2) Take a few minutes to discuss how you feel about each other and your relationship. Include in this discussion how you feel about yourself.

Giving and receiving this positive feedback may have been very difficult for you. But I'm sure you found that you could both give and receive. Despite your discomfort, you probably felt pretty good. Hopefully you will share your perceptions of others when you observe them doing something that you like. It is not desirable to do this continuously since that would lessen the value of the feedback. But it is desirable to give positive feedback when you feel the benefit of that little extra effort and concern from others.

There are some things about you that your partner would like to see you change. Generally, these are not expressed openly. But from now on, in your relationship this will become the rule rather than the exception. Let's begin this now. Do Exercise 6.12.

Exercise 6.12

In this exercise you and your partner will use "live" data to build a more cooperative relationship. You will use the skills you learned in Chapters 5 and 6. Turn back to page 119 now and reread the guidelines for giving and receiving feedback.

Take two minutes in silence to think about your relationship with your partner. Think about his behavior and how you feel about his behavior.

Starting with you, A, make the following statement: "One thing which you could do to improve our relationship is . . ." and tell a specific behavior that A could do differently. Make your request consistent with the guidelines for giving feedback.

B, when A expresses his request, respond with "What I think you mean is . . ." and continue until you understand precisely what A is requesting. Then add "My reaction to that is . . . ." Use the guidelines for receiving feedback.

Continue the process of negotiation until a decision is made, a commitment is obtained, and appreciation expressed for both the feedback and the possible change.

Paraphrase the instructions. Check with your partner. Begin.

Reverse the process. B, express a request to A. A, receive. Use the guidelines set forth above.

---

(1) Tell your partner how you felt during the several parts of the exercise. What did you learn about yourself? Your partner?

(2) Take a few minutes to discuss how you feel about each other and your relationship. Based on your experience, how do you feel about sharing feedback to resolve conflict in the future? Include in your discussion how you feel about yourself.

There is no way to know the outcome of your negotiation for change. While it is important that each of you make some changes to accommodate the other person, the key is how you negotiated. Hopefully you did this in a way that communicated respect, understanding, and acceptance of both yourself and your partner. You may have found that you were unwilling to make the change requested. This is your prerogative along with the responsibility of being aware that if you do this behavior with your partner, you may be producing conflict. You may have found that your partner was unwilling to make the change you requested. This may necessitate experiencing conflict sometimes. This may mean you will need to become a little less sensitive. With or without change, hopefully the experience was satisfying and marked the beginning of a new cooperativeness in your relationship.

SUMMARY

Conflict is the emotional state you experience when the behavior of another person interferes with your behavior. Conflict resolution is an attempt to reconcile differences in order to reduce the conflict you feel. The concepts of shared responsibility and perceptual imperfection are keys to satisfactory resolution of conflict.

Your initial efforts at resolving the conflict you feel must begin with direct expression of feelings or expression of feelings using metaphor. This is necessary but not sufficient since most of the responsibility is projected to the listener. The following components must be added:

(1) a behavioral description of the situation or behavior that you think produced the conflict you feel;

(2) a prescription of what the other person could do differently or how the situation might be changed to help you with your problem;

(3) an explicit statement or a manner of communicating that suggests your perception is not perfect and that you may have read more into the situation than was really there.

The little conflicts that you have ignored in the past are best dealt with before they accumulate. Involve the other person in decisions about conflicts you feel about him.

You experience more than conflict in relationships (though it may not seem that way sometimes). You experience good feelings when people do behavior that you like. But most of us have learned to respond to people only when they foul up or produce conflict. It is important to respond to the things that people do that please you. In this way the frequency of "responsible" behavior will increase and the frequency of "irresponsible" behavior will decrease.

From a purely pragmatic point of view, it is important that others learn to express their feelings and thoughts directly without assistance. This will maximize resource use in a social system. A person learns to influence instead of responding passively to his world.

However desirable it is that people express their feelings directly, many of us have not learned to do so. In fact, we have been punished for doing so; we have learned to feel guilty for feeling. Some people, however, take the risk and express their feelings directly if the environment is perceived as relatively safe—if they see others doing likewise and if they are assured that they will be heard, their ideas and feelings used, and their efforts recognized.

Your efforts at requesting direct expression of feelings must begin with you directly expressing your feelings. Include all components to maximize the probability that your messages can be heard. If you feel a conflict, it is your problem and it may be only your problem.

It is important that individuals learn to express their feelings directly and without assistance. You can reduce another person's dependency on you for expressing his feelings by reinforcing him when he does so and requesting that he do so in the future without waiting to be asked. You cannot coerce people into expressing their feelings but you can provide an atmosphere in which they experience the freedom to do so or not at their discretion.

If direct expression of feelings is not effective in changing behavior that you feel produces conflict in you, you can ignore or extinguish the behavior while simultaneously giving attention to behavior that is more effective.

The behaviors that produce conflict in you probably produce conflict in others. If you want another person to stop doing a specific behavior you must stop doing it yourself. The admonition "Don't do as I do; do as I say" is unfair (it will produce conflict) even if you have the authority position that precludes challenge.

When you are involved in a disagreement over a topic or issue with another person and are unable to reconcile your differences, there are several strategies you can use. You can bring in a third party to view your behavior or to bring more data to bear on the issue. A mutually acceptable definition of the problem without "win" or "lose" explicitly stated or implied is very important. Minimizing the areas of disagreement, maximizing the areas of agreement, and listing circumstances acceptable for accommodation may also be helpful. Reverse role-playing and recess for cooperative activities may be effective.

Become aware, experiment in situations where you have a realistic chance of success, but don't learn to swim in the middle of a large, deep lake. As you experience success in dealing with less serious (less threatening) interpersonal problems, you will acquire the confidence to proceed to the more difficult problems. Start small, but think and plan big.

Summarizing Exercise

Once again let's review your learning. Alternately respond to each of the following statements. Include (1) the concepts you may have learned, (2) the meaning of those concepts for you, and (3) the implications of the concepts and the behaviors for you in your relationship with your partner and others. The listener should use the skills he has learned thus far and he should add what he remembers and the personal meanings and implications for him.

B. Explain the distinction that was made between conflict and conflict resolution. Illustrate this explanation.
A. Describe and demonstrate several behaviors that may produce conflict in relationships.
B. Demonstrate expressing your feelings to deal with behavior that interferes with your behavior: (1) feelings expressed physically; (2) feelings expressed indirectly; (3) ambiguous, incomplete, vague state-

ments, or statements without perceptual qualification. Explain the probable effects on the receiver.

A. Explain and demonstrate the behaviors you could use if your efforts to deal with the conflicts you feel precipitate another behavior that produces conflict for you.

B. Demonstrate the process called extinction.

A. Explain circumstances under which a question might be called non-facilitative. Demonstrate several facilitative questions.

B. Expressing feelings is a form of giving feedback. Explain the obligations for both the sender and receiver of feedback.

A. Give an explanation of the probable effects on a receiver if you request a frame of reference for a question. Demonstrate requesting a frame of reference.

B. In reconciling interpersonal problems, give an explanation of the probable consequences of (1) procrastinating in dealing with the problem and (2) discussing the problem with a third person.

A. Give an explanation and demonstrate a way to help a person learn to deal with his problem with a third person.

B. You are arguing with another person about a topic. Explain the effects on this person of (1) coming down, mirroring, and then paraphrasing; (2) coming down, expressing feelings directly, and requesting a discussion of the relationship.

A. Explain several specific strategies you might use to resolve conflict when both people in a relationship are behaving effectively, but an impasse is reached.

FOR FURTHER READING

References are grouped by subject on pages 208-215. For further reading on the concepts covered in this chapter, see references under these headings:

Behavior-Communication Paradox and Values
Commitment, Action, and Interpersonal Contracts
Communication Theory: Norms, Roles, Expectations, Interaction
Human Development and Normalcy
Interaction Analysis
Interpersonal Problem Solving: Feelings, Feedback, and Conflict
    Resolution
Modeling and Reinforcement
Nonverbal Communication
Openness, Authenticity, and Trust in Relationships
Perceptions of Self and Others
Responsibility in Relationships
Self-Disclosure

SYSTEMATIC BEHAVIOR CHANGE III

Listed below are the behaviors that were the focus of your learning in Chapters 5 and 6. Once again record the frequency that your partner does each of the behaviors with you or with others for seven days. Two observation schedules are presented on the following pages for your use. As before you can record each behavior or each conversation. Enter your totals on the Progress Chart at the end of each day. Discuss your progress with each other each day.

Direct expression of feelings: In my relationships with others I will directly express my feelings. If another person is involved in the conflict I feel, I will describe the behavior that I perceive to interfere with my behavior. I will prescribe the behavior change that would help me either at the outset or when another person requests it.

Receiving expressed feelings: When I hear another person expressing his feelings directly, I will paraphrase the feelings he is expressing without defending, apologizing, or in any way deprecating the other person's feelings.

Facilitating direct expression of feelings: When I observe others expressing their feelings indirectly, I shall express my feelings, describe the behavior I see and/or the feeling state that I infer, and request that the person help me by expressing his feelings directly. When the person complies, I will paraphrase his feelings without deprecating his feelings.

Reward direct expression of feelings: When a person expresses his feelings, I shall express appreciation for this behavior.

Asking and requesting facilitative questions:
(1) Before I ask a question I will provide the listener with the frame of reference for the question.
(2) When another person asks me a direct question, I will request a frame of reference for the questions before I respond.
(3) If I wish to express a feeling about the behavior of another person, I will not entrap the person by asking the type of question that may precipitate a lie.

Facilitative conflict resolution: When I am engaged in an argument with another person, I will:
(1) come down in affect and summarize for understanding as a means of working through the conflict, moving later to a discussion of "how" we reconcile our differences;
(2) come down in affect, express my feelings directly, and request a discussion of how we reconcile our differences.

Receiving feedback: When someone gives me feedback directly or in the form of direct expression of feelings, I will paraphrase for understanding and:

(1) if the feedback is positive, express appreciation for the feedback and accept the feedback without embarrassment or any deprecation of the feedback;

(2) if the feedback is negative, consider making the requested change without defensiveness. Should I choose not to make the requested change, I will explain to my partner my thoughts and feelings. Should I choose to make the requested change, I will request assistance as I feel the need. Under either circumstance, I will express appreciation for the feedback.

Giving feedback: When I give feedback to another person directly or in the form of direct expression of feelings, I will request paraphrase for understanding if necessary and:

(1) allow the person to experience freedom in making the change or not as he chooses;

(2) paraphrase his thoughts or feelings as he considers the change, offer assistance as required, and express appreciation for his consideration whether or not the change is made.

Requesting effective messages: When another person is sending incomplete or ambiguous messages that produce conflict in me I shall express my feelings directly, describe the behavior, and request change.

Sending effective messages: When I am speaking I shall speak for myself, speak to the person I wish to respond, and qualify my statements as my experience or my perception.

TALLY CHART

Behavior \ Day	1	2	3	4	5	6	7
Direct expression of feelings							
Receiving expressed feelings							
Facilitating direct exp. of feelings							
Reward direct exp. of feelings							
Asking & requesting facilitative questions							
Facilitative conflict resolution							

PROGRESS CHARTS

Direct expression of feelings

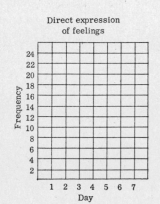

Receiving expressed feelings

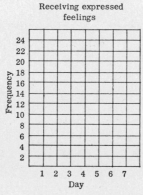

Facilitating direct expression of feelings

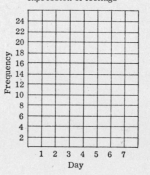

Reward direct expression of feelings

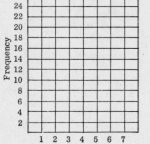

Asking & requesting facilitative questions

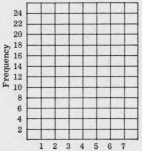

Facilitative conflict resolution

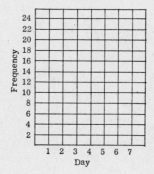

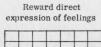

TALLY CHART

Behavior \ Day	1	2	3	4	5	6	7
Direct expression of feelings							
Receiving expressed feelings							
Facilitating direct exp. of feelings							
Reward direct exp. of feelings							
Asking & requesting facilitative questions							
Facilitative conflict resolution							

PROGRESS CHARTS

Direct expression
of feelings

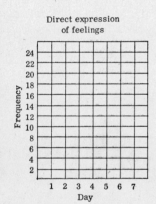

Receiving expressed
feelings

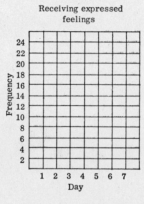

Facilitating direct
expression of feelings

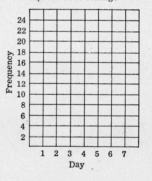

Reward direct
expression of feelings

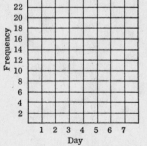

Asking & requesting
facilitative questions

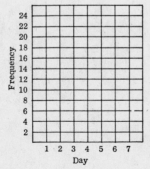

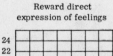

Facilitative conflict
resolution

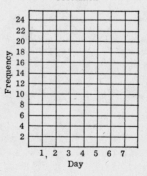

TALLY CHART

Behavior \ Day	1	2	3	4	5	6	7
Receiving feedback							
Giving feedback							
Requesting effective messages							
Sending effective messages							

PROGRESS CHARTS

Receiving feedback

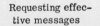

Giving feedback

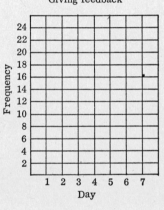

Requesting effective messages

Sending effective messages

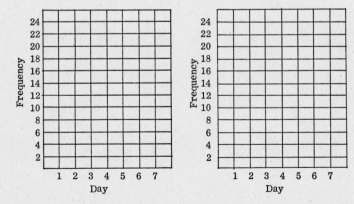

TALLY CHART

Behavior \ Day	1	2	3	4	5	6	7
Receiving feedback							
Giving feedback							
Requesting effective messages							
Sending effective messages							

PROGRESS CHARTS

Receiving feedback

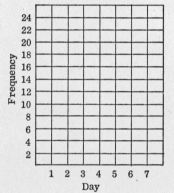

Giving feedback

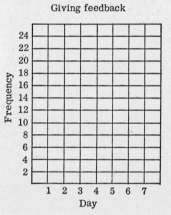

Requesting effective messages

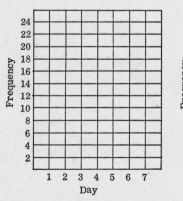

Sending effective messages

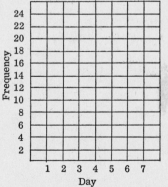

CHAPTER SEVEN

Intervention in Your Social Systems

You will need approximately $1\frac{1}{2}$ hours to get the maximum learning from this chapter.

In the preceding chapters the focus for your learning was developing skills and understanding why these skills are probably more effective than those you have been using. If you use these skills, the quality of your relationships may improve. However effective these skills may be, there are other aspects of interpersonal relationships and social systems that will help you use the skills to the advantage of all.

THE INDIVIDUAL IN THE SOCIAL SYSTEM

As you and your partner worked through this book, you built a social system. In your system each person was a resource for the other. As you learned the skills and the concepts, you helped each other. You may have differed at times, but the goal was helping each other and the relationship was constant. Although you may have formed a more cohesive social system, the uniqueness that is each person was not lost. Your individuality was enhanced by the quality of your relationship. Most social systems do not promote the development of the system and the development of the individuals within that system simultaneously.

It is quite common to hear a social system described as "it," "they," "them," "we," or "us." A social system is a collective unit. It is comprised of individuals who always wish to retain their identity as individuals while belonging to the collective. As a social system gets large, this becomes very difficult. But evidence suggests that if the social system treats the individual as the unique person he feels himself to be, the individual will more readily support the social system and will be more productive in the social system. These are practical reasons for respecting the individual within a social system. There is the further reason that is often lost in a pragmatic, utilitarian society: each human being deserves his right to dignity as an individual.

These are words that most social systems readily espouse. Unfortunately the reality often falls short. Let's see how we might make this view operational in a business meeting, classroom, or family forum. Let's characterize the system as follows:

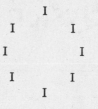

In the above diagram each person is designated as "I." Each member of a group is an individual who can serve a leadership function. Suppose a member of a group has information or a skill (resource) that meets some problem confronting the system and he makes that resource available to the system. At that moment he is the leader. As he makes his contribution he has the right to be heard and understood. He also has the authority to yield when he is finished or to continue. If another person seeks to express his comment (resource), only the speaker can authorize his entry. (This would not preclude helping someone express himself or paraphrase comments.)

Often the speaker is talking to another member. Together they constitute a subsystem that has the floor. Let's diagram the subsystem as follows:

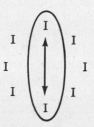

Should another person seek entry, he should respect the rights of the individuals that comprise the subsystem and request entry. All this formality and recognition of individual rights serves to encourage participation as individuals feel some control over the dynamics of the interaction.

It is possible that an individual may ramble on and on, but it is more likely to happen in a system where there is competition rather than cooperation, where members do not feel heard and their ideas are not considered seriously. Rambling does not reduce the speaker's right, but you may have to interrupt with direct expression of your feelings. "John, I'm becoming impatient. I think I understand your position.

Could I check to be sure I understand you and then could I respond?" In your initial efforts to promote a cooperative norm and respect for individual rights, you will be fighting old habits that develop when interaction is competitive. "I sure don't get to speak very often around here, so now that I have the chance, I had better make the most of it." In time this will change as ease of entry increases and people feel understood.

The individuals in a system are most effectively arranged in a circle. This is probably the most functional arrangement for promoting member-to-member interaction. Every other form tends to promote member-to-leader interaction. If members are seated around a rectangular table or stacked in rows and columns, the typical flow of communication will be through the leader. The circle serves other important functions. If each member is responsible for his behavior and the impact of his behavior on others, he should be in a position to observe each other person. Further, nonverbal behavior can be observed. These nonverbal signals may communicate an unspoken feeling or thought that the system needs to hear. King Arthur had a good idea with his round table.

As the leader of a system you can establish this circular arrangement of members and a more effective norm of communication. As the leader you are responsible for promoting respect for individual rights and the best use of the system's resources. By using the skills you have learned in this book, you can intervene to promote this norm. Your primary concern is "how" the group goes about its defined task. Several case studies are presented on the next few pages. These illustrate ways you might intervene to promote efficient use of resources and respect for individual rights.

Case Study 1

Read the following interventions aloud.

Leader or "I get uncomfortable when I can't see every person in our
member: our group without leaning forward or backward. It would
           help me if those of you along the side of the table would kind
           of "belly-out" in the middle so we form a rough circle.
           Thank you. Can everybody see each other person without
           straining? Good."

Leader: "Somehow I'm bothered by the formality of our sitting around
           the table. Let's take our chairs to this open area and form a
           circle so I can see every other person more easily. I can
           see it will be more difficult to take notes, but we could use
           note pads. Would that be okay? Good. Thank you."

> Analyze the behavior of the person who made the two interventions in Case Study 1. What are the possible effects if the interventions were made by (1) the leader and (2) a member.

Assuredly, these two interventions would be easier for a leader to make. His perceived authority will promote cooperation with the request despite anxiety on the part of some members of the system. The table structure and rows-and-columns structure provides a security for certain members. You may have noticed someone in a front row seat stand up and take a pot-shot at a comment made by someone in the back and then sit down abruptly leaving the other person hanging. He could make his statement with a certain impunity since he did not have to observe the effects of his behavior on the other person. A similar phenomenon can be observed as one member makes a comment to another two seats down the same side of a table.

A similar kind of intervention is made in Case Study 2. This time the intervention is made to promote individual rights to hold or relinquish the floor.

Case Study 2

Read the following dialogue aloud.

Teacher 1 (Helen): "I really like the idea of team teaching. It sounds like a real opportunity to learn more about teaching."

Principal: "You really like the idea. It will give you a chance to see other teachers in action and perhaps get new ideas."

Teacher 1 (Helen): "Exactly."

Principal: "Okay. Could I respond?"

Teacher 1 (Helen): "Sure!"

Principal: "Thank you."

Teacher 1 (Helen): Speaking to Teacher 3 (Bill). "Bill, I like the idea of having teachers work together in the same class. It seems like this would allow more time for individual attention."

Teacher 2 (Mary): "I agree that it would be a good idea, but I'm not sure that it is economically feasible, and . . . ."

Principal: (Interrupts) "Excuse me, Mary. I'm uncomfortable. I'm not sure Helen and Bill were finished. Would you check with them to see if they have something more to say before you come in? Thank you."

> Analyze the behavior of each member of both parts of Case
> Study 2. Specifically analyze the intervention by the princi-
> pal and possible effects of his intervention on Teacher 1,
> Teacher 2, and the group as a whole.

In Case Study 2 the leader intervened to establish the norm of
respecting individual rights. In the first part he demonstrated that he
was not immune from the rule he would like to see established. In the
second part he expressed his feelings, described the situation that he
felt influenced his feelings, and requested assistance from Mary. It
is likely that Mary may be somewhat embarrassed, but she probably
will check it out. She also has been sensitized to watch more closely
in the future. The leader did not do the job for Mary but used his
authority position to request that Mary intervene. Three or four such
interventions by the leader and the norm may be established to the
point where the speaker will indicate "I'm finished." This norm also
serves to legitimatize a comment if one member is interrupted by
another. "Mary, I'm not quite finished. Could you wait? Thank you."
When checking to see if another member is finished speaking is not
legitimatized, interruptions pile upon interruptions and competition may
become the norm.

A similar kind of intervention soliciting paraphrase can quickly
establish the norm of paraphrasing for understanding before responding.
Consider Case Study 3.

Case Study 3

Read the following interaction aloud.

Roy: (Talking to the class as a whole) "I think that World War
            II could have been avoided, but it was used as a means to
            get out of the depression and to build a new faith in Amer-
            ica."
Cleo: "I don't think that it was deliberately started . . . ."
Teacher: (Interrupts) "Excuse me, Cleo. Before you give your
            ideas let me check to be sure I understand what Roy said.
            Okay, Cleo?"
Cleo: "Okay."
Teacher: (Teacher paraphrases) "Thanks, Cleo. Roy, I hear you
            saying that America did not have to get involved in World
            War II, but because the depression was lingering on, we
            used this as an opportunity to get back on our feet econom-
            ically."

Roy:	"Yes, but America's spirit was low also."
Teacher:	"So you are saying that it also gave our spirit a shot in the arm."
Roy:	"Yes."
Teacher:	"Okay, Cleo. <u>Thanks</u> for waiting. You started to say that you didn't think it was deliberately started."
Cleo:	"Yeah, I think we would have been involved no matter what. Germany was a threat to the rights of all people. Japan had a totalitarian system that was bent on territorial expansion."
Marguerite:	"I rather agree with both of you . . . ."
Teacher:	"Marguerite, excuse me. Before you share your comment could you tell Cleo what you understood her to say before you respond and check with her to be sure you understood."
Marguerite:	"I guess so. She said that . . . ." (Paraphrases)
Teacher:	"Thank you, Marguerite. Now I would like to hear your comment."

Analyze the behavior of each person. Specifically analyze the interruptions by the teacher and the probable effects (immediate and long term) on students to whom the intervention is directed.

The manner of the teacher's intervention was quite similar to that used by the principal in Case Study 2. A different behavior was sought in this case. Other than respecting individual rights to be understood and establishing a cooperative norm, the paraphrase serves other purposes in all settings. It states the observation in a different way—a way that may help another person understand if he did not understand the first explanation. Further, pausing to paraphrase will tend to offset the quick response that can lead to attempts at conflict resolution through argument and interrupting behavior.

If the teacher intervenes a few times in this manner, the norm will quickly be established—if for no other reason than to get the teacher off the students' backs. But eventually the students will learn to like the reciprocal respect that they experience in the norm. Again, paraphrase is not always necessary but becomes necessary when emotional tones suggest an argument may be coming.

If all this sounds like a lot of work, it is. <u>Your</u> <u>attention</u> <u>must</u> <u>be</u> <u>directed</u> <u>to</u> <u>the</u> <u>way</u> <u>members</u> <u>interact.</u> You know you want cooperative interaction respecting individual rights. You intervene to promote this. For awhile you may have to live with an air of impatience to get on with the task.

In the teaching situation, for example, learning will probably proceed more efficiently than before if the teacher establishes a norm of cooperative interaction respecting individual rights. Students may learn more efficiently instead of "covering the material." The teacher may find that he needs to lecture less and he may just find that he enjoys teaching more when the norm in the classroom is cooperative rather than competitive. This norm of cooperative interaction can also be established in business settings to bring about more cooperation and corresponding satisfaction. If this norm is established at home, the "inevitable" conflict that is so "natural" in any family may decrease markedly.

With all of your attempts to change the norm of interaction in your social system, you may wish to help others learn as you have done. If you are in an authority position, you can establish the kind of interaction you would like to see by explaining to the group in advance what your role is and asking others to have patience with you as you intervene. Until they learn, however, you probably will need to make interventions like those illustrated in the case studies. The other group members may even help you if they know what you are doing.

If you are not in an authority position, your task is much more difficult. You must constantly use behavior consistent with the norm you would like to see. When the opportunity presents itself, you can make many of the interventions illustrated above. Without an authority base, you may have to intervene as illustrated in Case Study 4.

Case Study 4

Read the dialogue aloud.

Two individuals are talking at the same time. This represents a conflict for you and you interrupt:

> "Excuse me. Could I stop you for a moment? Thank you. I have a problem. I want to hear both of you, but when you are both talking at the same time, I can hear and understand neither of you. It would help me if only one of you would speak at a time. Will you do this?"

The chances are good that they will comply.

> "Thank you."

Let's look at another situation. The interaction is getting a bit heated. People are responding irrelevantly, interrupting each other, etc. You could attempt a shift from discussion of the topic to a discussion of the way each person is behaving.

"I have a problem. I am impatient with the way we are trying to resolve our differences. We seem bent on putting each other down. It would help me if we could talk about how we could reconcile our differences in a different way."

Or you could begin to do the behavior that each person needs to do to resolve the conflict by a means other than argument.

"John, before you come in let me check to be sure I understand what Harry is saying. Okay? Thanks." (Paraphrases)

> Analyze the interventions made above. What are the probable effects of these interventions (immediate and long term) on the individuals and on the group?

In the second intervention Harry feels heard. John is forced to hear indirectly. It brings about a pause in the argument. The tempo will be reduced when you pass the floor back to John. If you respond to your felt need to understand, the norm will be altered somewhat. Then again, there is a risk. They may reject you or attempt to involve you in the existing norm.

Yes, the task will not be easy, but the long-term payoff will be great for all individuals and thus for the social system. Let's examine another example to help you see how you might intervene to promote the cooperative norm that you might want. In this case let's focus on feelings expressed indirectly. Again, as either leader or member you can intervene as follows.

Case Study 5

Read the dialogue aloud.

Hilda: Frowning and shaking her head.
Leader: "Hilda, I'm concerned. You are frowning and shaking your head as though you disagree. Could you share your thoughts and feelings?"
Hilda: "Yes. I just don't feel that we should replace any more men on the production line. That is going to get us in trouble with the union."
Leader: "I understand you to say that . . . ." (Paraphrase; pause)
Hilda: "Indeed, yes. I think we should consider this before we make a decision."
Leader: (Paraphrase; pause) "Thanks for sharing that. It would help if you could give us your thoughts without my asking. Could you do this?"

> Analyze the probable effects (both immediate and long term) of the leader's intervention on Hilda and on other members of the group.

In Case Study 5 the leader was trying to establish the norm of directly expressing feelings and ideas. The nonverbal signal cued him that this person was a resource—had a question, feeling, contribution that might have a direct bearing on the quality of the decision. The leader concluded with a request to continue to do so. If Hilda felt heard, she probably will continue to do so. Others who observe may begin to speak out. The beginning of a new norm?

The next case study we will examine involves the feelings that Peter has about the behavior of another member of his family.

Case Study 6

Read the dialogue aloud.

Peter: Frowning, head lowered, looking out the top of his eyes, lips set firmly.

Mother: "Peter, I have a problem. You look angry."

Peter: "Why should I be angry? Who cares?"

Mother: "You sound really upset about something. It would help me if you could tell me about it."

Peter: "It's Charlie. Every time I say something he has to make faces and make fun of my ideas."

Mother: "So you are upset with Charlie. Could you tell him this instead of me?"

Peter: "Oh, he won't listen."

Mother: "You are really concerned that he won't listen. You would tell him if you could be sure he would listen."

Peter: "Yes, but he won't listen."

Mother: "Why don't you ask Charlie if he will listen?"

Peter: "Okay. Charlie, will you listen to me and not make fun of me like you usually do?"

Charlie: "Me listen to you? You just have dumb ideas."

Mother: "Charlie, you didn't answer Peter's question."

Charlie: "Okay, I'll listen."

Mother: "Good. Thank you. Peter, do you suppose you could tell Charlie how you feel and what he does that makes you feel that way without punishing him? He has agreed to listen."

Peter: "I get so mad. When I say something that I am excited about you make me feel dumb."

Charlie: "I don't either. You are just too touchy."
Mother: "Charlie, could you just tell Peter what he told you?"

> What is the mother trying to accomplish? Analyze Mother's
> interventions in terms of the probable effects on Peter and
> Charlie.

This case is particularly tough. When feelings smolder a long time
(as seems to be the situation with Peter) the feelings are dominant.
Mother could have paraphrased Peter's feelings in greater depth, but
this would not have helped the problem with Peter. Thus, her interventions sought to develop a cooperative, mutually respectful norm between
Peter and Charlie. As another alternative Mother could have paraphrased the feelings of both boys to model what they need to do. As both
Charlie and Peter feel heard by someone, their feelings will be less
intense. They may be in a better position to hear each other and to
describe the behavior of the other that they would like to see changed.
It won't happen through this one interaction, but given a consistent
approach by Mother and Father when this kind of conflict resolution
occurs, the norm will gradually be established. Mother and Father can
add to the learning considerably if they reconcile their own differences
fairly with their children present.

There is another intervention opportunity that will contribute much
to respecting individual rights, building individual strengths, and promoting unity within (rather than dividing) the social system. Read and
analyze Case Study 7.

Case Study 7

Read the interactions aloud.

Pauline: "I want to go to the zoo first and then go to the museum."
Otis: "Naw. It's too cold to go to the zoo now. Isn't that right,
            Ms. Jones?"
Ms. Jones: "Otis, your statement really puts me in a bind. You are
            asking me to agree with you and even if I do, this will not
            settle your differences with Pauline. Work it out with her.
            You can do it without my help. Will you try?"
Otis: "Well, I guess so."
Ms. Jones: "Good."
(From this point Ms. Jones will intervene only to help them fight fairly.)

Otis: "Naw. It's too cold to go to the zoo now. Isn't that right,
            Ms. Jones?"

Ms. Jones: "I can give you my opinion. But right now I suspect that if I
            disagree with you, you will become angry with me. I just
            won't give you my opinion unless you can assure me that you
            will respect it as my opinion and not get angry with me if I
            disagree with you."
Otis: "Okay."
Ms. Jones: "Pauline, I need that assurance from you as well."
Pauline: "Sure."
Ms. Jones: "Could one of you tell me what it is that you are agreeing
            to. Otis?"
Otis: "You want to be able to state your opinion without us getting
            angry with you if we disagree."
Ms. Jones: "Yes. Is that what you understood, Pauline?"
Pauline: "Yes. You don't want to be in a bind."
Ms. Jones: "Right."

Analyze Otis' request in terms of his own capacity to deal with
interpersonal problems. What would the effects be on Pauline,
Otis, and others in the system if Ms. Jones had taken a position? What is Ms. Jones' long-term goal? Under what conditions will Ms. Jones take a position? Analyze how she went
about that.

Divide and conquer works well in military operations. It is similarly
devastating to relationships. If Ms. Jones had responded to Otis'
request, Otis would not have learned that he can deal with his own interpersonal conflicts. Also, depending on her response either the relationship between Ms. Jones and Otis or Ms. Jones and Pauline would have
been damaged. Certainly the relationship between Otis and Pauline
would not have been helped regardless of Ms. Jones' opinion. Indirectly,
Ms. Jones' intervention may have been the beginning of their learning to
ask questions or express requests that do not create double binds for the
receiver. Ms. Jones sought a verbal, explicit contract before venturing
her opinion. The verbal response of understanding and commitment
before a group of peers is a tremendously motivating (coercive) force to
honor the contract as stated. It is necessary to observe the nonverbal
behavior of those who make such a commitment to be sure they are comfortable with it and not doing it in response to group pressure. It is
okay not to want to make such a commitment. Correspondingly, it is
okay for Ms. Jones not to venture her opinion unless she can be assured
that she can do so independently. She was asserting her right to be
treated as an individual. She also modeled for others.
Each of the case studies in this chapter illustrates how interventions

can be made to promote the desired norm of communication that respects individual rights and thus makes the social system more effectively attain its goals. It is important to remember that your interventions to promote this norm constitute a value judgment on your part. No norm of communication is in itself right or wrong. Any norm of communication is effective or ineffective relative to how well it serves the purposes for which it was intended—for individuals and for social systems.

Let's move on to another area that needs to be considered to help social systems function more effectively.

GOAL SETTING

A social system can make the most efficient progress toward attaining its goals when the goals are explicitly stated in ways that can be measured. In Chapter 5 when you were learning to express your feelings directly you learned to give precise behavioral descriptions and behavioral prescriptions for desired behavior change. This is the level of precision you should seek in stating goals. A goal describes a situation that does not currently exist but that would exist if the activities of a social system are successful. If goals are not precisely stated, not only will progress toward goals be impeded but members of the system may have ambiguous feelings about participating.

A. "Do you know why he called this meeting?"
B. "No, but he never calls a meeting unless something is wrong. The government cut back on funds recently. I wonder if there will be any layoffs."
A. "Do you think that is what it's about? I hope not. I have so many bills. I've only been here for six weeks. I'll be one of the first to go."

If the announcement of a meeting would include a bit of information about the purpose of the meeting, much of this could be avoided. Few people respond well when they are unclear about what will happen to them. Ambiguity builds anxiety. An overload of anxiety affects productivity and morale.

A goal is stated in future tense. It describes the desired future state if the activities of the social system are successful. Let's look at some goals that are fairly precise and measurable.

If we are successful, at the end of the meeting (class period, production year, family forum, counseling session):

"We will have made a decision about whether we will use team-teaching in Peabody Junior High School in the next school year."

"We will have heard each student's opinion about the causes of World War II."

"Each student will verbally recite conjugations of the French verbs etre, avoir, and pouvoir in present, past, and future tenses."

"We will have increased sales volume by two million dollars."

"We will have made a decision about reassigning salesmen to new territories or retaining them in their present territories."

"We will have decided which cities we will visit on our vacation, how much time we will spend in each city, and how much money we can afford to spend on the vacation."

"Each member of the staff will:
(1) express his thoughts and feelings directly without assistance from other members of the staff;
(2) paraphrase the ideas and feelings communicated to them;
(3) check with the speaker to be sure the interpretation was accurate and to be sure the other person is finished speaking before responding."

"Distribute to the members of the staff a list of goals to be attained at the weekly staff meetings. This list will be in the hands of each person no later than two days before the meeting."

"You will be walking up to people, introducing yourself, and initiating conversations rather than waiting for others to come to you."

"You will earn a grade of B or higher in math class."

Very often goals are stated in terms of activities: "Discuss the Jones contract." Members would be more likely to contribute their opinions if the goal were stated like this: "We will have heard members' opinions about the best strategies to employ in attaining the Jones contract for our firm."

Consistent with concern for individual rights, individuals should be involved in determining goals for the system. This can be accomplished if the leader takes some initiative. Each member of a system has information that is relevant to the successful functioning of that system. Memos are notoriously ineffective in obtaining information about the concerns of individual members. Requesting information in a large group will gain a few ideas but only from the more verbal members. Your initial efforts (should you find yourself as "leader" of a group) may require one-to-one or small group contacts. This will communicate that you really want the members' ideas. This will be reinforced as their ideas are used. As you hear their ideas, formulate goals with them.

"We will have discussed several examples to illustrate how a person can intervene in an ongoing social system to change the norm of communication." "We will have heard ideas from each member about the alternatives available to us to train the workers to use the new machines." "We will have made a decision about the kind of dog we will get."

It is possible that a goal may seem functional for an individual, but within the context of the system it may not be feasible. Requesting participation in goal definition should include a discussion of goal feasibility. As an individual participates in the discussion of his goal he will become aware of constraints that may render his goal infeasible. In the future his suggestions may be more compatible with reality as he becomes informed.

A parallel activity might be used. As a part of involving others in defining goals, the leaders of a system could communicate constraints and limits (as they perceive them). This information may serve to develop goals that are not only innovative but feasible.

Problems are more effectively dealt with and are seen as less formidable when they are precisely defined. Compare these two problems. "Everything is going wrong!" "The car won't start! I got fired! My hair is a mess! I failed my exam." It sure sounds as though everything is going wrong, but the solution seems much easier in "Get the car repaired, get a new job, wash and comb your hair, and prepare more adequately for the next exam" than in "Everything is going right."

At the beginning of every class, meeting, or family forum it is useful to check that all people agree on the goals. "I imagine you are wondering why I called you together" is best eliminated. But a restatement of the goals as you see them and verification from other members will help jog memories a bit. Similarly, a review at the end comparing goals with accomplishments is an excellent basis for reviewing the procedures used to conduct the class, meeting, or forum.

DEFINING PROCEDURES

A precise statement of goals is only a first step. Any social system needs to establish formal procedures about how it will proceed to accomplish tasks. This means more than ordering the topics to be discussed. It describes the ground rules the group will use in the interaction. Group meetings often bog down simply because there is no explicit set of procedures. Each member conducts the discussion in his own unique way. Each member has his own private plan that to him is a logical progression toward the goal. But unless the group can agree on a common plan, there will be chaos resembling the cacophony of tuning up before a symphony concert. A group may decide upon this way of proceeding, but it should be by design and not by default.

Robert's Rules of Order is one set of procedures. Unfortunately this system limits member-to-member discussion considerably and depends heavily on control from the chairman. Ideally, the procedures are defined by the group for the purpose of accomplishing the immediate task. Ideally each member would be responsible to stay within the bounds of the procedures and help each other member stay within the bounds. This avoids dependency on the leader.

Suppose the goal is stated: "We will have heard each student's opinion about the causes of World War II." We ask the next question. How shall we go about this? Should each student speak in turn around the circle? Should each student speak as he feels the urge? Who begins? Do we proceed clockwise or counter-clockwise? Do we react to each student's contribution right after we hear it, or do we wait until we have heard from all students?

Whatever procedures emerge from the system, it is important to successful resolution of differences that understanding be separated from evaluation. Understanding each person's opinion in depth will show more similarities than differences. Disagreeing on a small portion of a statement reinforces the norm of disagreeing and gives rise to a competitive, argumentative norm. Seeking understanding in depth before evaluating serves to point up similarities and to cool off the rash judgments which give rise to competition. An anecdote might illustrate this for you.

> Thomas Jefferson and Alexander Hamilton were relaxing after having dinner together. The coffee had been poured. As was the custom at that time Alex poured his coffee into his saucer. He asked, "Tom, why should we have two houses in the legislature? It seems it would be very inefficient and a waste of money and manpower."
>
> Tom paused, looked at Alex as he leaned back in his chair, and asked, "Why do you pour your coffee into your saucer?"
>
> Alex responded with a puzzled look on his face, "To cool the coffee, of course."
>
> Tom smiled triumphantly. "So we also must cool the legislation."

As we would cool the legislation, so we must also cool the evaluation that is so quick to spring up in many of us. Taking the time to explore an idea in depth through paraphrase and discussion of how it might be made to work would lead to an informed statement on its feasibility rather than a rash, flippant judgment. Some very improbable ideas may become very feasible and advantageous. In addition, when a member's ideas are given thoughtful consideration as opposed to snap judgments he is more likely to actively participate in and support the social system.

NORM OF COMMUNICATION

So we have well defined problems and goals and a set of procedures that seem functional for the task of the group. What is missing? We still need to promote development of a norm of communication that maximizes individual rights and resource utilization for the social system. You as leader and you as member can do this through interventions like those exemplified in the beginning of this chapter. Another activity can help promote the desired norm of communication: a review of the procedures and an assessment of the progress made toward defined goals with an opportunity for members to express feelings and give feedback. If each member would respond to the following questions after a meeting, progress would be made (slowly but surely) toward finding the most functional norm of communication for the group's task.

(1) What did I do today that I particularly liked?
(2) What behavior did I do today that I would like to change and that I will work on in our next session?
(3) What behaviors did other members of the group do that I liked?
(4) What behaviors did other members of the group do that I felt interfered with the progress of the group?

The behavior of members who respond to these questions might look like the following.

"I really worked on attending to people when they spoke today. It seems that I was able to stay with this task during the entire session. Did you feel as though I was attending well to you? It would help me if you could share your observations."

"I was not pleased with the amount of preparation I did for the meeting. There were times when I just could not make a contribution because I had not read all the memos. I was also not pleased with the way I was too quick to evaluate when I disagreed with a part of the speaker's statements. I want to work on understanding and I will make a deliberate effort to increase the frequency of paraphrasing in our next session."

"Bill, I think you paraphrased very well today. You did not paraphrase when it was obvious. It seemed you were able to discriminate when further clarification was needed and paraphrased to do this."

"Harriet, it would help my relationship with you and possibly help me in the meetings if you could share your feelings and ideas directly. I am somewhat distracted when I observe a nonverbal signal. I get the impression you have something to say and this is later confirmed when you express yourself. However, in the interim I find it very distracting.   Could you help me and do this?"

As the leader who wants to make the norm of communication most effective for all members, you will need to begin. Model what you want the others to do. It would serve no purpose to "make" each member take his turn. This only increases tensions and produces resistance, thereby lowering your power of influence. However, if you make each of the four statements about your own behavior and if you solicit feedback regarding others' perceptions of your behavior and receive this feedback well, the probability is increased that others will take the risk.

Initial efforts at this activity and at defining a set of procedures are often made with "we" statements. This is low risk—and correspondingly unproductive. It is akin to "they" statements. "Why don't they do something?" "They are always doing that." "We must go there some time." "We should be better prepared." "We must quit going off the task." These statements are not effective simply because nobody is assuming the responsibility. You can take these "we" statements and transform them—if you are willing to be the "I" of the "we." (If you make someone else the "I," you are setting a trap and that's decidedly unfair.) "That's a good idea. I will be more prepared next time. How about the rest of you?" "If I see us getting off the task, I will intervene to bring us back. I will need help. Will the rest of you do this also?"

As members publicly agree to the goals, set of procedures, norm of communication, and changes in behavior in the presence of others, you have mobilized the pressure of the peer group. Although members may feel free to choose, as other members of the group comply with the request, the pressure for all members to comply increases greatly. You must attend well to individuals as they verbalize a commitment. If their nonverbal signals suggest discomfort with the commitment, check it out and again let them experience freedom to choose or not. "John, I'm uncomfortable. I hear you saying you agree, but at the same time you seem uncomfortable with it. It would help me if you could share your thoughts and feelings." As you do this, you may elicit information to amend the agreement somewhat—more probably in the direction of a better decision for the group—and as you do so you are moving in the direction of a consensus decision.

CONSENSUS DECISIONS

Most people throw up their hands in dismay at the thought of getting a consensus decision. "We have a hard enough time getting a simple majority." If problems are defined in win-or-lose, either-or terms, the best that can be hoped for is a simple majority. If the norm of communication is one that exaggerates differences, does not separate understanding from evaluation, and emphasizes competition, you'll be lucky to get a majority. If members are not consulted in the process of goal and procedure definition, the majority will probably be the best you can attain.

But one fundamental problem with the majority decision is that there is always a disgruntled minority. Even though we have been taught to accept majority decisions, the minority never completely supports nor expends full energy to implement the majority decision.

Consensus does not mean full agreement. It means a decision that members are comfortable with and that members will support. Consensus does not mean polarizing the group and then having one side try to persuade (coerce) the other side to abandon its position. Compromise is implicit in the consensus decision.

If the norm of communication includes cooperation, respect for individual rights, and felt responsibility for self and others, the polarization accompanying most decision-making efforts will be minimized. The skills you have learned in this book approximate this cooperative norm. The collaborative activities and intervention activities you have learned in this chapter will supplement your use of the skills. The guidelines for giving and receiving feedback mentioned in Chapter 6 describe the attitudes and skills necessary for attaining consensus decisions. Consensus decisions result from the "how" of interaction, from the "how" of system resource use, and from "how" well individual dignity and rights are respected. These variables transcend specific issues. They allow each person his individual identity while allowing others their identities. This is basic to attaining a consensus.

As you return to your individual social systems, you cannot expect these ideals to be attained overnight. In fact, these ideals are probably not perfectly attainable. But they can be approximated as you use the skills in each of your relationships, as you intervene into your ongoing social systems to help others learn these skills. Learn to define problems, set goals, and define procedures. Evaluate the interaction and procedures in your social system. Apply the new skills. The effort required will be great. Sometimes you will fail, but you will observe a gradual transition to the ideal. Admittedly this ideal is a value choice. Only as you experience this ideal can you decide whether it fits your own values.

Summarizing Exercise

Time for review again. Respond to each of the following statements. Include (1) the concepts you may have learned, (2) the meaning of those concepts for you, and (3) the implications of the concepts and the behaviors for you in your relationship with your partner and others. Add what you remember and personal meaning and implications for you when your partner has finished.

A. Give an explanation of how respecting individual rights, promoting understanding, and using individual resources can pay dividends for a social system.

B. Demonstrate requesting permission to intervene into an ongoing conversation. What is the probable effect on the receiver when you request or when you do not request permission to intervene?

A. Explain why interventions to promote a specific norm of communication constitute a value judgment on your part.

B. Explain the advantages of setting specific goals and the possible disadvantages of not setting specific goals. Demonstrate how you might intervene to promote setting specific goals.

A. Explain the effects of defining a common set of procedures for a class, group, meeting, or forum. What are the probable effects if agreement on a common plan is not obtained?

B. An important ingredient for a set of procedures is separating understanding from evaluation. Explain the consequences if these are separated in the discussion plan and if they are not.

A. Explain the immediate and long-term effects on group members if at the end of the class, group, meeting, or forum you and other members self-disclose how you saw yourself and give feedback to others.

B. Explain how effective definition of the problem and an effective norm of communication can facilitate progress toward consensus decisions.

FOR FURTHER READING

References are grouped by subject on pages 208-215. For further reading on the concepts covered in this chapter, see references under these headings:

Attitude, Behavior, and Social Change
Commitment, Action, and Interpersonal Contracts
Communication Theory: Norms, Roles, Expectations, Interaction
Defining Procedures
Goal Setting
Idealized Relationships: Respect, Dignity, Values
Interaction Analysis
Interpersonal Problem Solving: Feelings, Feedback, and Conflict
    Resolution
Leadership, Decision Making, and Organization Development
Modeling and Reinforcement

SYSTEMATIC BEHAVIOR CHANGE IV

Listed below are the behaviors that were the focus of your learning in Chapter 7. Once again record the frequency that your partner does each of the behaviors with you or with others for seven days. Two observation schedules are presented on the following pages for your use. As before you can record each behavior or each conversation. Enter your totals on the Progress Chart at the end of each day. Discuss your progress with each other each day.

Goal setting: Before beginning a class, meeting, forum, or group discussion, I will state the goal(s) of the group as I understand it. I will state the goal in the form of the desired future state if the group is successful. I shall request that other members of the group define the goal(s) as they perceive it. We shall negotiate until a common goal statement has been reached.

Plan procedures: Before beginning a class, meeting, forum, or group discussion, I will offer an explicit plan or procedure for the group to follow in accomplishing its goal. I will solicit alternative plans from other group members. We shall negotiate until a common plan of action has been attained.

Request permission to intervene: When I am in a class, meeting, forum, or group discussion, I will respect the rights of individual members by recognizing they have the floor. I shall request permission to intervene should I wish to comment and wait until I am reasonably sure others are finished before commenting.

Intervention for resource utilization: I shall intervene in the class, meeting, forum, or group discussion to promote respect for individual rights, maximum resource utilization, and the development of an effective norm of communication.

Expressing action plans: When I am in a class, meeting, forum, or group discussion and a specific set of activities outside the group has been identified, I shall tell the group what I will do, when I will do it, and when I will report on the progress of the task. I shall request that other members make similar statements of commitment.

Review goals, plan, and communicate: At the end of a class, meeting, forum, or group discussion I shall initiate the following activities:
   (1) Review the accomplishments relative to the goals that were set.
   (2) Review the procedures used to make progress toward goals.
   (3) Share what I did that I liked and what I did that I would like to do differently.
   (4) Tell others what they did that I liked and what I perceived them to do that they could do differently to help the group's progress.
   (5) Request that others self-disclose and give feedback.

TALLY CHART

Behavior \ Day	1	2	3	4	5	6	7
Goal setting							
Plan procedures							
Requesting permission to intervene							
Intervention for use of resources							
Expressing action plans							
Review goals, plan, and communicate							

PROGRESS CHARTS

Goal setting

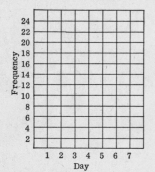

Plan procedures

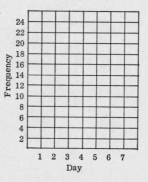

Request permission to intervene

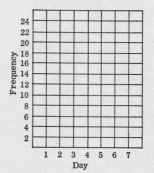

Intervention for resource utilization

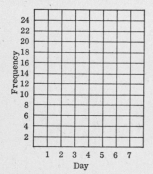

Expressing action plans

Review goals, plan, and communicate

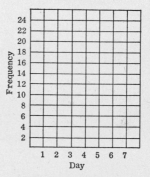

TALLY CHART

Behavior \ Day	1	2	3	4	5	6	7
Goal setting							
Plan procedures							
Requesting permission to intervene							
Intervention for use of resources							
Expressing action plans							
Review goals, plan, and communicate							

PROGRESS CHARTS

Goal setting

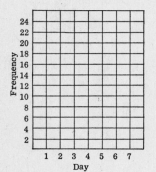

Plan procedures

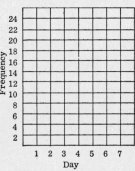

Request permission to intervene

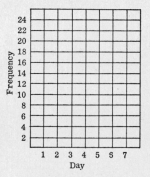

Intervention for resource utilization

Expressing action plans

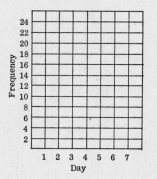

Review goals, plan, and communicate

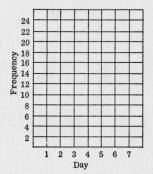

CHAPTER EIGHT

Application from Different Perspectives

At the beginning of this last chapter, I am vividly aware of how much more it would be useful for you to know. You, too, may be feeling the need to know more. Yet, there is another reality. You will need to learn a great deal on your own initiative—through your own efforts and through the exciting process of trying out new modes of communication and learning from your successes and failures. In any case you should not be deprived of the personal satisfaction and the growth that you will experience as you attempt to influence your world.

You will encounter many problems that you won't know precisely how to deal with as you attempt to influence your world. While the skills you have learned will be useful to you in most interpersonal situations, your particular environment is uniquely important to you. While no prescriptions apply to all possible situations, I can alert you to ways of applying the skills in a few selected situations. That is the purpose of this chapter. Specifically, we will analyze how you might use these skills as a student, teacher, parent, and/or administrator. Take whatever ideas seem to fit you and apply them to your own situations. Read them all. There are some ideas that may appear in each analysis that may be useful to you.

STUDENT

In most school situations, the student is in a very low "power" position. As a student you sometimes may feel completely at the mercy of your school and class environments. To some extent this is true, but the amount of influence you have in your classrooms is related directly to "how" you attempt to exert that influence.

Over years of experience, some teachers may have become very sensitive to attempts to influence in ways that could be construed as "disruptive." Similarly, many teachers are sensitive to influence in ways that may make them lose face. As a result, many classrooms have acquired an atmosphere that may best be described as psychological warfare. Indirect expression of feelings on the part of teachers and students is the norm. This gives rise to game-playing and psyching-out activities on the part of both the teacher and the students. A philosophy of many teachers is "If you give them an inch, they will want a foot." In response, the students may seek to stretch the inch into a foot, especially in a coercive classroom. Unfortunately, this often backfires, for as the inch stretches to two inches by methods that threaten the teacher's need for order, the students may end up by losing part of the original inch!

Another part of the gamesmanship makes changing the norm of communication difficult. As the teacher becomes fair game, other students will expect you to follow the crowd. You may even find yourself leading the charge. In some classrooms, the only satisfactions that students receive is upsetting the teacher, and the peer pressure to do so is very difficult to resist.

The above description may not fit any class that you have. Fortunately, it is not the existing norm of most classrooms.

Let's take a few of the skills you have learned and see how they might help your classrooms become more satisfying for you. In your classes, try attending well to your teacher. You will very quickly notice that your teacher will direct much of his attention to you. Contrary to some popular opinions, teachers are human beings and feel important and worth listening to when people attend to them.

Now let's add seeking clarification. In most traditional classrooms, teachers prefer that you raise your hand. First, you must ask for clarification only when you really don't understand words or phrases that need clarification. Mirroring is appropriate here. When asking for clarification you should make your request maximally facilitating. Give it a frame of reference and phrase it so that you are asking for help. "Ms. Wilson, you used the word 'parenthetically.' I'm not sure what that word means. Could you help me?" Most teachers will be glad you asked and will tell you so. Other teachers may respond very defensively. To protect themselves (for their own "need to explain perfectly the first time") they may think you "should know if you had been paying attention." They might say, "Look who doesn't know what 'parenthetically' means. How many times have we used the word and he is just asking now?"

At this point you will need to call on all your patience and fight the urge to fight back. If you respond defensively you will ultimately lose. The teacher is the "boss" and always has the ultimate weapon of expulsion to bring into the battle. But, stay by your guns and try to accept the teacher's impatience and need to put you down. "Yes, I realize that I probably should have asked earlier. But I didn't. I really would appreciate it if you would help me before we go any farther." You will get a response. It might not be given consistent with the spirit of the sincerity you feel in asking, but it will be a start. If you get a response, paraphrase the response to be sure you understand. "I understand you to say that . . . ." Follow this with a reward. "Thank you, that helps." Seek clarification whenever you feel the need. Don't seek clarification to show up the teacher; if you do, your nonverbal behavior will carry this motive and the teacher is likely to respond defensively. As your sincerity and desire to learn come through, the teacher's attitude and behavior will change slowly but surely.

You used paraphrasing in the above situation as the teacher responded to your question. Paraphrasing is useful in another way in the classroom. Some teachers lecture interminably. They literally throw the whole load at you at once. But many lectures are carefully planned. Concepts are often clearly isolated to make them more understandable. Many teachers will pause appropriately and ask for questions at what to them is an appropriate spot. When you have this opportunity use it; ask questions if that is what you need. This is also an excellent time to do a summary paraphrase of what the lecture material meant to you (how you interpreted it). If the teacher does not pause and offer an opportunity for questions, raise your hand whenever you feel the need to check your understanding and paraphrase. "It would help me if I could summarize what you have said so far. Is that okay?" The chances are good the teacher will grant your request. "Thank you. I understand that you said . . . ."

Some teachers have a bad habit of not waiting until you are finished speaking. They may anticipate the end of your question or paraphrase and end it for you. Sometimes they do this accurately. Sometimes they do not. After teaching a class for several years, teachers tend to hear the same or similar questions at the same point in the course. If their anticipation is not accurate, so indicate. "I'm not sure I made myself clear. Let me phrase it another way." Having anticipated incorrectly the first time, the chances are good a teacher will wait until you finish the second time around. After he responds to your paraphrase or question by giving additional information or elaborating, again paraphrase. When the transaction is finished, reward. "Thanks for helping me."

As you ask questions and paraphrase you are doing more than helping yourself. You are helping others in the class—students who did not know the meaning of "parenthetically" but were afraid to ask or students who wanted to verify their understanding but were afraid to and didn't know how to do this. Your paraphrase and the teacher's response to your questions typically involve different words which may help others to understand better. There is another valuable payoff for you; you probably will need to study less for your exams outside of class.

From your position as a student, expressing your feelings directly is a bit tricky. You can very easily express your positive feelings directly. This you should do when you feel satisfied with the experience.

As you express your positive feelings directly, the teacher will have some data with which to determine the most effective class activities. Over time, the frequency of those activities you like will gradually increase. As the frequency of activities you like increases, there will be a corresponding decrease in activities you dislike.

In your initial efforts, your negative feelings are probably best expressed when the teacher provides you with the opportunity. You can seek to make opportunities when it is legitimate to express negative feelings. "Mr. Jones, would you consider giving us some time to discuss how we can learn this material better?" Some teachers will feel very threatened by a suggestion like this. Most teachers spend a great deal of time and energy preparing for their classes and they are pretty ego-involved in the result of their best efforts. Some teachers, though, will seize upon this opportunity to obtain data to make the class experience more meaningful. This kind of teacher is probably uncomfortable developing methods without feedback and will appreciate it very much.

There is no way to know which kind of teacher you have. But if you are going to express your feelings, express them directly rather than indirectly. Indirect expression of feelings begets indirect expression of feelings. Direct expression of feelings may beget indirect expression of feelings but at least one of you is responding openly.

All teachers provide some opportunities for you to offer your comments. If you use these opportunities effectively to help the teacher, yourself, or the relationship you have with the teacher rather than to punish or put down, slowly but surely the gamesmanship in that classroom will decrease.

There are limits to what the teacher can do. The school may have rules. A teacher of history is responsible to the community to see that you learn history. The principal of the school may have definite ideas as to which teaching methods may be employed. But there is an area of freedom—human interaction.

Despite opinions and experiences to the contrary, teachers are human beings. They are more similar to you than different. They recall quite vividly the things they did to their teachers and do their best to avoid being put in similar binds. You can help your teachers to learn more effective ways to interact in the classroom, but it will be no easy task. You might say, "Why should I help them?" That is an excellent question. Probably the best answer is that this may be the only way you can actually help make school something exciting and worthwhile rather than something to avoid or at best passively accept.

THE TEACHER

If you have read the preceding section, you can anticipate some of the comments that will follow. The previous discussion was pretty hard on you, the teacher. Most of you won't fit the worst teacher described, but at times each of us is a bit of the worst teacher despite our best intentions.

One of the realities is that by the time students reach you they have learned the gamesmanship in the classroom from other teachers. Unfortunately, many of us view students as "That's the way they are." True, that is the way they are, but they have learned to be this way. They can learn to be different. Helping them change will take time and much effort, but it is worthwhile if teaching can then be more satisfying and if your students can enjoy learning.

If you can implement the skills you have learned in this book, you will experience a more "open" approach to teaching. As you use these skills you will begin to depart from the traditional stereotype of a teacher—a person who tries to unscrew the tops of students' heads and pour! Your students can play an active role in their learning rather than a passive-reactive role. In your classroom, students can participate in setting learning goals and developing classroom activities. They can feel responsible for the effect of their behavior on other students and you. They can experience freedom and responsibility as they work cooperatively rather than competitively. The open expression of thoughts and feelings can become more frequent as students recognize and respect reciprocally the validity and imperfection of perceptions. Control through threat of failure or imposition of punishments can cease to exist.

If you are somewhat cynical about whether this ideal can be achieved, I certainly can't blame you. No doubt you have tried. Maybe when you announced to the class what your intentions are, the students didn't believe you. They have heard other teachers describe how they wanted "free" discussions. The students too have learned to be cynical. And you certainly don't receive any help from those more experienced teachers who tried and failed. They sit in the wings waiting for you to fail and get these dreams out of your system.

So you attempt to implement the dream. The inch is given and the students, experiencing freedom from the traditional coercion, take the full foot. To them it rather feels like taking off a pair of tight shoes after spending a long day standing on their feet. All too often the result is chaos, intervention by the principal, a few expulsions, and the withdrawal of the inch. They will have proved to you that they are beyond hope. "That's the way they are." You will have proved to them that you are just another teacher who backs down from what was promised. We have gone the full circle. The experienced teachers once more have their suspicions confirmed.

The norm of interaction you learned earlier in this book would promote the experiencing of freedom with reciprocal responsibility, respect for individual rights and group cooperation. This norm of interaction may fit your ideal classroom. Can this ideal be achieved? Probably not perfectly, but it can be approximated. Should you work toward this ideal? This you will need to decide relative to your own value system. Should you choose to try, two ways you might proceed are presented below.

You should realize at the outset that your students will need to learn how to make this idealized system work. Through a series of steps you should gradually increase the freedom that you allow. Neither you nor your students are equipped to begin swimming in the middle of the Atlantic! If you have been lecturing, continue to lecture, but break your lecture into small pieces. After each, request paraphrase of the students' understanding. Reward the fact of response separately from the correctness of the response. As you hear interpretations different from what you intended to communicate, show your gratitude. "John, that wasn't what I thought I communicated. I guess I didn't make it clear. Thanks for helping me. Let me try again."

You may even delay lecturing at all until you know what the students don't understand. The only thing a teacher needs to explain are those things students don't understand. It is amazing how teachers complain that their students don't prepare; but students often don't need to prepare. The teacher will cover the same material that is in the chapter, relieving them of that responsibility. Some teachers even make students read in class time, again relieving students of the responsibility of studying on their own and relieving teachers of the necessity of lecturing. Those who previously prepared now see it isn't necessary.

If students are not prepared, class time is probably best spent in discussing the relationship between teacher and students, classroom procedures, etc. As a teacher you should express your feelings directly together with behavioral description, behavioral prescription, and an opening for negotiation. Students should be allowed to express their feelings with impunity. While the goals for a specific class may be prescribed by the community or school authorities, the means (procedures) for attaining the goals allow room for negotiation. If you use the guidelines for giving and receiving feedback and intervene to help the students follow the guidelines, you and your students can arrive at a set of mutual expectations and commitments to behave consistent with these expectations. As procedures and goals (whenever possible) evolve through mutual comfort and negotiation, they are more likely to be respected. When you set up all rules, procedures, and goals by yourself, they become fair game and you have no legitimate basis for confrontation except your authority base. When mutual expectations and

commitments are obtained, you and your students have a legitimate
basis for confrontation. Recall that your anger may be inappropriate
if expectations have not been discussed, agreed upon, and accepted
by all parties. Expectations mandated from your authority base are
less likely to be honored and usually can be enforced only through threat
of punishment.

But back to the lecture. As you give explanations or lecture,
observe your students carefully. Watch for nonverbal signals. These
nonverbal signals may (and probably should) interfere with your lecturing behavior. You should pause to deal with "your problem" by asking
the student to verbalize the thoughts or feelings behind his nonverbal
behavior. As the student responds, attend well, paraphrase for understanding as necessary, and allow him to finish before you respond.
Respect the student for helping you with your problem and helping himself to learn. Reward his responses and request that he continue to
verbalize his thoughts and feelings (by raising his hand if you wish).
Respect the validity of his perception.

You can begin to establish this norm of respect by the way you handle one student belittling the question or comment of another student.
"I am irritated. You are laughing. John's question is important to
him and to me. It would help me if you could accept that what he has
to say is important to him and not laugh when he speaks. Would you
do this?" Here you might solicit verbal responses from students,
requesting commitment or their feelings about your request. Again
listen well and paraphrase for understanding.

In the situation just described, John will feel heard by you, but he
will also feel a powerful force that affects him beyond the class hour—
pressure from peers. If you take the time to request and allow students
to verbalize their reactions to your request, he will hear both support
for continuing to ask questions and comments from those who don't like
to waste time with "stupid" questions. Don't argue with the students.
If you argue, you may "win" the battle because you have the authority,
but you lose the war. Students will feel: "We're free to respond as long
as we don't disagree." Instead, do with them what you did with John—
hear and understand. Paraphrasing is not a skill to use only when students agree with you. It is most important that you paraphrase when
they do not agree with you. You may not be able to comply with their
requests. Students can accept this if you do comply when you can, if
they feel understood, and if you level with them. Students can well
appreciate being in the double-bind of conflicting demands.

If students learn to respond and verbalize their thoughts and feelings,
they may begin to argue as the group polarizes on the issue. Arguments
may break out. A bit of chaos? You bet it is. But it is a basis on
which to build the norm of respect for individuality. "Stop. I've got a
problem. I want to hear each of you. I can't hear when you are shout-

ing and two people are speaking at once. Could one person speak at a time? Peter? Mary? Good. Thank you." Now again you model paraphrasing and respect for the opinions of individuals. "Your obligation is not to agree with each other, but to understand each other." As you paraphrase, Peter and Mary will hear each other—similarities as well as differences.

You will need patience to influence interaction and promote the guidelines for giving and receiving feedback in conflict resolution. When an impasse is reached, students will look to you to make a decision—to take their responsibility for resolving the problem. You could do this, but the consequence is maintaining their dependency as you intervene to rescue. Your role is that of the mediator, the "third party" we discussed in Chapter 6.

The process of establishing the norm will be time-consuming. In the meantime you will not cover the subject matter as fully as you would like. You will have to accept that this activity will pay dividends in the future and decide whether you are willing to sacrifice the goal of subject matter learning momentarily to promote another kind of learning. The philosophy and objectives of your school probably suggest that this kind of learning is important. The philosophy and objectives of your school probably resemble the following:

> Education must include more than the acquisition of facts. It
> must be an instrument through which people release the tremen-
> dous creative potential that was born into all of us. We must
> help our young develop compassion, concern for others, faith
> in themselves, the ability to think critically, the ability to love,
> the ability to maintain physical and psychological health, and
> the ability to remain open to other people and new experiences.

Your school may well give you a legitimate basis for the activity of developing this new norm of communication.

Let's go back to the beginning of the class. Before you begin the class, you have some objectives in mind. Present these to the class. "At the end of this class, if we are successful each student will . . . ." Solicit additional objectives from your students and include these among those that are required of you as a teacher of your subject matter in your school.

Further, present your plan of activities to the students. Again, solicit alternatives from your students. Not all alternatives will be acceptable or consistent with making progress toward the desired classroom atmosphere. For example, some students will want to continue in the passive role and request that you lecture the entire period.

Students will probably suggest activities that you feel will not work. As a member of the class group you might express your feelings, but if the students feel strongly, sometimes they should be allowed to try

and fail. You could use failure as an excuse for withdrawing the privi-
lege or you could use it to help students explore why they failed and how
they can make appropriate changes. You should treat failure not as a
basis for punishment but as an opportunity for learning. Similarly,
students will suggest activities that you know are beyond the boundaries
of the rules of the school and community. You may work with them to
help move the boundaries back a bit to accommodate the activity. But
what is most important is that you hear their ideas and, whenever feasible, that you use their ideas.

At the end of each class, plan time to evaluate the progress made
toward goals, the set of procedures used, and the behavior of you and of
your students. Conclude by defining objectives for the next day, planning
activities, exchanging feedback, communicating changes in behavior that
you will make, and hearing changes in behavior that students will make.
(See Chapter 7.) Your first few attempts will consume much time.
Efficiency will come as the norm of communication changes.

If you are teaching elementary school in a self-contained classroom,
the basic format is the same but much more complex. Begin by present-
ing the overall plan for the day. Before each learning period, present
objectives and activities for the period. At the end of each period, set
aside time to evaluate progress toward goals, activities, and behavior.

You might begin to help students learn skills for conducting effective
group discussions by forming a circle. A circle of thirty students? Why
not? It is at least as effective as rows and columns of thirty students.
As you form the circle so that each can see the other, students can
observe how their behavior affects other people. In this kind of setting
you come down to their level at least physically. Gradually you promote
student-to-student interaction. You intervene with the conflict you feel
when they fail to attend, paraphrase, or express their feelings directly.
Intervene to promote respect for individual rights and to enforce individual responsibilities. In your initial efforts you are modeling. Students
will usually comply with your requests. Their perception of you as an
authority figure buys you this much. They will also comply with your
demands, but when you demand you relieve them of the responsibility
they will feel when they experience a choice.

After a while you will need to intervene less often. Students will
anticipate your intervention and begin to do the behavior that you were
doing or that you requested previously. Further, they will experience
having some control over their world. They will experience being
understood, understanding, and respect.

When students have begun to internalize the skills in their interactions
with you, they can begin to use them independently of you and to use each
other as sources of feedback. You might even set up a fishbowl structure.
Split your group in half. An inside group will conduct the discussion. An
outside group will observe the "how" of interaction. Initially assign one

person to observe one person. This may seem threatening, but most students handle it well if you support them in the activity, model the activity, and share the guidelines for giving and receiving feedback. As senders they must send feedback. As receivers they should hear, not necessarily use. At the end of the discussion, each person in the inside group evaluates his own behavior. Then each person in the outside group communicates to the student he was observing (1) the behavior that he perceived was helpful or effective and (2) the behavior that he perceived as ineffective and how it could be done more effectively. In this way students learn to give and receive feedback. After the feedback, the students should have the opportunity to discuss whether they want to make the changes consistent with the feedback.

Your class may be too large for one group. You may choose to form groups of four or five students with an equal number observing. This will increase the amount of participation per student and give the observer much more data. This method makes your supervision much more difficult. You might choose to use both—first the larger group and then the smaller.

With time the students will learn to participate in discussions and observe the "how" of the discussion simultaneously. When this happens, they are ready to use groups as a part of the learning process.

There are advantages to having students help other students. The explanation a student may give another student may be much more effective in promoting understanding than any explanation that you might give. This may threaten some teachers, but remember your goal is to promote learning. If there is no learning, can you call what you are doing teaching? You might ask, "Isn't this placing an unfair burden on the 'brighter' student?" The best response is another question: "Didn't you learn your subject much better when you taught than before?"

The most critical variable is your behavior. You must do consistently what you would have your students learn. There must be no double standards. Your students take their cues from you. Typically their behavior is in response to your behavior. There is no way you can establish this norm from a "Do as I say, not as I do" position.

Probably the fairest way to proceed is to expose your hand. Communicate to the students what you would like to accomplish and how you plan to go about it. You might begin by working through this book with your students. This is the most honest way to proceed, but it carries a higher risk. As your students learn what you have learned, the pressure for you to use these skills consistently will increase. By telling them what you are doing, you are committing yourself to follow through. Yes, you can use your authority to back down, but you will lose their respect. You can return to coercion and gamesmanship, but you probably will lose.

It will not be easy. There will be moments when it will take all of your energy to stay with it. But you may just experience a bit of the dream philosophy. You can help yourself if you work together with three or four of your colleagues. You may wish to meet regularly to give each other emotional support or a prod to keep trying. It has taken centuries to implant the traditional model. It may take a few weeks or months to promote the change.

The counselor in your school may be a definite resource to assist you in promoting a more cooperative norm in your classroom. Although you may not be aware of it (as he spends time in his office) he probably possesses a very high level skill in using the behaviors you have learned in this book. You might consult with the counselor as to how it is best to proceed in the context of your particular school. I suspect he would be pleased to assist you in any way you might choose.

THE PARENT

For you the task is both more difficult and yet easier. It is more difficult because of the frequency of contacts you have with your children. But for that same reason your task is easier. Since you are with your children for large portions of your day, the demands upon you to stay with the skills consistently will never cease. But because you are with them for so long, the amount of learning that can take place in a relatively short time is increased. When your children begin to do the behavior that you value, they will help you in the task.

A key variable is the quality of the relationship with your spouse. Your children imitate your behavior. If you think you do not have influence, just observe them closely and take a look at your own behavior. They do with each other and with you pretty much as you and your spouse do with each other and with them. This is the best reason for doing away with double standards; you cannot request from them what you do not do yourself. When you maintain double standards, you also maintain a destructive climate for your relationship with your children. How frequently have you observed or done the following? (Read them aloud.)

"When are you going to learn to say please?"

"If you want something, ask. Now give that back."

"It's about time you learned to say thank you."

Spanking the child and saying, "Now don't hit your brother."

"John, come in here. I don't want you to yell for me to come to you. If you want something, you come to me and ask."

I can't remember what it felt like to experience these as a child. I know very well what it feels like now—not very good. Question: Can you do to your children what you expect them to do? If you expect respect from them, can you respect them? If you expect them to understand and be influenced by you, can you understand and be influenced by them? If you expect them to pay attention, can you pay attention to them? If you expect them to respect your direct expression of feelings, can you respect theirs? These questions can go on and on. The answers you give are critical. They will determine whether your children will reflect your influence or the influence of others. There is no way you can coerce attitude change. You can coerce behavior change for a time, but only for a time. As your children experience freedom, choice, respect, acceptance, and understanding they will find it satisfying to relate to you and subsequently be influenced by you.

Let's see what this might look like in action. Many parents do not attend well to their children. Recall the conversation when your father was intent on reading the paper or your mother was preparing supper. Earlier in the book you learned how it felt when people were inattentive or gave you half attention. Many parents do this while expecting their children to attend to them. When you can't give attention, you must defer it while recognizing that what the other person has to say is important. This sounds like a formidable task, for children can make so many demands. Yet, it is remarkable how they can wait until later if "later" comes and they can have their parents' undivided attention. Similarly, we must not expect our children to give us full attention on demand. We can request their attention but it is unfair to interrupt. We must realize that painting a picture or repairing a broken airplane are as important to them as our need to get to the theatre on time, to get dinner prepared, or to finish writing checks for the month. The tasks are different, but relative to each person's unique world, they are equally important.

Similarly, as we talk to our children it is important that we look at them to observe the effect of our message. Your children will reciprocate and look at you when they talk to you if you listen actively and empathetically. Relative to the development of your child, what is important to him is important to you.

As children talk to us, we often get impatient when they fumble for words to express themselves. We are too quick to rescue and put words into their mouth. We risk making assumptions and depriving the child of the satisfaction that comes from successfully communicating by himself. This could well influence his self-confidence.

How quick we are to voice our discontent when our children interrupt us. Yet how frequently we listen until we find something to disagree with or make the assumption that we know what he is going to say. Again the double standard. Too often we "rescue" in response to our impatience rather than allowing a child to express himself.

A frequent complaint of parents is that children do not come to them with their problems. The truth is our children try, but we do not recognize them as problems. Often children will express their problems to us indirectly in the form of questions. John may ask, "Is Mary's piece of cake bigger than mine?" Look beyond the words to the conflict he may be feeling. It probably is irrelevant whether Mary got a larger piece of cake or not. "Yes" will answer the question, but will not address the concern. Attend beyond the question to the nonverbal—the tone, the facial expression. This always takes precedence. "Let's see. It does look bigger. You're concerned because Mary has a larger piece of cake and you're wondering why Mary's piece should be larger than yours?" Children often interpret the size of a piece of cake as the manifestation of love. As you attend and paraphrase his concern at needing to be loved, you address a possible hidden question: "Do you love me as much as you love Mary?" Your ability to understand his concern may address this much better than "I love you." A typical response of "Don't worry about it, you will get a larger piece next time" just doesn't make it. Helping the child feel understood with an accompanying hug or squeeze may address the concern directly. "Gee, I guess it is. I sure didn't intend to make yours smaller. I guess I didn't measure very well." This coupled with understanding communicates that the parent is not perfect. As the child sees a less than perfect parent, he may be better able to accept his own imperfections.

Children would bring more problems to us if we did not punish them for doing so. A child may break a favorite toy. He feels badly about it. He did not intend to break it; his ability to discriminate strong from weak, fragile from sturdy may be less than perfect. When they are young our children tell us about broken toys. "Look, Mommy. Bwoke." As they grow older they stop doing this, probably because they begin to get lectures. They are asked "Why did you do it?" Most children don't know why they did it. They don't <u>intend</u> to break it. Literally, it serves no purpose to kick a person when he's down. If you see a child feeling badly, paraphrase the feelings you see or hear. "You are feeling down because you broke your toy. It is a shame." "You liked your toy and you will miss it." Without understanding, the harangue about the value of a dollar and the admonition to be careful next time are meaningless. By communicating understanding, the harangue and the admonition are not necessary. Besides, if he risked coming to you with a problem and you punished him, he probably won't come to you again. He will, instead, hide the broken toy.

Parents frequently provoke their children into lying about problems. We may observe that the child's bed is not made. Do we tell him? Oh, no. We try to trap him. "Did you make your bed?" If you know the answer to the question, don't ask the question. "I notice your bed has not been made yet. When do you think you can do it?" You have communicated to him that he did not live up to his responsibility. This is not negotiable. When he will do it is negotiable.

There are limits and these can be enforced quickly and meaningfully with understanding. "Knives are pretty and shiny, but they are not for playing with." No lecture on cutting yourself or doctor bills is necessary. "It is okay to be angry with your sister, but you don't hit your sister." "Cars are for riding in, but not without your seatbelt fastened."

If you reread the situations presented above, you will see the common theme of respect and understanding that allows for individuality and for self-expression within limits. The consistent application of the skills in your relationship with your spouse will yield much in terms of better relationships with your children.

THE ADMINISTRATOR

If the task of developing more effective norms of communication is difficult for teachers and parents, the task becomes more difficult for the executive-administrator-employer. In general, the larger the organization and the more complex the structure of the organization, the more complicated the task. Further confounding factors are the number of subsystems in the organization and the number of subsystems (stages or departments) between the people occupying the lowest level positions and the person in the top executive position. It is beyond the scope of this guide to provide anything but a few thoughts for a beginning. To learn more about large, complex organizations, it is advisable to read extensively in the areas of organizational development and leadership.

We can explore some of the possible ways you as a leader in your organization can intervene to promote more effective communication. As a beginning, you must remember that your decision to promote more effective communication constitutes a value judgment and is somewhat less than democratic, although the goal is to move toward a more democratic leadership style. More specifically, if you use the skills that you learned in this book, you will be interacting with the people in your organization in a way that will move them toward cooperation, utilization of resources, respect for individual rights, and openness.

There are very pragmatic reasons for promoting more democratic leadership and open communication within an organization.

(1) Decisions made with the involvement of all personnel resources available will probably be decisions that will most effectively move the organization toward its goals.

(2) Decisions made with the involvement of and use of the ideas of resource personnel will probably produce greater satisfaction with the decision and with the organization.

(3) Decisions will probably have a greater chance for successful, efficient implementation if the changes emerge from the felt needs of the resource personnel and if they are involved in the process of making the decision.

Should you see these long-term goals as desirable, a few suggestions about how you might proceed are presented below.

If your organization is large and/or complex you realize that your efforts may not be sufficient. You must identify from your organizational charts those key employees who link the highest and lowest positions and/or who link subsystems or departments within a level of your organization. These people must develop similar skills to increase the flow of accurate information both up and down the organization.

You must begin by changing your own attitude and behavior. Your willingness to participate in communication training with other members of your organization will go far toward building better relationships with them. This will not be easy for you. If the communication has been less than open in the past, employees may unload all their repressed feelings about your past behavior. Not all of this is personal. Much has accumulated over the years from other "bosses." As was the case with the teacher in the preceding section, it will take a great deal of patience, understanding, and tolerance on your part to deal with the concern directly and fairly. The employees need to vent their feelings, but they also need to describe the behavior that is involved in their feelings and prescribe the behavior change that would help them in their relationships with you. There is potential for constructive change, but there is also potential for change for the worse. Clearly, you should engage a professional in organizational development and interpersonal communication to assist you in this enterprise.

Most organizations are characterized by a predominant downward flow of communication with minimal upward flow of information—one-way communication rather than two-way communication. Memos and directives maintain this most effectively. As a beginning you might replace memos and directives by communication of ideas in face-to-face contacts. This will allow you to observe and to solicit reactions from those who are affected by the decision. It is highly desirable that these ideas be solicited before a decision is made. If you obtain the ideas from resource personnel before making a decision and include in the communication of the decision how the ideas solicited were accommodated and why other ideas could not be accommodated, the members will note that their ideas were considered and in some instances used. Literally, they will have controlled their work environment to some degree.

This involvement in the decision-making process may be threatening to both you and those you consult. By deliberately reaching out you may obtain negative information that previously you didn't receive. It will be extremely difficult to hear well in this situation. You may be inclined to "shut off" this negative information when it becomes too much to use. This will be especially true if members have not been given the opportunity to communicate upward for some time. However, the intensity of negative feelings tends to drop considerably when members observe you hearing and using the information that you obtain.

It will be difficult for the members of the organization as well if this is new behavior on your part. They may have built a dependency on your assuming authority and making decisions for them. There is a certain comfort for them; they are relieved of responsibility. Further, they may fear reprisals if they share negative information. Recall that many of us have learned that we may be punished for feelings, especially negative feelings. Your biggest challenge will be in helping them become more open with you. You may feel defensive. This is okay and probably should be communicated, but it should not preclude hearing well and shutting off the information that your organization needs so badly for long-term efficiency and productivity.

A key component in your behavior change is direct expression of your feelings rather than indirect expression of your feelings. This behavior will allow others to see that you are a human being like them and will serve to model the legitimacy of open expression of feelings in formal channels of communication rather than the informal (grapevine) channels.

Another key component is extensive use of paraphrase and requesting paraphrase. As you may recall from previous discussions, this serves several purposes—understanding and feeling understood. Paraphrase is a fundamental skill in resolving conflicts. As you paraphrase you include both similarities and differences. You promote a cooling-off period instead of the listen-until-you-disagree so often observed in conversations. You will need to paraphrase extensively to obtain accurate information and to model paraphrasing behavior. Your perceived status and the rewards that those below you assign to your status makes you a potent model. As you model paraphrase, you allow others to see that it is okay to interpret inaccurately. The goal is not to look good but to understand.

People lower in the organizational hierarchy will have greater success promoting effective communication with those below them than with those above them in the organization. The structure imposed from higher in the organization may preclude some activities on your part. For example, it might be very functional for you in production to communicate directly with the person in charge of sales. Your superior might insist that he deal directly with each unit without face-to-face contact between the units. This is unfortunate, for direct communication is necessary and will develop through the informal channels. Often this isolation of units is an attempt to maintain tight control.

The fear of loss of control usually comes from equating control with authoritarian rule and coercion. Here lies the fundamental paradox that you have read at several points earlier in the book. Before you apply these skills, you must be convinced that the greater the experience of freedom you provide to those under you and the greater they experience their ability and corollary responsibility to effect changes in their work lives, the greater influence you will have.

Democratic administration seems less efficient than authoritarian procedures. However, when the quality of decision, the quality of procedures for implementation, and the satisfaction with involvement in making the decision are considered, the probability is high that there will be greater efficiency in the long haul. Stated differently, the efficiency question is best asked relative to the time between posing the problem and implementation of a satisfactory solution rather than solely from the perspective of the time required to make a decision.

Is this model of management for you? Only you can decide this. You might experiment a bit and experience the results. Use these skills with those members of your organization with whom you come in contact. You might slowly expand the number of members you contact. Begin slowly, knowing that they have to learn to accommodate you. Some of the intervention strategies described in Chapter 7 might help you in this task. Extend to them the same patience you will need to feel with yourself. Sometimes you will forget the specific skills in the heat of a crisis, but as you become aware of what you might have done differently, these lapses will occur less frequently. As other members of your organization begin to reciprocate, you will find your task much easier. As other members of your organization are trained, you will not be alone in your task.

Summarizing Exercise

A and B, each of you select one or more of the roles discussed in this chapter and explain the following to your partner:

(1) How you might use the skills in that role.
(2) The difficulties you may encounter as you attempt to influence the norm of communication.
(3) The attitude you will need to be effective in influencing change in the norm of communication.

FOR FURTHER READING

References are grouped by subject on pages 208-215. For further reading on the concepts covered in this chapter, see references under these headings:

Acceptance and Understanding
Attitude, Behavior, and Social Change
Commitment, Action, and Interpersonal Contracts
Communication Theory: Norm¯, Roles, Expectations, Interaction
Idealized Relationships: Respect, Dignity, Values
Interpersonal Problem Solving: Feelings, Feedback, and Conflict
  Resolution
Leadership, Decision Making, and Organization Development
Modeling and Reinforcement
Openness, Authenticity, and Trust in Relationships
Parent-Child, Marriage Relationships
Teacher-Student Relationships

IN CLOSING

Hopefully this book has provided you with an exciting and satisfying learning experience. More importantly, I hope you have acquired some skills to make your relationships more satisfying. Whether or not that goal was attained is a shared responsibility—between my efforts to provide adequate experiences for you to acquire new skills and your efforts in the experiences and at implementation.

A summary list of behaviors and a summary tally sheet are presented in the Appendix. Keep in mind that this list is by no means complete. Further, recall that these behaviors describe a value judgment about human interaction. (There are many other styles of behavior, as we know.) If your values fit those espoused in this book you might want to begin your efforts using the behaviors as prescribed. Let me remind you, though, to modify the behaviors in your own unique style to your own unique environment. I do hope you try. I feel you will find it well worth the effort. Thanks for your best efforts and patience.

A final exercise brings this book to a close. In Exercise 1.2 you recalled specific situations that you experienced in relationship with others. Turn back to page 5 and repeat Exercise 1.2.

How do you feel now about your relationships with others?

If you have been using the skills (relative to the amount of application you have tried and the amount of time elapsed since you began), you may notice a change in your level of satisfaction and your ability to influence your relationships.

SUGGESTIONS FOR CONTINUING RENEWAL

Changing your behavior and the norm of communication in your social systems can be extremely lonely. Thus, even though you and your partner have completed the initial task together, your relationship should be maintained for the near future. Successes can be more significant and failures less devastating if you support each other in the difficult but exciting task ahead. I suggest that you continue to meet with your partner at least once a week for formal progress reports. (If possible meet daily at first and gradually increase the intervals between meetings.) Make this meeting a regular part of your life. I suggest the following goals for each meeting.

(1) Both of you will have shared your interpersonal experiences since the last meeting—activities and feelings, successes and failures. Specifically each of you will share:
   (a) What you did during the week that pleased you.
   (b) What you did that you would like to change.
   (c) Any problems with specific individuals that are particularly difficult and that require special consideration.

(2) Both of you will have provided assistance to the other as needed (both as requested and perceived).

(3) Both of you will have shared (a) the behaviors you will work on before your next meeting, (b) specific interpersonal problems that you will deal with, and (c) a commitment to report progress at your next meeting.

(4) Both of you will have offered to assist the other before the next meeting (observing, interim meetings, feedback, etc.).

(5) Both of you will have shared the following information regarding the interaction that occurred during the meeting:
   (a) What behaviors you did today that you liked.
   (b) What behaviors you did today that you would like to change.
   (c) What your partner did today that you liked.
   (d) What your partner did today that you would like to see him change.

(6) The two of you will have established a definite time and place for your next meeting.

(7) The two of you will have evaluated the procedures you used in your meeting.

You might use these guidelines and have your first meeting now. If you cannot do it now, decide when you can meet. To get you started, you might read the summary list of behaviors on pages 194-197 and identify those behaviors that may be difficult for you. It is easy to work on behaviors that are not particularly troublesome. Challenge yourself to take the necessary risks (behaviors that are not comfortable for you but that you feel would help your relationships) to build the quality relationships you desire.

The behaviors you select must be stated positively. ("I will check to see that people are finished speaking before I respond" rather than "I will stop interrupting people.") Discuss each behavior with your partner and assess your level of proficiency with that behavior. As you do this, you have started to make progress toward the first goal stated on page 191.

I'm inclined to say good luck to you, but luck or chance has very little to do with success in building satisfying relationships. The key ingredient is you—your efforts, your perseverance, and your relationship with your partner.

Appendix

SUMMARY LIST OF BEHAVIORS

1. Empathetic attention as listener: When I am listening to someone speak I shall behave in a manner apparently consistent with the person's mood. I mirror or reflect on my face and through my gestures the feelings that I observe in the person's behavior or that I hear the person expressing.

2. Active listening: When someone is speaking to me I will look directly at the person, observe his posture, facial expression, and tone of voice, and I will indicate by words that I understand what he is saying and seek clarification when necessary.

3. Attention as speaker: When I am speaking to a person(s) I will look directly at the person(s). I shall observe his posture, facial expression, and the effect of my message and the manner of delivery of my message on the person(s).

4. Deferring attention: When someone starts to speak to me and I am not able to attend as well as I would like, I will explain my circumstance to the person, affirm my interest in hearing what he has to say (if I am interested), and arrange a time when I can attend more fully.

5. Seeking clarification: When I am listening to someone speak, I will mirror those words or phrases that are not clear in meaning to me.

6. Showing respect through silence: When I am listening to someone speak I will respect his choice as to whether he wants to discuss his situation in greater depth. I will allow him to experience freedom to elaborate by showing nonverbal empathy and understanding but will use no words.

7. Paraphrase of feelings and thoughts: When I am listening to someone speak and I observe that the message is important to the speaker, I will paraphrase the thoughts and feelings he has expressed in the sequence in which he has presented them. As I paraphrase I shall not agree or disagree, explore motivation, or evaluate. My sole goal is to understand and help the speaker feel understood. Understanding of feelings shall take precedence over understanding the thoughts or ideas.

8. Requesting paraphrase: When I am talking about something important to me, I will ask for a paraphrase of my message to be sure I have made myself clear.

9. Rewarding effective behavior: When another person is doing an effective communication behavior, I shall thank or otherwise show appreciation for his having done the behavior.

10. Summary paraphrase: When I am listening to several people speaking, I will paraphrase the comments of each individually or paraphrase in summary as seems appropriate for the situation.

11. Acknowledge message received: When I do not paraphrase, I shall verbally communicate to the speaker that his message has been heard.

12. Direct expression of feelings: In my relationships with others I will directly express my feelings. If another person is involved in the conflict I feel, I will describe the behavior that I perceive to interfere with my behavior. I will prescribe the behavior change that would help me either at the outset or when another person requests it.

13. Receiving expressed feelings: When I hear another person expressing his feelings directly, I will paraphrase the feelings he is expressing without defending, apologizing, or in any way deprecating the other person's feelings.

14. Facilitating direct expression of feelings: When I observe others expressing their feelings indirectly, I shall express my feelings, describe the behavior I see and/or the feeling state that I infer, and request that the person help me by expressing his feelings directly. When the person complies, I will paraphrase his feelings without deprecating his feelings.

15. Reward direct expression of feelings: When a person expresses his feelings, I shall express appreciation for this behavior.

16. Asking and requesting facilitative questions:
    (a) Before I ask a question I will provide the listener with the frame of reference for the question.
    (b) When another person asks me a direct question, I will request a frame of reference for the questions before I respond.
    (c) If I wish to express a feeling about the behavior of another person, I will not entrap the person by asking the type of question that may precipitate a lie.

17. Facilitative conflict resolution: When I am engaged in an argument with another person, I will:
    (a) come down in affect and summarize for understanding as a means of working through the conflict, moving later to a discussion of "how" we reconcile our differences;
    (b) come down in affect, express my feelings directly, and request a discussion of how we reconcile our differences.

18. Receiving feedback: When someone gives me feedback directly or in the form of direct expression of feelings, I will paraphrase for

understanding and:

(a) if the feedback is positive, express appreciation for the feedback and accept the feedback without embarrassment or any deprecation of the feedback;

(b) if the feedback is negative, consider making the requested change without defensiveness. Should I choose not to make the requested change, I will explain to my partner my thoughts and feelings. Should I choose to make the requested change, I will request assistance as I feel the need. Under either circumstance, I will express appreciation for the feedback.

19. Giving feedback: When I give feedback to another person directly or in the form of direct expression of feelings, I will request paraphrase for understanding if necessary and:

(a) allow the person to experience freedom in making the change or not as he chooses;

(b) paraphrase his thoughts or feelings as he considers the change, offer assistance as required, and express appreciation for his consideration whether or not the change is made.

20. Requesting effective messages: When another person is sending incomplete or ambiguous messages that produce conflict in me I shall express my feelings directly, describe the behavior, and request change.

21. Sending effective messages: When I am speaking I shall speak for myself, speak to the person I wish to respond, and qualify my statements as my experience or my perception.

22. Goal setting: Before beginning a class, meeting, forum, or group discussion, I will state the goal(s) of the group as I understand it. I will state the goal in the form of the desired future state if the group is successful. I shall request that other members of the group define the goal(s) as they perceive it. We shall negotiate until a common goal statement has been reached.

23. Plan procedures: Before beginning a class, meeting, forum, or group discussion, I will offer an explicit plan or procedure for the group to follow in accomplishing its goal. I will solicit alternative plans from other group members. We shall negotiate until a common plan of action has been attained.

24. Request permission to intervene: When I am in a class, meeting, forum, or group discussion, I will respect the rights of individual members by recognizing they have the floor. I shall request permission to intervene should I wish to comment and wait until I am reasonably sure others are finished before commenting.

25. Intervention for resource utilization: I shall intervene in the class, meeting, forum, or group discussion to promote respect for individual rights, maximum resource utilization, and the development of an effective norm of communication.

26. Expressing action plans: When I am in a class, meeting, forum, or group discussion and a specific set of activities outside the group has been identified, I shall tell the group what I will do, when I will do it, and when I will report on the progress of the task. I shall request that other members make similar statements of commitment.

27. Review goals, plan, and communicate: At the end of a class, meeting, forum, or group discussion I shall initiate the following activities:

    (a) Review the accomplishments relative to the goals that were set.
    (b) Review the procedures used to make progress toward goals.
    (c) Share what I did that I liked and what I did that I would like to do differently.
    (d) Tell others what they did that I liked and what I perceived them to do that they could do differently to help the group's progress.
    (e) Request that others self-disclose and give feedback.

SUMMARY TALLY SHEET

Behavior \ Day	1	2	3	4	5	6	7
1. Empathetic attention as listener							
2. Active listening							
3. Attention as listener							
4. Deferring attention							
5. Seeking clarification							
6. Showing respect through silence							
7. Paraphrase of feelings and thoughts							
8. Requesting paraphrase							
9. Rewarding effective behavior							
10. Summary paraphrase							
11. Acknowledge message received							
12. Direct expression of feelings							
13. Receiving expressed feelings							
14. Facilitating direct expression of feelings							
15. Reward direct expression of feelings							
16. Asking & requesting facilitative questions							
17. Facilitative conflict resolution							
18. Receiving feedback							
19. Giving feedback							
20. Requesting effective messages							
21. Sending effective messages							
22. Goal setting							
23. Plan procedures							
24. Requesting permission to intervene							
25. Intervention for use of resources							
26. Expression action plans							
27. Review goals, plan, and communicate							

REFERENCES AND BOOKS FOR FURTHER READING

The references are listed alphabetically on pages 201-207 and by subject matter on pages 208-215.

1. Abrahamson, M., Interpersonal Accommodation (New York: Van Nostrand, 1966).

2. Anderson, A., A Conceptual Model for Counseling (Unpublished manuscript, 1968).

3. Anderson, A., Goals and Objectives in Counseling Groups (Unpublished manuscript, 1968).

4. Argyle, M., The Psychology of Interpersonal Behavior (Baltimore: Penguin, 1967).

5. Aspy, D., Toward a Technology for Humanizing Education (Champaign, Ill.: Research Press, 1972).

6. Bandura, A., "Behavioral Modifications Through Modeling Procedures," L. Krasner and L. Ullmann (eds.), Research in Behavior Modification (New York: Holt, Rinehart and Winston, 1969).

7. Bandura, A., Principles of Behavior Modification (New York: Holt, Rinehart and Winston, 1969).

8. Baker, L., and Wiseman, G., "A Model of Interpersonal Communication," Journal of Communication, 1966, 6:172-179.

9. Bennis, W., Benne, K., and Chinn, R., The Planning of Change (New York: Holt, Rinehart and Winston, 1966).

10. Bennis, W., Schein, E., Steele, F., and Berlew, D. (eds.), Interpersonal Dynamics (Homewood, Ill.: Dorsey Press, 1968).

11. Berenson, B. and Carkhuff, R. (eds.), Sources of Gain in Counseling and Psychotherapy (New York: Holt, Rinehart and Winston, 1967).

12. Berne, E., Games People Play (New York: Grove, 1964).

13. Blocher, D., "Issues in Counseling: Elusive and Illusional," Personnel and Guidance Journal, 1964, 43:796-800.

14. Blocher, D., Developmental Counseling (New York: Ronald Press, 1966).

15. Blocher, D., Dustin, R., and Dugan, W., Guidance Systems (New York: Ronald Press, 1971).

16. Blocher, D. and Shaffer, W., "Guidance and Human Development," D. Cook (ed.), Guidance for Education in Revolution (Boston: Allyn and Bacon, 1971).

17. Borton, T., Reach, Touch and Teach (St. Louis: McGraw-Hill, 1970).

18. Bradford, L. (ed.), Group Development (Washington, D.C.: National Training Laboratories, National Education Association, 1961).

19. Bryan, J. and Loche, E., "Goal Setting as a Means of Increasing Motivation," Journal of American Psychology, 1967, 51:274-282.

20. Carkhuff, R., Helping and Human Relations, Vol. II (New York: Holt, Rinehart and Winston, 1970).

21. Cathcart, R. and Samovar, L., Small Group Communication (Dubuque, Iowa: W. C. Brown, 1970).

22. Cartwright, D. and Zander, A. (eds.), Group Dynamics: Research and Theory, Third Edition (New York: Harper and Row, 1968).

23. Combs, A. (ed.), Perceiving, Behaving, Becoming (Washington, D.C.: Association for Supervision and Curriculum Development, 1962).

24. Combs, A., Avila, D., and Purkey, W., Helping Relationships: Basic Concepts for the Helping Professions (Boston: Allyn and Bacon, 1971).

25. Corsini, R. and Cordone, S., Role-playing in Psychotherapy: A Manual (Chicago: Aldine, 1966).

26. Dale, E., Building a Learning Environment (Bloomington, Ind.: Phi Delta Kappa, 1972).

27. Della-Piana, Gabriel, How to Talk with Children (and Other People) (New York: John Wiley & Sons, 1973).

28. Dreikurs, R., Children: The Challenge (New York: Hawthorne Books, 1964).

29. Dustin, R. and George, R., Action Counseling for Behavior Change (New York: Intext Educational Publishers, 1973).

30. Elms, A., Role-playing, Reward and Attitude Change (New York: Van Nostrand, 1969).

31. Gardner, J., Self-renewal: The Individual and the Innovative Society (New York: Harper and Row, 1964).

32. Gelso, C., "Two Different Worlds: A Paradox in Counseling and Psychotherapy," Journal of Counseling Psychology, 1970, 17:271-277.

33. Gergen, K., The Psychology of Behavior Exchange (Reading, Mass.: Addison-Wesley, 1969).

34. Gibb, J., "Defensive Communication," The Journal of Communication, 1966, 11:141-148.

35. Gibb, J., "Defense Level and Influence Potential in Small Groups," L. Petrullo and B. Bass (eds.), Leadership and Interpersonal Behavior (New York: Holt, Rinehart and Winston, 1961).

36. Gibb, J., "Sociopsychological Processes of Group Instruction," N. Henry (ed.), The Dynamics of Small Groups, Fifty-ninth yearbook, National Society for the Study of Education, 1960, 115-135.

37. Ginott, H., Between Parent and Child (New York: Avon Books, 1965).

38. Ginott, H., Between Parent and Teenager (Toronto: Macmillan, 1969).

39. Glasser, W., Reality Therapy (New York: Harper and Row, 1965).

40. Glasser, W., Schools Without Failure (New York: Harper and Row, 1969).

41. Good, T. and Brophy, J., Looking in Classrooms (New York: Harper and Row, 1973).

42. Gordon, T., Parent Effectiveness Training (New York: Peter Wyden, 1971).

43. Gorman, A., Teachers and Learners: The Interactive Process of Education (Boston: Allyn and Bacon, 1969).

44. Hackney, H. and Nye, S., Counseling Strategies and Objectives (Englewood Cliffs, N.J.: Prentice-Hall, 1973).

45. Hall, E., The Silent Language (Greenwich, Conn.: Fawcett, 1959).

46. Hamachek, D., Encounters with the Self (New York: Holt, Rinehart and Winston, 1971).

47. Harris, T., I'm OK, You're OK (New York: Harper and Row, 1967).

48. Hayakawa, S. (ed.), The Use and Misuse of Language (Greenwich, Conn.: Fawcett, 1962).

49. Hill, W., Learning thru Discussion (Beverly Hills: Sage Publications, 1962).

50. Hollander, E. and Hunt, R. (eds.), Current Perspectives in Social Psychology, Second Edition (New York: Oxford, 1967).

51. Hollander, E. and Hunt, R. (eds.), Current Perspectives in Social Psychology, Third Edition (New York: Oxford, 1971).

52. Homme, L., How to Use Contingency Contracting in the Classroom (Champaign, Ill.: Research Press, 1971).

53. Hoopes, M., Scoresby, A., and Fuhriman, A., Communication Exercise (Unpublished manuscript, undated).

54. Houts, P. and Serber, M. (eds.), After the Turn-on, What? (Champaign, Ill: Research Press, 1972).

55. Ivey, A., Normington, C., Miller, C., Morrill, W., and Haase, R., "Micro-counseling and Attending Behavior: An Approach to Pre-practicum Counselor Training," Journal of Counseling Psychology (Monograph), 1968, 15:1-12.

56. Johnson, D., Reaching-out: Interpersonal Effectiveness and Self-actualization (Englewood Cliffs, N.J.: Prentice-Hall, 1972).

57. Johnson, D., The Social Psychology of Education (New York: Holt, Rinehart and Winston, 1970).

58. Johnson, D., "The Use of Role Reversal in Intergroup Competition," Journal of Personality and Social Psychology, 1967, 7:135-141.

59. Jourard, S., The Transparent Self (New York: Van Nostrand, 1964).

60. Jourard, S., Self-disclosure (New York: John Wiley & Sons, 1971).

61. Jourard, S. and Overlade, D. (eds.), Reconciliation, a Theory of Man Transcending (New York: Van Nostrand, 1966).

62. Joyce, B. and Weil, M., Models of Teaching (Englewood Cliffs, N.J.: Prentice-Hall, 1972).

63. Kell, B. and Mueller, W., Impact and Change: a Study of Counseling Relationships (New York: Appleton-Century-Crofts, 1966).

64. Kibler, R., Barker, L., and Miles, D., Behavioral Objectives and Instruction (Boston: Allyn and Bacon, 1970).

65. Knox, D., Marriage Happiness (Champaign, Ill.: Research Press, 1972).

66. Krumboltz, J., "The Parable of the Good Counselor," Personnel and Guidance Journal, 1964, 43:118-124.

67. Krumboltz, J. and Thoresen, C., Behavioral Counseling: Cases and Techniques (New York: Holt, Rinehart and Winston, 1969).

68. Learning Technology Incorporated, How to Talk with Children about Sex (New York: John Wiley & Sons, 1973).

69. Leppitt, R. and Hubbell, A., "Role-playing for Personnel and Guidance Workers: Review of the Literature with Suggestions for Application," Group Psychotherapy, 1956, 9:89-114.

70. Lippitt, G., Leadership in Action (Washington, D.C.: National Training Laboratories, National Education Association, 1961).

71. Luft, J., Of Human Interaction (Palo Alto, Cal.: National Press, 1969).

72. Mager, R., Goal Analysis (Belmont, Cal.: Fearon Publishers, 1972).

73. Maslow, A., Toward a Psychology of Being, Second Edition (New York: Van Nostrand, 1968).

74. Matson, F. (ed.), Without/Within: Behaviorism and Humanism (Monterey, Cal.: Brooks/Cole, 1973).

75. May, R., Psychology and the Human Dilemma (Princeton, N.J.: Van Nostrand, 1967).

76. Mill, C., Selections for Human Relations Training News (Washington, D.C.: National Training Laboratories Institute for Applied Behavioral Science, 1969).

77. Mowrer, O., The New Group Therapy (Princeton, N.J.: Van Nostrand, 1964).

78. Newcomb, T., "The Prediction of Interpersonal Attraction," American Psychologist, 1956, 11:575-587.

79. Northam, S. (ed.), Interpersonal Communication Participant Materials (Portland, Ore.: Northwest Regional Educational Laboratory, 1971).

80. Ohlsen, M., Group Counseling (New York: Holt, Rinehart and Winston, 1970).

81. Otto, H. and Griffiths, K., "A New Approach to Developing Student's Strength," Social Casework, 1963, 45:119-124.

82. Patterson, C., Theories of Counseling and Psychotherapy, Second Edition (New York: Harper and Row, 1973).

83. Patterson, G., Families (Champaign, Ill.: Research Press, 1973).

84. Peter, L., Individual Instruction (St. Louis: McGraw-Hill, 1972).

85. Pfeiffer, J. and Jones, J., A Handbook of Structured Experiences for Human Relations Training, Volumes I, II, III (Iowa City, Iowa: University Associates, 1969, 1970, 1971).

86. Pietrofesa, J., Leonard, G., and Van Hoose, W., The Authentic Counselor (Chicago: Rand McNally, 1971).

87. Rogers, C. and Roethlisberger, F., "Barriers and Gateways to Communication," Harvard Business Review, 1972, July-August, 28-35.

88. Rogers, C., "Two Lectures Delivered on the Nellie Heldt Lecture Fund," Becoming a Person (Oberlin, Ohio: Board of Trustees of Oberlin College, 1954).

89. Rogers, C., On Becoming a Person (Boston: Houghton-Mifflin, 1961).

90. Rogers, C., "Interpersonal Relationships: Year 2000," Journal of Applied Behavioral Science, 1968, 4:265-280.

91. Rogers, C. and Stevens, B., Person to Person: The Problem of Being Human (Lafayette, Cal.: Real People Press, 1967).

92. Ruesch, J. and Bateson, G., Communication: The Social Matrix of Psychiatry (New York: W. W. Norton and Company, 1968).

93. Satir, V., Conjoint Family Therapy (Palo Alto, Cal.: Science and Behavior Books, 1967).

94. Satir, V., Peoplemaking (Palo Alto, Cal.: Science and Behavior Books, 1972).

95. Schmuck, R. and Schmuck, P., Group Processes in the Classroom (Dubuque, Iowa: W. C. Brown, 1971).

96. Seeman, J., "Toward a Concept of Personality Integration," American Psychologist, 1959, 14:633-637.

97. Shoben, C., "Toward a Concept of the Normal Personality," American Psychologist, 1957, 12:138-190.

98. Shostrom, E., Man the Manipulator (New York: Bantam, 1968).

99. Smith, G. and Phillips, A., Me and You and Us (New York: Peter Wyden, 1971).

100. Stevens, J., Awareness: Exploring, Experimenting, Experiencing (Palo Alto, Cal.: American West Publishing Co., 1971).

101. Tannenbaum, A., Social Psychology of the Work Organization (Belmont, Cal.: Wadsworth, 1966).

102. Umans, S., The Management of Education (New York: Doubleday, 1971).

103. Wallen, J., Emotions as Problems (Portland, Ore.: Northwest Regional Educational Laboratory, 1967).

104. Wallen, J., <u>Paraphrase: A Basic Communication Skill for Improving Interpersonal Relationships</u> (Portland, Ore.: Northwest Regional Educational Laboratory, 1968).

105. Wallen, J., <u>The Constructive Use of Feelings</u> (Portland, Ore.: Northwest Regional Educational Laboratory, undated).

106. Watson, G. (ed.), <u>Change in School Systems</u> (Washington, D.C.: National Training Laboratories, National Education Association, 1967).

107. Watson, G. (ed.), <u>Concepts for Social Change</u> (Washington, D.C.: National Training Laboratories, National Education Association, 1967).

108. Watzlawick, P., Beavin, J., and Jackson, D., <u>Pragmatics of Communication</u> (New York: W. W. Norton, 1967).

109. Weick, K., <u>The Social Psychology of Organizing</u> (Menlo Park, Cal.: Addison-Wesley, 1969).

110. Zifferblatt, S., <u>Improving Study and Homework Behaviors</u> (Champaign, Ill.: Research Press, 1971).

111. Zimbardo, P. and Ebbesen, E., <u>Influencing Attitudes and Changing Behavior</u> (Reading, Mass.: Addison-Wesley, 1969).

GUIDE TO FURTHER READING IN SELECTED AREAS

The content in the various topic areas may overlap. The reader may find it beneficial to read in several topic areas which may be related.

Acceptance and Understanding

  5. Aspy, pp. 81-96
 24. Combs, Avila, and Purkey, pp. 210-230, 234-246
 27. Della-Piana, pp. 26-40
 28. Dreikurs, pp. 90-91
 56. Johnson, pp. 141-157
 86. Pietrofesa, Leonard, and Van Hoose, pp. 50-69

Attitude, Behavior, and Social Change

  9. Bennis, Benne, and Chinn, pp. 192-267, 317-370
 20. Carkhuff, pp. 263-282
 22. Cartwright and Zander, pp. 74-79, 247-249, 389-397, 463-464
 29. Dustin and George, pp. 71-94
 30. Elms, all
 47. Harris, pp. 54-64
 51. Hollander and Hunt, pp. 92-125, 332-342, 359-405, 421-429,
      435-462, 533-549, 629-636
 54. Houts and Serber, pp. 45-72
 76. Mill, pp. 3-9
106. Watson, all
107. Watson, all
110. Zifferblatt, all
111. Zimbardo and Ebbesen, all

Behavior-Communication Paradox and Values

  9. Bennis, Benne, and Chinn, pp. 580-618
 13. Blocher, pp. 796-800
 32. Gelso, pp. 271-277
 47. Harris, pp. 211-267
 71. Luft, pp. 153-168
 75. May, pp. 1-22
 92. Ruesch and Bateson, pp. 3-11
108. Watzlawick, Beavin, and Jackson, pp. 48-50, 187-229

Commitment, Action, and Interpersonal Contracts

20. Carkhuff, pp. 116-128
22. Cartwright and Zander, pp. 468-471
28. Dreikurs, pp. 162-171
29. Dustin and George, 71-94, 119-148
52. Homme, pp. 17-59
74. Matson, pp. 92-98
110. Zifferblatt, all

Communication and Human Relations Training Exercises

43. Gorman, pp. 63-119
53. Hoopes, Scoresby, and Fuhriman, all
79. Northam, all
85. Pfeiffer and Jones, all
99. Smith and Phillips, all

Communication Theory: Norms, Roles, Expectations, Interaction

4. Argyle, pp. 13-67
8. Baker and Wiseman, pp. 172-179
10. Bennis, Schein, Steele, and Berlew, pp. 13-43, 65-69, 121-163
12. Berne, pp. 1-20
14. Blocher, 3-13, 45-84, 160
15. Blocher, Dustin, and Dugan, pp. 144-178
20. Carkhuff, pp. 3-18, 283-289
21. Cathcart and Samovar, 240-250, 278-288
23. Combs, pp. 35-39
31. Gardner, all
33. Gergen, pp. 34-70, 75-77, 82-83
34. Gibb, pp. 141-148
47. Harris, pp. 1-53
48. Hayakawa, pp. 29-100
50. Hollander and Hunt, pp. 318-328
51. Hollander and Hunt, pp. 199-202, 211-218, 254-261, 279-297
71. Luft, pp. 3-11
74. Matson, pp. 11-25, 47-53
75. May, pp. 25-54
78. Newcomb, pp. 575-587
87. Rogers and Roethlisberger, pp. 28-35
90. Rogers, pp. 265-280
93. Satir, pp. 63-90
95. Schmuck and Schmuck, pp. 1-14, 84-102
98. Shostrom, pp. 3-32
108. Watzlawick, Beavin, and Jackson, pp. 19-71, 118-148

Defining Procedures

22. Cartwright and Zander, pp. 125-135
49. Hill, pp. 22-31

Goal Setting

14. Blocher, p. 157
19. Bryan and Loche, all
22. Cartwright and Zander, pp. 22-24, 49-52, 91-92, 119-124, 401-415, 419-424
29. Dustin and George, pp. 43-70
44. Hackney and Nye, pp. 22-27, 66-101
64. Kibler, Barker, and Miles, pp. 28-110
66. Krumboltz, pp. 118-124
72. Mager, all

Human Development and Normalcy

14. Blocher, pp. 45-71
16. Blocher and Schaffer, pp. 117-123
46. Hamachek, pp. 1-130
96. Seeman, pp. 633-637
97. Shoben, pp. 138-190

Idealized Relationships: Respect, Dignity, Values

15. Blocher, Dustin, and Dugan, pp. 120-143
24. Combs, Avila, and Purkey, pp. 65-69
29. Dustin and George, pp. 1-42
46. Hamachek, pp. 225-253
73. Maslow, all
82. Patterson, pp. 521-540
86. Pietrofesa, Leonard, and Van Hoose, pp. 146-161
88. Rogers, all
90. Rogers, pp. 265-280
91. Rogers, pp. 13-46
98. Shostrom, pp. 33-78

Interaction Analysis

5. Aspy, pp. 15-30
12. Berne, pp. 23-65
18. Bradford, pp. 37-59
43. Gorman, pp. 120-164
47. Harris, pp. 65-113

Interaction Analysis (continued)

71. Luft, pp. 11-76
79. Northam, pp. 217-241
84. Peter, pp. 47-82
94. Satir, pp. 59-79
108. Watzlawick, Beavin, and Jackson, pp. 149-186

Interpersonal Problem Solving: Feelings, Feedback, and Conflict Resolution

5. Aspy, pp. 69-80
9. Bennis, Benne, and Chinn, pp. 147-192, 486-526
10. Bennis, Schein, Steele, and Berlew, pp. 60-65
18. Bradford, pp. 69-72, 80-93
21. Cathcart and Samovar, pp. 72-102, 143-148
27. Della-Piana, pp. 48-82
28. Dreikurs, pp. 86-91, 106-115, 145-161
39. Glasser, pp. 63-166
42. Gordon, pp. 103-264
54. Houts and Serber, 89-108
56. Johnson, pp. 85-115, 159-169, 195-225
57. Johnson, pp. 153-179
58. Johnson, pp. 135-141
61. Jourard and Overlade, pp. 13-76
67. Krumboltz and Thoresen, pp. 429-470
79. Northam, pp. 41-87, 101-170, 198-217, 296-311
80. Ohlsen, pp. 116-129, 164-192
83. Patterson, pp. 89-132
94. Satir, pp. 80-122
101. Tannenbaum, pp. 33-56
103. Wallen, all
105. Wallen, all
108. Watzlawick, Beavin, and Jackson, pp. 72-118

Leadership, Decision Making, and Organization Development

9. Bennis, Benne, and Chinn, pp. 11-108
10. Bennis, Schein, Steele, and Berlew, pp. 139-153
15. Blocher, Dustin, and Dugan, pp. 33-88
21. Cathcart and Samovar, pp. 347-425
22. Cartwright and Zander, pp. 301-315, 319-326, 351-379, 381-387
33. Gergen, pp. 84-88
35. Gibb, pp. 66-81
51. Hollander and Hunt, pp. 495-532, 559-597, 605-619
57. Johnson, pp. 124-139, 250-284

Leadership, Decision Making, and Organization Development (continued)

 70. Lippitt, all
 71. Luft, pp. 97–124
 95. Schmuck and Schmuck, pp. 26–44, 123–141
101. Tannenbaum, all
102. Umans, all
109. Weick, all

Modeling and Reinforcement

  1. Abrahamson, pp. 13–20, 33–40
  6. Bandura, pp. 310–340
  7. Bandura, all
 11. Berenson and Carkhuff, pp. 261–284
 27. Della-Piana, pp. 52–98
 29. Dustin and George, pp. 95–118
 41. Good and Brophy, pp. 113–160
 56. Johnson, pp. 171–193
 62. Joyce and Weil, pp. 271–292
 65. Knox, pp. 2–3, 22–33
 67. Krumboltz and Thoresen, pp. 25–78, 87–130, 166–264
 68. Learning Technology Incorporated, pp. 73–74
 83. Patterson, pp. 9–88
 84. Peter, pp. 155–175

Nonverbal Communication

  1. Abrahamson, pp. 31–33, 40–45
 10. Bennis, Schein, Steele, and Berlew, pp. 197–205
 21. Cathcart and Samovar, pp. 260–265
 45. Hall, all
 71. Luft, pp. 153–168
 79. Northam, pp. 87–100
 92. Ruesch and Bateson, pp. 23–26
100. Stevens, pp. 77–78, 113–116

Openness, Authenticity, and Trust in Relationships

 46. Hamachek, pp. 228–229
 56. Johnson, pp. 43–59
 59. Jourard, all
 68. Learning Technology Incorporated, pp. 3–10
 76. Mill, pp. 75–76
 77. Mowrer, pp. 65–71
 79. Northam, pp. 171–197

Openness, Authenticity, and Trust in Relationships (continued)

89. Rogers, pp. 107-124
91. Rogers, pp. 47-88
98. Shostrom, pp. 145-178
100. Stevens, p. 64

Parent-Child, Marriage Relationships

10. Bennis, Schein, Steele, and Berlew, pp. 90-104
27. Della-Piana, all
28. Dreikurs, all
37. Ginott, all
38. Ginott, all
42. Gordon, all
46. Hamachek, pp. 131-175
47. Harris, pp. 126-195
65. Knox, pp. 52-58
68. Learning Technology Incorporated, all
80. Ohlsen, pp. 193-239
93. Satir, all
94. Satir, all
98. Shostrom, pp. 79-135
99. Smith and Phillips, all
100. Stevens, pp. 189-199
110. Zifferblatt, all

Perceptions of Self and Others

4. Argyle, pp. 117-132
21. Cathcart and Samovar, pp. 58-62
24. Combs, Avila, and Purkey, pp. 13-14, 82-101, 144-157, 187, 297-300
46. Hamachek, all
51. Hollander and Hunt, pp. 152-165, 298-321
57. Johnson, pp. 82-99
61. Jourard and Overlade, pp. 134-145
81. Otto and Griffiths, pp. 119-124
86. Pietrofesa, Leonard, and Van Hoose, pp. 19-42
94. Satir, pp. 20-29
100. Stevens, pp. 5-7, 26, 29

Problems in Understanding Words

48. Hayakawa, pp. 11-25
51. Hollander and Hunt, pp. 193-198, 219-232
100. Stevens, pp. 96-112

Relationship Building Skills: Attending, Listening, Understanding

    4. Argyle, pp. 105-115
    5. Aspy, pp. 15-30, 49-68
   11. Berenson and Carkhuff, pp. 71-86, 285-301
   14. Blocher, pp. 143-155
   20. Carkhuff, pp. 81-102
   21. Cathcart and Samovar, pp. 251-259
   24. Combs, Avila, and Purkey, pp. 185-209
   27. Della-Piana, pp. 1-40
   29. Dustin and George, pp. 1-42
   37. Ginott, pp. 21-40
   42. Gordon, pp. 29-102
   44. Hackney and Nye, pp. 40-50
   46. Hamachek, pp. 225-253
   54. Houts and Serber, pp. 109-122
   55. Ivey, pp. 1-12
   56. Johnson, pp. 117-139
   63. Kell and Mueller, all
   76. Mill, pp. 45-50
   79. Northam, pp. 19-40
   80. Ohlsen, pp. 1-3
   86. Pietrofesa, Leonard, and Van Hoose, pp. 123-136
   94. Satir, pp. 30-58
   95. Schmuck and Schmuck, pp. 44-64
  100. Stevens, pp. 33-35, 116-121
  104. Wallen, all

Responsibility in Relationships

   22. Cartwright and Zander, pp. 175-180, 184-189, 503-511
   24. Combs, Avila, and Purkey, pp. 188-189, 248-270
   37. Ginott, pp. 79-103
   39. Glasser, pp. 15-41
   40. Glasser, pp. 1-24, 186-204
   75. May, pp. 161-181
   77. Mowrer, pp. 9-13, 58-64, 100-103
  100. Stevens, pp. 49, 74-76, 87-90

Role-Playing

   25. Corsini, all
   30. Elms, pp. 1-13, 47-65, 92-133, 168-192
   69. Leppitt and Hubbell, pp. 89-114
   80. Ohlsen, pp. 150-163
  100. Stevens, all

Self-Disclosure

56. Johnson, pp. 9-41
59. Jourard, all
60. Jourard, all

Teacher-Student Relationships

  5. Aspy, all
17. Borton, all
22. Cartwright and Zander, pp. 251-257
26. Dale, all
27. Della-Piana, all
36. Gibb, pp. 115-135
39. Glasser, pp. 154-166
40. Glasser, pp. 25-32, 112-185
41. Good and Brophy, pp. 1-66
43. Gorman, all
46. Hamachek, pp. 174-223
49. Hill, all
51. Hollander and Hunt, pp. 77-85
52. Homme, all
57. Johnson, all
62. Joyce and Weil, pp. 36-47, 75-92, 210-211, 233-264
64. Kibler, Barker, and Miles, all
67. Krumboltz and Thoresen, pp. 87-165, 249-264
68. Learning Technology Incorporated, all
89. Rogers, pp. 279-313
95. Schmuck and Schmuck, all
98. Shostrom, pp. 110-119

Index